PENGUIN BOOKS

Amazing Dog Stories

Vickie Davy is a founding director of PetRescue. After leaving a successful career in advertising and marketing, she helped to build PetRescue into Australia's largest online animal welfare organisation. Vickie is also a qualified behavioural dog trainer, and she lives in Melbourne with her partner and daughter.

Saskia Adams is a freelance writer and editor. She spent ten years working at Penguin Books before her ever-increasing number of rescue animals necessitated a treechange to the Yarra Valley. In 2011 Saskia co-founded Forever Friends Animal Rescue Inc., which has saved and rehomed over 2500 dogs, cats, puppies and kittens from death row in pounds and shelters. Her other books include *Unconditional Love: PetRescue's Great Animal Stories* and *Dogs That Make a Difference*.

PetRescue.com.au
Amazing Dog Stories

Edited by
Vickie Davy and Saskia Adams

PENGUIN BOOKS

PENGUIN BOOKS

UK | USA | Canada | Ireland | Australia
India | New Zealand | South Africa | China

Penguin Books is part of the Penguin Random House group of companies
whose addresses can be found at global.penguinrandomhouse.com.

First published by Penguin Group (Australia), 2011
This edition published by Penguin Group (Australia), 2016

Copyright © this collection Penguin Group Australia 2011
Copyright © in individual stories and photographs remains with the authors

The moral right of the authors has been asserted

All rights reserved. Without limiting the rights under copyright reserved above,
no part of this publication may be reproduced, stored in or introduced into a retrieval
system, or transmitted, in any form or by any means (electronic, mechanical,
photocopying, recording or otherwise), without the prior written permission
of both the copyright owner and the above publisher of this book.

Cover design by Karen Scott © Penguin Group (Australia)
Text design by Cathy Larsen © Penguin Group (Australia)
Cover and title page photographs by Shannon Plummer
Typeset in Stone Serif Medium by Post Pre-press Group, Brisbane, Queensland
Printed and bound in Australia by Griffin Press, an accredited ISO AS/NZS 14001
Environmental Management Systems printer.

National Library of Australia
Cataloguing-in-Publication data:

Pet rescue's amazing dog stories : true tales of second-chance dogs and the
lives they changed / edited by Vickie Davy, Saskia Adams.
9780143573715 (pbk)
Dogs – Australia.
Dog rescue – Australia – Anecdotes.
Davy, Vickie.
Adams, Saskia.

636.70832

penguin.com.au

Contents

Foreword by Dr Katrina Warren	vii
Introduction	1
Saving the Day	5
Best of Friends	29
Who's Rescuing Who?	69
Just for Fun	93
Not Quite Perfect	119
Superdog!	151
Special Seniors	171
Lending a Hand	189
Dogs Overcoming the Odds	203
Part of the Family	225
When it's Just Meant to Be	245
Use PetRescue to Find Your New Best Friend!	274
How Else Can You Help Rescue Pets?	276

Foreword

In Australia it is estimated that we currently euthanase around 120 000 healthy, homeless pets annually, which is not only a national epidemic but plain unnecessary. Hundreds of thousands of us buy puppies and kittens each year from pet stores, backyard breeders and even online, without realising that there is always an abundance of wonderful, healthy but homeless puppies and dogs, cats and kittens, of all shapes and sizes, waiting to be adopted via PetRescue, and at their local pound and shelter.

People often assume that homeless pets must have something wrong with them, but this is rarely the case. Many rescue pets in need of homes are in that position because their owners' circumstances changed and they could no longer care for them, or because their person never came looking for them after they strayed. Further, some in our community do regard pets as disposable items, and when the new puppy or kitten is no longer as cute as it was at eight weeks old in the pet-shop window, it is abandoned.

In January 2010, my beloved Border Collie Toby passed away and he took a little piece of my heart with him, forever. Toby was my companion for fourteen years. He was my best friend: beside me through my relationships, my developing career, holidays, the birth of my daughter and so much more. I miss him each and every day. Toby brought sunshine to my life – he had the special quality of making everyone who met him smile.

I have a very busy household, with a beautiful young child and a very mischievous cat called Mr Fox, but something was missing. There is something truly special about the wag of a tail as you walk through the front door. My house no longer felt like a home and I craved some canine company. However, I didn't feel that I was ready to commit to another dog. So, I decided to foster a four-legged through Golden Retriever Rescue (GRR) – a wonderful organisation that finds 'forever homes' for hundreds of abandoned Goldies around New South Wales each year.

I had a long list of prerequisites for a potential pooch entering my home: they needed to be great with children, with other dogs and with cats. Moreover, because I am living in a high-density area, it was important that the dog didn't bark much. I was prepared to wait until the right canine came along, and it didn't take long.

Riley was found dumped outside Griffith Pound and collected by GRR, who rushed him to their vet. The poor boy was emaciated, covered in fleas and had horrific open wounds on each of his legs where he had been tied up by all fours. He could barely walk due to an infected grass seed in one of his paws but it was his eyes that told his story – they were the saddest eyes that I have ever seen, and they stared through me to my core. He needed urgent help. . . and love.

I brought Riley into my home and we started the journey towards his recovery. As he lay with his head on my lap, I questioned how anyone could ever hurt an innocent animal in this way. He was so gentle, and through it all he managed to wag his tail every time I stroked his fur. I promised him that no one would ever hurt him again and I told him over and over that he was a good boy. He just looked up at me as if to say, 'Thank you so much.'

It has given me enormous satisfaction to help Riley get his life back on track. He has put on 10 kilograms, his awful wounds have healed and he has gradually lost the sadness in his eyes. His coat now looks wonderful and has developed a rich golden colour. He looks like the happy young Golden Retriever that he deserves to be. It is clear he is now feeling good about himself and he makes human and canine friends wherever he goes.

While I have no doubt that I have contributed to helping Riley heal, he has also been an integral part in helping mend my broken heart and closing the gaping wound left by Toby, and for that I am extremely grateful.

In addition to this, a very special and unexpected relationship has developed in my home and it has been heart-warming and very entertaining to watch. My cat, Mr Fox, welcomed Riley as if he was one of his own. Mr Fox followed Riley everywhere when he arrived and within a couple of days, they were playing together and grooming each other as though they were lifelong pals. Now, they often sleep on the same bed, snuggled up and spooning each other! It's adorable. Mr Fox also views Riley's tail as his ultimate play toy and is often seen launching and attacking the Golden Tail as it swings from side to side. Riley doesn't mind at all – I think he loves the attention.

Riley isn't going anywhere – I'm officially a 'foster failure' and have offered Riley a forever home with me. He truly is a special dog – a testament to the canine species, that they can endure so much and still have the ability to forgive and love again. Adopting Riley was a huge decision and commitment, but I am overjoyed to offer him a safe home. I realise that he is never going to be Toby the Wonderdog, but he is Riley the Wonderful Family Dog, and he suits where I am at in my life right now.

The fostering process was incredibly rewarding and something I highly recommend. How better to test whether you're ready for pet ownership, or whether a new dog or cat will fit well into your household? It's a bit like try before you buy! Most rescue groups provide 24/7 back-up and advice, and all you need to supply is food, exercise and cuddles. If you'd like to know more, please visit PetRescue's other great website, PetFoster.com.au.

Incredible as it seems, each and every dog featured in this book was unwanted at some point. Most were saved and rehomed by the hundreds of tireless rescue groups operating in every state around Australia. Their volunteers work around the clock to save as many lives as they can, usually digging deep into their own pockets to do so. Please find out what groups are working in your area and support them. There are over one hundred doggy stars on the following pages who are only here today because of these organisations.

Above all, please consider a rescue pet for your next four-legged family member. Not only will you never regret it – they will never stop loving you for it.

Dr Katrina Warren

Introduction

Dogs who save lives; dogs who love unconditionally; dogs who overcome the odds, dogs with jobs; dogs with special skills and dogs who are *just dogs*. We received hundreds of contributions to our *Amazing Dog Stories* from all over Australia, and although each story was different, they all had two things in common: every one of these dogs was once homeless, and every adopter said they now couldn't imagine life without their rescue pet.

PetRescue was founded in 2003 to give homeless pets a second chance, and to date we have helped over 300 000 rescue pets find loving families. Our vision is to give every rescue organisation, every foster carer and every single one of the community's homeless pets a way to reach out to and engage with the Australian public. The first big step towards realising this vision was the launch of PetRescue.com.au. PetRescue statistics speak for themselves, with visits to the website from potential adopters rocketing to 24 000 per day, proving that more and more animal-loving Australians are choosing to adopt a rescue pet!

PetRescue is the central place for the huge network of compassionate, community-based animal rescue groups, offering diverse rehoming programs, campaigns and support. Over 900 rescue groups, pounds and shelters across Australia proudly call themselves PetRescue members and each one works incredibly hard to save the lives of homeless animals.

But why are so many pets homeless?
To anyone who has ever experienced the joy of an adopted animal, it seems unbelievable that over 250 000 of these pets will be euthanased in shelters and pounds across the country each year. While it can be tempting to blame these deaths on cruel or callous owners, the truth is pets lose their homes for myriad reasons.

Healthy, friendly pets end up in care when human relationships break down, owners move interstate or overseas, people get sick and can't care for their pet, and when owners don't understand the commitment or choose the wrong pet for their circumstances. Giving these pets a second chance is the mission of PetRescue and every single one of our members.

Hundreds of thousands of Australians bring a new canine into their families every year; however, a lack of awareness results in too few people choosing to adopt a rescue dog. PetRescue is working hard to promote the 'adoption option', asking families to open their hearts and homes to needy pets. We believe pet lovers are the answer to saving the life of each and every healthy companion animal in this country.

The joy of second chances
On a daily basis our rescue pets show us their incredible resilience, their capacity to love, to forgive, and to rise above circumstances that would have many of us two-leggeds utterly beaten. They remind us to find wonderment in the smallest things, and wake up every day with a smile.

The rescue dogs starring in this book are young, old, big, small, pedigree and mixed breeds. They are alive now thanks to the wonderful volunteer-run rescue groups, progressive pounds and shelters, and the big-hearted families who saved them.

We hope these stories will inspire you to not only adopt your next pet, but to support rescue groups across the nation in their vital work.

It was a joy compiling this book – the only sad moment we had was knowing we couldn't include every story. To all who contributed – thank you. Your rescue dog's tale might not have made it through this time, but we shed many an appreciative tear reading about how much you love your four-legged friend, and we agree with you wholeheartedly that your rescue dog is a star.

We'd like to leave the last word to Anne, who wrote in about her rescue dog called Raphy:

He is the nicest dog and we are absolutely amazed that there is even one person on this planet that didn't want him. Through no fault of his own Raphy found himself homeless and, yes, we rescued him, but he has given us so much more in return. He spreads love and joy wherever goes and what he gives, he gives unconditionally. Aside from the fact he's helped heal some broken hearts in our family, he hasn't done any heroic deeds or performed amazing stunts. He's just Raphy.

Vickie Davy & Saskia Adams

Introduction

Dogs who save lives; dogs who love unconditionally; dogs who overcome the odds, dogs with jobs; dogs with special skills and dogs who are *just dogs*. We received hundreds of contributions to our *Amazing Dog Stories* from all over Australia, and although each story was different, they all had two things in common: every one of these dogs was once homeless, and every adopter said they now couldn't imagine life without their rescue pet.

PetRescue was founded in 2003 to give homeless pets a second chance, and to date we have helped over 300 000 rescue pets find loving families. Our vision is to give every rescue organisation, every foster carer and every single one of the community's homeless pets a way to reach out to and engage with the Australian public. The first big step towards realising this vision was the launch of PetRescue.com.au. PetRescue statistics speak for themselves, with visits to the website from potential adopters rocketing to 24 000 per day, proving that more and more animal-loving Australians are choosing to adopt a rescue pet!

PetRescue is the central place for the huge network of compassionate, community-based animal rescue groups, offering diverse rehoming programs, campaigns and support. Over 900 rescue groups, pounds and shelters across Australia proudly call themselves PetRescue members and each one works incredibly hard to save the lives of homeless animals.

But why are so many pets homeless?
To anyone who has ever experienced the joy of an adopted animal, it seems unbelievable that over 250 000 of these pets will be euthanased in shelters and pounds across the country each year. While it can be tempting to blame these deaths on cruel or callous owners, the truth is pets lose their homes for myriad reasons.

Healthy, friendly pets end up in care when human relationships break down, owners move interstate or overseas, people get sick and can't care for their pet, and when owners don't understand the commitment or choose the wrong pet for their circumstances. Giving these pets a second chance is the mission of PetRescue and every single one of our members.

Hundreds of thousands of Australians bring a new canine into their families every year; however, a lack of awareness results in too few people choosing to adopt a rescue dog. PetRescue is working hard to promote the 'adoption option', asking families to open their hearts and homes to needy pets. We believe pet lovers are the answer to saving the life of each and every healthy companion animal in this country.

The joy of second chances
On a daily basis our rescue pets show us their incredible resilience, their capacity to love, to forgive, and to rise above circumstances that would have many of us two-leggeds utterly beaten. They remind us to find wonderment in the smallest things, and wake up every day with a smile.

The rescue dogs starring in this book are young, old, big, small, pedigree and mixed breeds. They are alive now thanks to the wonderful volunteer-run rescue groups, progressive pounds and shelters, and the big-hearted families who saved them.

We hope these stories will inspire you to not only adopt your next pet, but to support rescue groups across the nation in their vital work.

It was a joy compiling this book – the only sad moment we had was knowing we couldn't include every story. To all who contributed – thank you. Your rescue dog's tale might not have made it through this time, but we shed many an appreciative tear reading about how much you love your four-legged friend, and we agree with you wholeheartedly that your rescue dog is a star.

We'd like to leave the last word to Anne, who wrote in about her rescue dog called Raphy:

Saving the Day

Dogs are known for their loyalty and unconditional love, but it's their intelligence and courage that see them come to the aid of their beloved human families, at times endangering their own lives. Here are inspiring tributes to some four-footed heroes.

No Price on Love

Jetta had saved my two girls – how could I not save her?

It began when we were living in the suburbs, and wanted a Kelpie dearly but knew we couldn't put such an energetic dog in a small backyard. So when we came across a beautiful 75-acre rural property at Clonbinane for sale with abundant native flora and fauna, a large dam near the house and a variety of fruit trees, we knew we had to grab the opportunity with 'both paws'!

By the time we moved in, our daughters Miah and Kali were three years and twelve months old respectively. It was time for a dog to join our family! And when I saw a 'Free to Good Home' ad for an unwanted five-month-old Kelpie Labrador mix, I knew straight away this was the dog we'd been waiting for. In her photo the beautiful black girl had large chocolate-brown eyes and a gentle expression.

When we arrived to meet the pup after the two-hour drive, a black streak ran up to me and slid to a stop at my feet as soon as we got out of the car. Kali wriggled out of my arms and reached down towards the dog. I was worried the pup would start jumping on her, spotting a potential playmate, but the little black one simply licked Kali's hand and gently wagged her tail. Needless to say, we soon left with the newest member of the family, utterly delighted.

She had simply been called 'Pup' by her former owners, so the first thing was to name her. I decided that this jet-black dog would be called Jetta. From the first moment we arrived home she settled into our lives and routine, becoming one of the kids. Jetta soon determined the children were her priority and she followed them everywhere. If they spilt up she would follow the youngest closely, and if a car came up our driveway and the kids were there she would position herself between the girls and the moving vehicle. I was absolutely thrilled at the intelligence and protectiveness Jetta showed towards our girls.

This was proven in an unforgettable way only two weeks after she joined the family. While hanging out the washing, I suddenly heard my girls screaming. It sounded as if their voices were coming from the dam. Heart pounding, I sprinted towards the sound and as I drew closer, I saw my girls being nipped on their bums and herded back towards the house by Jetta. As I caught up to them, shouting and asking what on earth they'd been doing, the story gradually came out through their tears.

Miah related how she and my other little devil had snuck out the front door and down towards the dam while I put the washing out the line. Jetta followed at their heels, trying to herd them back. When they ignored her and tried to run past, she started nipping at them. Thinking their new dog was going to eat them, they screamed and started back towards the house.

My heart still pounding, I couldn't believe that an untrained five-month-old dog had the understanding and intelligence to know my young girls should be kept away from our deep dam at all costs. I had no doubt Jetta had saved the girls from drowning that day. From that point on, Jetta was spoilt rotten at every opportunity. We clearly had a *very* special dog.

Time marched on, and on 7 February, 2009, a scorching-hot day, we were enjoying Miah's fifth birthday party at home when smoke suddenly filled the sky. Panicked, we did out best to find out where the fire was coming from, but there was little information. After many phone calls we were told the fire was in Kilmore, a twenty-minute drive away and heading away from us, but to get the grandparents and kids out as a safety precaution. As we packed some party food and an overnight bag, my partner Royce started our fire plan. I was calling Jetta to get into the car with us when Royce told me to leave her with him as she gets car sick, and that he would keep an eye on her. The fire surely wouldn't come near our place.

So I left with the kids and grandparents, thinking we'd be back in the morning. Little did any of us know what was about to unfold.

Within four hours, everything changed. The winds had altered direction and the fire was turning around, heading straight back to our place. We were half an hour's drive away at a friend's house, and all telecommunications were down. The TV news showed the mountain we lived on up in flames, and I had no idea if Royce and Jetta were all right. My head was spinning. It was the longest night of my life.

I woke to a text message the next morning from our neighbour's son saying 'Royce and Jetta burnt but okay, everything else gone'.

I raced to Kilmore hospital. Royce was heavily medicated for burns to his feet, and the doctors reassured me they were doing all they could to keep him comfortable. Knowing Royce was in good hands, I called our local vet where Jetta had been taken. *Please God, please make Jetta be all right . . .*

'We're worried about her breathing,' the vet told me over the phone. 'We don't know if it's smoke inhalation or burns affecting her lungs, so we need you to take her to an animal hospital where they have an oxygen kennel.'

I said I'd be there right away. When I arrived and they brought Jetta out, I couldn't believe my eyes. My poor baby was in bad shape. I raced her to the animal emergency hospital at Essendon and trembled while the vet on duty told me they were very sceptical of her survival, and recommended I put her to sleep.

Jetta was part of our family, only eleven months old, and had saved our two girls. Moreover, we'd just lost our home. I just couldn't do it. We'd already lost too much – we weren't losing Jetta too.

The vet said the next forty-eight hours would be critical, and if she survived that period we could re-examine the options. But the cost was going to be substantial.

'Just do whatever she needs – I'll find the money somehow,' was my reply, but in reality I had no idea how we would even afford to rebuild our house, let alone pay Jetta's vet bills.

Our girl survived the first forty-eight hours but was put on a morphine drip for the pain. She had extensive burns to her face and eyes, neck, belly, legs and paws. Royce told me Jetta had hidden under the house (her safe place) when the fireball hit, while he was still inside. After the curtains and furniture caught fire, Royce ran down to the dam and held his breath underwater as the fire front passed directly over the water's surface. Shouting for Jetta to join him, she came out from under the house, but she was confused and tried to go back. When she heard the koalas screaming (we had two females and their babies living in the gums surrounding our house), Jetta ran down to the dam, and Royce waded out and dragged her in, wetting her burns. They stayed there for a few hours together and watched the rest of our home burn to the ground.

The following days became a blur, visiting Royce in hospital in Kilmore and then Jetta in Essendon 60 kilometres away. I also had to try piecing our lives back together and keeping the girls in some kind of routine while camping at my mother's house.

Then, I heard the RSPCA had opened their Werribee vet hospital to the animal fire victims for free. I rang and spoke to them and they were happy to arrange transport of Jetta from Essendon to Werribee. I had mixed feelings, though – relief that the financial burden of Jetta's care would be lifted, but anxiety that Werribee would be too far for me to visit her regularly. I rang Essendon and left a message that Jetta would be moved, only to have them call back within ten minutes, saying no. Moving her would be detrimental to her care, particularly if she didn't have contact with her family to keep her going. 'Leave her here, and we will cover all costs,' the vet said.

Stunned, I wanted to cry. I couldn't believe their generosity.

Neither could Jetta, I think, because from that point on she slowly surprised everyone. Her recovery speeded up and although she was in pain, she did not fret and would wag her tail and look expectantly at me every time I visited. Our girls and other family members also came to see her; my Aunty Linda gathered donations from all her animal-loving friends and even sent out a global email asking for contributions towards Jetta's care. The hospital staff themselves were amazing, donating their time and some of their wages into the hospital's 'Jetta Fund', which was written up on a clipboard near our girl's enclosure. Once when I visited they hid the clipboard and when I tried to give them some money from a bushfire grant I received they wouldn't accept it. So I decided the only thing I could do for the wonderful staff was to bring them a big box of Krispy Kreme doughnuts every time I visited! I got accused of making them put on weight, of course, while they tucked in.

Jetta's treatments were lengthy and varied as the staff experimented with various creams and medications. As a dog with her injuries would normally have been put to sleep, Jetta was an important case study in severe burns for the vets. At first we were told she would be completely blind, her hair wouldn't grow back and that she would need skin grafts for her paw pads. Remembering Jetta's love for my family, my response was always the same: 'I want her to have a good quality of life – until she's shown that she can't recover, we will give her every chance.'

Then, more miracles occurred. We began to realise Jetta *did* have some vision. She was able to navigate around the hospital without bumping into things and would look straight at you when you were talking to her. Hooray! Next, we found her pads didn't need to be grafted after all – they were healing rapidly themselves. If that wasn't enough, then her fur started to grow back. I believe Jetta's own attitude played a huge part in recovery. She wanted to live; she wanted to be a normal dog again. She was so patient with the vets prodding and poking her, and once she was off the morphine drip and able to hobble around the hospital, she acted like she owned the place!

In the end, Royce was in hospital for two weeks – Jetta for two months. At her last bandage change at the vet hospital I hid a bunch of Krispy Kreme doughnut vouchers in thank-you cards for all the wonderful staff that helped ensure Jetta survived.

Since then, our girl has had to have one of her eyes removed as it was causing her pain. But she has sight in her other eye, and can still fetch a ball and avoid stepping on the kids' toys. We were told her remaining sight will probably fade as she ages, more rapidly than that of other dogs. She still has problems with her paw pads and nails – she can't walk on gravel or rock without pain, so we avoid those surfaces. But apart from that she is in perfect health – even if she is a little chunky! – and her personality hasn't changed a bit, except now she loves riding in the car: no more car sickness!

In October 2010 we welcomed a chubby eight-week-old black Kelpie into our family. Jetta tended to sleep away her days and we thought a new friend might give her a new lease on life, plus be a guide for her when she no longer has any vision left. It was the right decision – the dogs have been inseparable from day one. Called Rainbow, or Bow for short, the new addition has taught Jetta how to be more playful and active again, and Jetta has taught Bow how to have at least two naps a day! Even though we are still living in a shed on our property and don't know how to fund the rebuilding of our house and Jetta's ongoing medical costs, we are happy.

I will never regret pushing for Jetta's survival. Not only has it saved the life of a loving soul who saved our own daughters from drowning that day, but I have had the privilege of feeling the huge compassion and generosity of my fellow humans since Black Saturday. So many friends, family and strangers came to us in our time of need, going well beyond the call of duty. For that and more, I am eternally grateful.

Renee, Victoria

Hot Fudge Hero

Fudge was a feisty little dog, small in stature and big in attitude. With a chequered brown-and-gold coat and soft brown eyes, he was a magnet for all who entered the Sunshine Coast Animal Refuge. But under the cute facade lay a dog who made the great escapee Houdini look like an amateur. There wasn't a fence that Fudge couldn't climb or a garden he couldn't tunnel out of. He had been rehomed three times to new owners who were given warnings of the dog's incredible skills. But inevitably the phone would ring and a voice from the council pound would say, 'Guess who we've got?'

Time was running out for Fudge. The head ranger stomped over to our refuge and barked at everyone that Fudge's days were numbered. 'My officers,' she said, 'have better things to do than chase around, picking up stray dogs.' No one felt inclined to point out that that was exactly what they were employed to do!

Strict rules were put in place. His next rehoming had to be his last. Weeks turned into months. Offers for him were made regularly but we just didn't feel the homes being offered would be escape proof.

One Friday morning a middle-aged couple with a physically disabled adult son in a wheelchair came into the office. They were looking for a companion dog. As the father filled in the normal paperwork required, he explained that his son was physically fragile and unable to handle anything too big. The mother piped up, 'Nothing too yappy either. I can't stand yappy dogs.'

The young man was obviously eager to see the dogs. 'Hi,' I said, touching his hand, 'I'm Tricia. How about you and I wander through while your parents finish the forms?' He gave a lopsided grin and replied, 'Good idea. I'm Toby.'

We trailed past the pens but surprisingly none of the dogs seemed to appeal to Toby. I'd almost run out of dogs to show him when we reached young Fudge. Suddenly, Toby nearly fell out of his wheelchair. He pointed excitedly. Fudge, seeing he was once again the centre of attention, put on a pathetic act, whimpering and grovelling, until Toby's father demanded I bring him out. I tried to put them off, explaining Fudge's chequered history, but the father was firm. If Toby wants him, Toby shall have him.

We went into the 'meets and greets area' and I brought Fudge in on a lead. It was love at first sight. Fudge sniffed the wheelchair and jumped lightly onto Toby's lap and settled down. It was incredible – none of the volunteers had ever seen Fudge behave like this. He normally got so excited, he would almost knock a person over. It appeared that he sensed Toby was fragile and treated him accordingly.

After many warnings about his previous escapades, Toby and his parents took Fudge home. All the volunteers held our breath, but as the weeks passed and Fudge did not return, we let him pass into history.

Months later, we heard in the local media that a small dog had alerted his disabled owner that his house was on fire and had dragged him from the burning building. We didn't give it a lot of thought until we saw the picture in the newspaper. There was young Fudge, sitting proudly on a beaming Toby's lap! He had apparently sensed the fire first and barked continually to warn his family. Having alerted the household to the danger, he grabbed Toby by his clothes and dragged him out of the house.

Work that day seemed lighter than normal. People smiled more. This was what made volunteering worthwhile. We felt we had achieved the impossible. Not only had we successfully rehomed a 'problem dog' but this time he had stayed put, brought joy to a young man's life, and by a heroic deed had even saved that life. So much for the council's head ranger! Good on yer, Fudge.

Tricia, Queensland

Mum of the Year

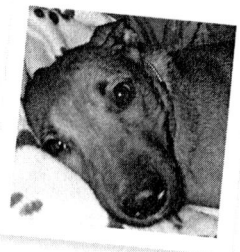

Ranger Gary found a sad and confused Staffy mix outside the Mildura Animal Shelter in the caged area called the 'mini pen'. Here, dogs are often dumped by their owners after hours, or placed as strays found wandering. It was clear this 18-month-old had recently been a mum, and her microchip revealed her name was Bella. When Gary rang the owner, he said he'd come get her. But he didn't, and the days dragged on.

The day after Bella's arrival, a litter of unwanted Labrador mix pups were dumped outside. As they were only about five or six weeks old – too young to be away from their mother – instead of letting them struggle to feed themselves in their own pen or, worse still, be euthanased, Gary had an idea: he would give them to Bella. Perhaps she would feed them and help save their lives?

Bella took them on without batting an eyelid. Gary noticed it actually lifted her spirits, as she'd been quite depressed the day before. This foster mum took excellent care of the pups for eight days, feeding and fussing, before they were adopted locally.

Bella then found herself alone and sad again, still waiting for her owner who kept saying he'd be in to collect her 'tomorrow'. But it was clear this was a Christmas present Bella just wasn't going to get. Then, on Christmas Eve, three little Staffy mix pups were dumped out the front. They were a little older – say, six or seven weeks – but smaller than the Labs. As the pound was due to be closed from the day after, Christmas Day until 2 January, Gary knew the best chance they had was if special Bella could also save them.

When Gary presented the puppies to Bella at her pen, she became excited. More babies to love! She took to the new litter with the same affection and care as she had done with the last.

Again, the cute and cuddly small ones found homes, and Bella was left alone. Seven weeks had passed and it was clear her owner was never coming to save her, nor was there any interest from the public in adopting her. That meant only one other fate lay in store for this loving and generous girl. That was when Sunraysia Animal Rehoming Group (SARG) stepped in, with some generous donations from our supporters. We would not let anything happen to Bella. It was time she had some foster care of her own!

We organised for local carers Pam and John to liberate Bella from her cage, and she went to a 5000-acre farm for some well-deserved R&R.

Pam and John soon discovered she adored water. But the best was yet to come. When the couple took her on a holiday to Rosebud on the Mornington Peninsula for a friend's birthday, a guest at the party fell in love with Bella, announcing he wanted to adopt her after just a day in her company. But did he choose Bella, or did Bella choose him? She wouldn't leave him alone! Bella followed Graeme all around the house and yard. Her foster parents told Graeme to think a little longer about it, but they got a call the next morning. Graeme had gone back to Melbourne but returned to Rosebud that day to collect her. The adoration was mutual.

Bella now divides her time with Graeme between Melbourne, Rosebud and Yarrawonga, depending on where the work is, as her new dad is a builder. She's a favourite on the work sites. One of the apprentices renamed her 'Bess' after Bessa Bricks – because not only is she the same colour, but she's shaped like one!

Being a water baby, the newly named Bess is also lapping it up on Graeme's boat and chasing seagulls on the beach. One of Graeme and Bess's tricks is for Graeme to pick her up and throw her into the air and catch her (she loves it!). Graeme's other Staffy dog, Bodie, has for fifteen years been much loved and spoilt – and after seeing Bess save the lives of so many puppies at the pound, we couldn't be happier that she's now reaping her own wonderful reward.

Carolyn Dufty, Sunraysia Animal Rehoming Group, Victoria

Snowy, my Guardian Angel

We fell in love with Snowy the day we met him. I knew he was meant to be with us. He was with the Greyhound Adoption Program (GAP) of South Australia and we were warned he was rather 'full on'. But the people who knew him back then are now surprised to see how much he has changed. Snowy is calm and loving, but that is not his only gift.

Shortly after adopting Snowy, we discovered he had an unexpected skill. He's more than just alert and protective: he's telepathic.

I was having difficulty with seizures at the time. We'd had a car accident and the seizures began following that. Always by my side, Snowy seemed to know when a seizure was imminent. He would go into protective mode, barking and whining to alert those in the house, then lying beside me until someone came to my rescue. If I was home alone, when I regained consciousness after the seizure, I would find I was safe and secure with Snowy lying alongside me, waiting until it was over. He would whine and bark at me until I came around, back into the world. He would even refuse to leave the room when the doctor or ambulance was called – my husband had to physically carry him away from me.

Snowy has been my guardian angel through those hard times, and is also there through the good. I no longer have seizures, but I know that if it happens again, he will be there with me.

I am now the coordinator for GAP in South Australia. I was so inspired by these beautiful dogs I wanted to be more involved with the initiative that finds them loving homes once their racing careers have ended. Snowy was my 'assistant' for four years, coming to work with me every day. He would sit in his favourite spot in my office, watching and greeting people that came and went within the Greyhound Racing building. The trainers and industry all knew him, and would stop in from time to time to say hello.

Snowy also came along to potential foster home inspections and helped me out with those. Always great with all other animals, he had the confidence to stand in front of me when meeting the existing pets of the house, which would tell me he was comfortable and that they would be of no harm to other Greyhounds. If he hid behind me and tried to avoid the other dog, then that indicated the dog might be too aggressive or a danger to another Greyhound. Snowy was very tolerant and his instincts where always correct.

Now almost fourteen, Snowy's days of being my assistant have ceased. He has slowed down a bit, is starting to lose his hearing and spends his days lounging on our bed with his other Greyhound friend, Hulk, until I come home from work.

I believe everything happens for a reason and Snowy was definitely meant to be with us. Every day I am grateful for GAP. If it wasn't for Snowy, I wouldn't now have the privilege of bringing happiness to other people who have also chosen to change their lives by adopting a Greyhound.

Angela Webb, Greyhound Adoption Program, South Australia

An Unforgettable Gift

When I went to the local pound to help look for a friend's lost dog, we didn't find him, but another dog found me. As I wandered around, I saw an Airedale Terrier mix standing to attention, focused on the gate of her pen and staring into the distance. When I asked the staff about her, they told me she'd been standing like that since her owner surrendered her eight days previously. The reason he had surrended her? He said he didn't want her any more because she could no longer have pups.

Her name was Brandy and she was scheduled for euthanasia the next day.

The vet felt she was about eight years of age, though the owner claimed she was only five. Looking at her, I desperately wanted to take her home, but Dan, my eight-year-old son, was terrified of dogs after being bitten by a Jack Russell at the age of four. I swallowed the lump in my throat, turned away and went home.

By the next morning, I still couldn't get Brandy's face out of my mind. I couldn't bear it any longer. I rang the pound and asked if I could come and see her. The receptionist told me she thought Brandy had already been taken to the euthanasia room. Heart pounding, I pleaded for her to check. Thank goodness this kindred soul agreed to put down the phone and run and see. With seconds to spare, she stopped Brandy being killed that day. The message then relayed to me was that I could come in to see Brandy, but I had to bring my children too, and be willing to accept the staff's decision if they felt she wasn't the right dog for us.

We piled into the car and raced to the pound. Soon after, we all nervously stood in the assessment area. Brandy had been brought in but again was standing to attention at the nearest gate and ignoring us – no doubt still loyally waiting for the owner who would never return. I had Dan hiding behind me and my other two children tentatively trying to attract Brandy's attention, to no avail. When instructed by the staff for us to move forward, Dan, with his fear of dogs, began to sob in terror.

Then something extraordinary happened.

Brandy's ears went up and she turned to us.

She watched Dan cry. Then she lay down on the ground. On her stomach, ever so slowly, she began to inch her way over towards my sobbing son.

When she reached him, she put her head on his feet.

Amazed, my other children and I started patting and making a fuss of Brandy – but it wasn't us she saw. She was only concerned with Dan, trying to tell him to not be afraid.

Two hours later, we drove home with our girl. It took Brandy a dedicated five weeks to cure my son of his terror. She continued to go down on her belly and inch her way over to him, until her head rested on his feet – hence we soon added 'Beetle' to her name. Not long after that, Dan would let Brandy rest her head on his legs, and within months, if I couldn't find Brandy, I just had to check under my son's blankets. If I couldn't find Dan, I would look for Brandy. Her patience and gentleness cured his fear forever.

My other favourite memory of Brandy-Beetle was when my cat Blonde had kittens. She was *not* a natural mother like Brandy. So I was not surprised when it was our dog, and not the kittens' mother, who cleaned them up at birth and did all the mothering from then on. However, the funniest sight would occur at feeding time. Brandy would go in search of the bleating kittens' mum – and the look on Blonde's face as Brandy dragged her back like a pup by the scruff of her neck from wherever she found her said it all: 'Not Again!'

But that wasn't all. Once Brandy had deposited Blonde into the kittens' box, the dog would hold the reluctant mother down with a paw so she couldn't get away until her kittens were thoroughly fed.

We had almost six years full of love and laughter with Brandy before a leaky mitral valve took her away. Right until her last days, if she knew any member of her family was sad or in pain, you would find her there, loving them, nurturing them, and not moving from their side until she was satisfied they were all right. Then she'd set out to make them laugh with a game of hide-and-seek. Nine years on, we still miss our girl and she remains in our laughter and many 'Remember when Brandy . . . ?' stories. I also often think of the receptionist who ran to the euthanasia room to save Brandy for us. You gave us all an unforgettable gift that day.

Joanne, Victoria

In the Line of Duty

A lost dog, a Koolie, was found wandering at a truck stop in central Victoria. As often happens, this dog ended up in the local ranger's van, heading for the pound. Now, let's be plain: these days if you are a working breed and find yourself at the mercy of the local council, life can be very short. Many pounds across Australia don't have the staff or funding to go to any great lengths to find abandoned dogs a home – the dog becomes another number in a small cage for a short while and then . . .

But Amber was lucky. The ranger was kind and astute enough to realise he had a special dog in that pound and it would be criminal for her life to be snuffed out. So he put in that little extra effort, and tracked down Koolie Rescue. We drove many kilometres to collect Amber from the pound, guaranteeing her safety. This one wouldn't be just another statistic.

Of course we're biased, but Koolies are exceptional dogs. Even when you've been written off by your owner and you've hit rock bottom, waiting for a quick end to a short life, that's when a Koolie goes beyond all expectations.

Amber took her second chance at life in both paws and ran. And she kept on running, until she found herself thousands of kilometres away, serving her country in Afghanistan!

About the time of Amber's rescue, we had been approached by a representative from the Explosives Detection Dog Unit of the Australian Army, based in Queensland. They outlined their need for a smart, responsive, quick learning dog, who could handle a long day's work in high heat and dust and still be agile and attentive to the job. He told us that it sounded like a Koolie could fill this job description very well. We could only agree!

But which dog? We soon noticed Amber was very willing to please, keen to play and socialise, and her favourite activity was a game of ball. Moreover, she was clever. She was the ideal candidate.

With much excitement on our part and hers, Amber headed off to Brisbane to commence training with the Australian Armed Forces. She took to her schooling with delight and relished the challenges, starting later in the course than the other dogs, but impressing her handler by finishing her education earlier than expected. Next stop for Amber? Overseas deployment.

In August 2010, Amber and her handler hit the scorching deserts of Afghanistan. She put her training to use, helping to keep our troops safe, and not returning home until about four months later. We got regular updates and news about how Amber was going, and could see how much she was relishing her new life.

Today, Amber continues her work with the Explosives Detection Dogs Unit and no doubt has new adventures ahead. And to think this special girl was once just another number inching ever closer to being recorded in the euthanasia column of a council pound. Amber is a hero, and although all that ranger did that day was to pick up the phone, we think he is a hero too.

Kerrie Challenger, Koolie Rescue, Victoria

Blood Hound

From abuse, through illness and abandonment, to saving lives. This is Silas's love story.

When I saw Silas's photo on PetRescue, I knew that he was the dog for me. Then I learnt that this Greyhound mix had tested positive for heartworm. It didn't change anything in my mind, for I had already fallen in love with him. I would save his life, even though he was on the other side of the country. So, with the help of Jetpets, he made the journey from Albury in New South Wales to Perth in Western Australia.

Little did I know that before us were a series of surprises that would culminate with my Silas helping save the lives of others.

Silas arrived, very shy, and absolutely terrified of men. He now had to live with two other dogs and five cats! Thankfully, he is a fan of cats. But whenever my friends came to meet him, he would run to the end of the house and hide. This was heartbreaking. I can only imagine what has happened to Silas in the past.

The first happy surprise was that Silas's positive heartworm test was a mistake. Three subsequent tests came back negative. There is a one-in-a-million chance of getting a false positive heartworm test!

Then came the second happy surprise. I had been warned that Greyhounds didn't come back when called. But as with the medical results, Silas defied diagnosis! Our first trips to the beach and the park saw him come straight back to me – a great accomplishment for his breed.

Then came the third surprise. My vet asked if Silas would be prepared to donate blood to patients in need, as Greyhounds are known for being especially helpful in this way. How could I say no? Silas doesn't mind at all, because after each time he donates he gets treated like a hero for a couple of weeks. I saved his life and now he has saved seven other dogs' lives and counting. Their owners cannot express their gratitude that their own beloved companions have been saved because of Silas's generous nature.

Silas continues to surprise us. He has pretty much overcome his fear of men, and is now doing well at obedience training. No one at our dog club can believe that I have had a Greyhound come such a long way in such a short period of time!

I can't express how grateful I am that Albury Dog Rescue could give me such a wonderful companion. Silas is a hero in my eyes.

Danielle, Western Australia

The Good Samaritan

It was a stifling hot January day when the nine puppies were born and taken straight to the cemetery. With their umbilical cords still in place, they were tied up in a hessian bag and dumped. Four would die quickly before a caring stranger found the five survivors.

The Papillon mix pups were rushed to a vet where they were immediately given the medical help they needed. The vet was then on the phone to a rescue group: 'We desperately need a surrogate mother to feed these puppies – can you help?'

But hopes were quickly dashed. The mother dog who came to their aid had very little milk left. In a race against time, my group – Newcastle Dog Rescue – was called in. There was good news. We did have a lactating mother! The only possible problem was that she was a cat . . . We had rescued loving mum Donatella and her six kittens from death row just days before.

The odds were against the motherless puppies, but we had to try. A kind volunteer made the lengthy trip in the middle of the night to take the helpless pups to the mother cat. On standby, we cared for her kittens while the much more vulnerable newborn pups were put next to their new 'mum'. Then came the long, slow sigh of relief as we watched the miracle unfold. The generous mother Donatella allowed the five little pups to snuggle up to her and select their teat.

She looked up at us: it was as if she was saving 'our' puppies out of gratitude for us saving her and her kittens.

Donatella could not be left with a mob of eleven small mouths to feed, so again the next day there was a race against time to find a loving lactating mother dog. There was one more disappointment with another canine mum whose lactation period was close to over. You can imagine our worry and frustration.

Again, our hearts calmed when another breeder came forward. Her dog had just given birth to one pup and still had colostrum in her milk! This was the opportunity of survival that the puppies desperately needed. As the excitement rose and the little ones started to gain weight, we gave thanks for their survival thus far. Then a great wave of sadness hit: the smallest pup passed away. He just hadn't been able to recover from the cruel ordeal he'd been through following his birth.

The four puppies who were left comforted us. We enjoyed a few weeks watching them grow and then move on to their forever homes, our love and hope going with them. Since that day, some of Donatella's own kittens have been lucky enough to find forever homes, while a couple are still waiting. We were again moved by this special mum's generosity when soon after the puppies' departure a litter of abandoned kittens were found, in need of a surrogate mum in order to survive. Once more, Donatella rose to the challenge, allowing them to drink from her and keeping them clean and warm. This special mum will now spend the rest of her days with her rescuer, who could never part with her, and she'll live out her life in the same love and warmth she has shown so many other innocent small creatures.

Donatella's four little puppies are now making their way in the world, hopefully they will never need a rescue group again. They will not remember the searing hot day they were dumped at the cemetery, the good Samaritan who found them, the caring vet who called us, and the surrogate mother dogs who did their best. And they will not remember the heavenly moment that a rescue cat called Donatella gave them her milk. Thank you, Donatella, for your gift.

Anne Ward, Dog Rescue Newcastle, New South Wales

Jasmine's Story

Jasmine, my grandparents' German Shepherd, never fails to rate a mention when my sisters and I drink one glass more than we mean to and start reminiscing about our childhood. Jasmine's long dead but we all still remember the wiry feel of her fur and her distinctive bark that went *Woo-woo-woo*, as if she were singing a sad song.

'Remember that time Jas saved your life?' Alice inevitably says to me.

Of course I do. Well, to be fair, I don't. I was a toddler – no, younger than that. However old you are when you're just learning to crawl.

I have no memory of it but it's part of our family's lore. That Time Jasmine Saved Bridget's Life.

Jasmine was six months old when my uncle Jim, still just a teenager, rescued her from a park. She was so skinny, her ribs corrugated her mangy fur, and she'd bitten bald a patch of skin on her thigh. She was very wary of strangers and once or twice she'd snarled at and even bit Uncle Jim. Jim's a pretty patient bloke, though, and he worked hard for a long time to win Jasmine's trust.

Jim eventually moved out of my grandparents' house to go to uni and to travel, but Jasmine stayed. Over time she became as loyal a companion as you could imagine, and very protective of my nan and grandpa. This last trait could go in both directions: there was no affection between Jasmine and the postman – which caused some nuisance as occasionally letters were withheld until the postie was feeling robust enough to face her – but Jasmine was greatly prized for her ability to frighten off door-knocking God-botherers. Her scars remained, however: she absolutely hated it whenever people waved around anything resembling a rod, which we took to mean she'd borne beatings, and she got freaked out by lots of movement. Whenever we kids ran around she'd nip at our heels. At Christmas or birthday celebrations when my cousins joined us at my grandparents' place, we'd make a game of it – who could outrun Jasmine's teeth?

Back when I was nine or ten months old, my grandparents would look after me during the day while Mum and Dad worked. My dear nan fretted that having a large intemperate dog around an infant was courting strife, but she needn't have worried. Jasmine treated me as if I were her pup: she was gentle and quiet and would follow me as I scooted around the house looking for entertainment. She'd also patiently endure my 'patting', which was typically so firm that it pulled back the skin from her forehead to show the lolly pink of her eyelids, or went roughly against the grain of her fur. I can't imagine Jasmine was very fond of either style really, so I count myself lucky that I still have all ten fingers.

One day the front door wasn't shut properly and, as that obviously proved too good an opportunity to ignore, I crawled out the doorway and down the front path towards the road. Not long after, with some alarm, my grandpa noted both the open door and my absence.

When he ran outside frantic, he saw me on the footpath, a metre or so from the road, with Jasmine standing over me.

She had the collar of my dress in her mouth and was attempting to pull me back towards the house. I looked dead keen to get away, as though the world's plushest soft toy – or whatever it is that nine- or ten-month-olds desire most in the world – was on the other side of that road. Meanwhile Jasmine, her jaw still firmly clamped on my dress, was doing her level best to stop me.

My grandpa swore he recognised the look in her eye, he'd seen it in the faces of those in the sweetie aisle at supermarkets: the exasperated parent dealing with a wilful child. After I'd been scooped up and brought safely inside – the door pulled firmly shut behind us – Jasmine was rewarded: an extra-large dinner and no patting from me for a while.

Bridget, Victoria

Best of Friends

They say a dog is man's best friend, but a dog's best friend could be almost anyone – great bonds are not bound by breed or even species. Dogs make for such good companions because they are so social and loyal, and this means they can display some extraordinarily selfless behaviour. They can be friend, babysitter, teacher or adoptive parent. Here are some inseparable duos.

A Pair of Diamond Hearts

Pic: David Ban

It was a normal day at Blacktown pound in western Sydney when a pair of ten-year-old dogs were brought in. One was a brindle Staffy Kelpie mix called Sparkles, and the other a white-and-tan Jack Russell mix called Lucky. Obviously they had come from the same home. Why they were surrendered is not clear – perhaps as often happens with older animals, their owner had passed away, and immediate family members sadly did not want to keep the dogs. They immediately became known only as 'Impound Number 06629' and 'Impound Number 06630'. This council's policy is for existing names not to be recorded on their website.

But volunteers at the pound soon noticed how much 06629 and 06630 doted on each other. Wherever one went, the other had to follow. One would get distressed if the other was out of view. Despite being in one of Australia's most unforgiving, busy and noisy pounds, they seemed quite happy to be there as long as they were together. They were both alert and happy, and Sparkles' happy 'moon' face shone from between the bars in the pen with her little mate. Their picture reminded me of a race horse and its companion pony.

Their mischievousness was evident. Of the 7977 animals that were impounded in Blacktown last year, Lucky and Sparkles were the only ones to discover the treats cupboard, which they raided together one day. A photo shows Lucky up on the top shelf of the cupboard – bottom in the air – shovelling treats out to her bigger sister Sparkles waiting down below. They truly were a team.

However, three days later, the unthinkable happened for Sparkles.

Her sister Lucky was taken. A Sydney rescue group chose Lucky for rehoming, but they had no room for her bigger sister. The pound thought that a pair of dogs, and particularly a pair of *older* dogs, would have no chance of being rehomed together. And Lucky *was* lucky to be rescued . . .

Sparkles waited in the pound alone, day after day, for someone to notice her. She began to lose weight and condition. Her expression became haunted. She developed bleeding sores all over her body from lying on concrete. Her fur began to fall out due to stress. Videos of her from this period show her in the exercise area scanning the horizon, paying no attention to other dogs around her, as if she was looking for her little mate. A kind person put another dog in her pen for company, but she continued to look devastated. She had lost the sparkle in her eyes.

Eventually the day came for her to be put on the kill list. She had run out of time. She was just another brindle dog. Nobody seemed to notice. Nobody seemed to care. Many a former loved pet leaves this pound in a black plastic bag; like a broken toy that nobody wants any more. Sparkles was now on death row, with only a few hours left to live.

All the while, I was watching and hearing about Sparkles' imminent fate via the internet from my home in rural Victoria, a long way away. What could I do? By now it was nearly Christmas, and I made a decision: whatever it took to save Sparkles from the pound I would do it. She would not end up as yet another statistic on a spreadsheet of a callous councillor; a victim of the senseless killing inherent in a heartless, archaic and ill-conceived council policy. I thought, No, not this one. You can't have her. I'll take her.

Getting her out of the pound and down to Victoria required every ounce of resourcefulness I had. But I was determined. Over the six weeks Sparkles had been in the pound she had developed behavioural and stress-related conditions. She no longer wanted to make friends with other dogs. She had developed separation anxiety. And yet she truly was the most loving and affectionate soul you could ever hope to meet.

She craved human affection and company with all her might. Her grief was palpable.

Once Sparkles arrived in Melbourne, I began my endeavours to find her a perfect home. I myself couldn't adopt any more pets. In the meantime, she passed through several kindly foster homes until I found an environment in which she began to stabilise. Not knowing her former name at that stage I named her Layla, which she instantly responded to. I believe naming an animal is a sign of respect, and to me it signified the first step towards giving this girl a new and brighter future. It saddens me that multitudes of innocent, healthy, adoptable animals go to their death in many pounds and shelters in Australia known only as 'Impound # XXXX'. It reduces them to a statistic while they are still breathing. They have done nothing to deserve to be stripped of their dignity in such a fashion. So Layla she became. A new name, a new life, and a new chapter. And she seemed very happy with that.

From the first few minutes I spent with her I knew I was in the company of a very special and loving soul. We bonded deeply and intensely. She would follow me around until I sat down and formed a lap upon which she would fall into a deep sleep. It was as if she *couldn't* sleep unless she had a warm and safe person to sleep *on*. I think it was the only time she could fully let go of her anxiety about her loss.

In the meantime, a miracle happened. I was *lucky* enough to discover the whereabouts of Lucky in New South Wales! She was still being cared for by Doggie Rescue who had got her out of the pound and she was now known as Teagan. As she was an older dog they had not yet been able to place her in a home. I began negotiations with Doggie Rescue to allow Teagan to come down to Victoria to be reunited with Layla in the hope they could be rehomed together. Layla was still grieving for her lost friend, and I was determined that these sisters be given the chance to be together again. We *had* to try.

With the help of a fantastic team of volunteers, this was arranged. Lynda drove all the way to New South Wales and back to retrieve Teagan – no small feat in itself – and we were all on the edge of our seat with the prospect of reuniting 'the girls'. However, just as Teagan arrived in Victoria, she become seriously ill. She was rushed to the animal hospital with hemorrhagic gastroenteritis. I was despairing – surely all our efforts to reunite these sisters would not end in tragedy?

Teagan was kept in hospital on a drip for several days. Thankfully, due to swift action on the part of her foster carer who was a vet nurse, and the excellent care of emergency staff, she recovered quickly and well – surprisingly so for an older dog.

However, I was now left with a vet bill of around $1500 on top of all the other expenses. But by now the girls had their own Facebook following, and many people were kind enough to donate money towards Teagan's vet bill. The support and dedication people have shown towards these dogs' plight along the way has been humbling.

Teagan proved herself to be a sweet and loving soul too, who wanted so badly to have her *very own human*. Her foster carers fell instantly in love with her, and she with them. Who couldn't love this bright little spirit, full of beans and 'all ears'?

The Big Reunion Day finally arrived, and my main team of helpers – Saskia, Lisa, Lynda and photographer David – gathered together at the doggie park where it was to take place. I was nervous – what if, after all our efforts, the girls had forgotten each other? What if Layla didn't want a bar of Teagan any more, like she was with some other dogs?

My fears were ill-founded. It couldn't have gone more beautifully. Layla recognised Teagan instantly and let out a cry. She wanted to jump all over her! Teagan (who had met many new dogs since being in the pound with Layla) was a little more reserved. However, by the end of their meeting, they jumped into the boot of my car together, and all our cameras and videos came out, as did the girls' grins. The photo you see at the start of this story shows the bond of great trust still existing between the two girls, the larger one quite happily allowing the smaller to stand underneath her belly; the smaller one feeling the safety of her sister's size and warmth above and around her. Many a tear was shed by the team.

The girls were together again. Against all odds, we had done it.

By their second meeting, Teagan was fully relaxed and at home in Layla's company again. She gave her kisses as if to say, 'G'day, Sis! Where've ya been?' We had made the dream of reuniting the girls a reality. The wait was worth it. We had put the sparkle back in their eyes!

One of the most poignant things to observe during the first week the girls spent together again was them sleeping on the same bed at night, and most touchingly of all, playing together. Separately, they were not interested in playing with any dog. Together, however, these old girls were now tearing around like a couple of youngsters, no doubt picking up their former roles in games of monsters and dragons known only to them, exactly where they had left off. To me this made the whole journey worthwhile. Sparkles and Lucky – now Layla and Teagan – are a team again. Their hearts are reunited.

The *Herald Sun* newspaper heard about this amazing story, and drove out to meet the girls. A four-hour photo shoot followed, and the pair ended up on page three – Layla and Teagan were famous! The photo showed Teagan kissing Layla, and the article invited readers who felt they could give these special girls a forever home to get in touch.

Recently, the girls were adopted by a wonderfully caring family. Finally they are well and truly loved, and can sleep safe in the knowledge they will never have to see the inside of a pound cell again. Now that these two mischievous little bouncing bunnies have been *lucky* enough to be brought back together, I can attest that the light which has always shone so powerfully from their hearts also *sparkles* brightly from their eyes once more. Sparkles and Lucky have truly lived up to their names. Shine on, you precious pair of diamond hearts!

JuJu, Victoria

Pocket Rocket

It was the photo of an adventurous young Australian Cattle Dog mix up a tree that first made me fall in love with Rocket. Only seven months old, he had a plaster cast on his front leg as he'd injured himself trying to jump into a puppy pen. This was clearly an adventurous little soul, just waiting to get out and explore the world!

When I first brought Rocket home, he jumped out of the car and promptly tried to assert his authority over our other dog, a 50-kilogram Malamute, Mika, nearly three times his size! Thanks to Mika's tolerance, they soon became firm friends.

Rocket continued to excel at jumping in his new home. He would often leap our fences just to prove he could do it, I think. After his escape, he'd go off for a swim in the nearby creek, visit the horses, or drop in on our next-door neighbours, get spoilt with dog biscuits there and then trot happily home. Too many dog biscuits soon meant that Rocket couldn't launch himself over the 5-foot-high fence any more, so our two dogs hatched a plan. Mika would dig a little hole under the fence for Rocket, Rocket would push through the wire first, and Mika would then follow.

Rocket's true nature was yet to shine, however. My daughter Tahlia was born just over two years ago, and from the beginning Rocket has adored her. When he first sniffed her in the baby capsule, his tail started wagging intently. Later, when he would hear Tahlia start to cry, he would run to get my attention and let me know she was awake. As she grew older and would crawl outside into the yard, Rocket would lie close to her and watch, almost as if he was admiring her, and always with a smile on his face!

Tahlia is now two and as she has continued to grow and develop,

Rocket has been with her every step of the way. Every morning when she wakes her first words are 'Roccy, pat!' She will go outside and put a 'saddlecloth' on him and 'bridle' around his neck and sit on him like she's riding a horse. He doesn't move a muscle – he loves every bit of attention she gives him. She leads him into her cubbyhouse, shuts the door, and when she gives him the signal he jumps out the window. They repeat this game over and over. If he's outside and we're inside playing, he will lie watching Tahlia through the window, wagging his tail at her. If he sees his little mate hurt herself or cry, he jumps up and runs back and forth, trying to get inside to comfort her. When we throw his ball, Rocket will not bring it back to us – though he'll return it to Tahlia every time.

Rocket comes with us every day when we feed the horses. We ride the quad bike down and Tahlia sits on it while I tend to the various tasks. Rocket stays by the bike, guarding Tahlia. If she climbs off the bike, he quickly warns me that she's on the move. Not only are these two the best of friends, but Rocket helps reassure me that my little girl is never alone.

It is so sad that many people give up their dog when they have their first child, assuming the dog will be a problem with a baby. Of course precautions need to be made, but with good advice, your rescue dog can end up being a third parent to your little one – and that is something that definitely comes in handy!

Nel, New South Wales

The Real-Life Milo and Otis

Pic: *Herald Sun*

So many abandoned, unwanted and dumped dogs and cats come into Pets Haven, the animal shelter I volunteer at in Woodend, Victoria, and they are all beautiful and special in their own ways.

But some are truly unforgettable.

One day a small, scruffy terrier – starving and suffering from a bad case of mange on her back, and a tiny eight-week-old kitten were found huddled together, alone and frightened, in an industrial area of Melbourne.

The pair had become so close during their ordeal, that the tiny kitten had begun suckling from the female dog. And whenever the kitten was taken too far away from her canine friend, she would cry until they were reunited. The terrier was so gentle and loving towards the kitten. She let her climb all over her. She had obviously had puppies before and had taken on the role of mother to the frightened feline.

But the story gets even more amazing. While in foster care, this beautiful dog also began nursing six, seven-day-old puppies and a few more orphaned kittens. She wouldn't let any of them out of her sight and guarded them with vigilance.

All the while, the one that never left her side was the kitten she had been rescued with. Their bond was undeniable, and it was decided it should never be broken.

Trish Burke from Pets Haven named the pair Milo and Otis, after the children's movie about the friendship between a dog and cat. The *Herald Sun* heard about the amazing pair, and their story was featured on the front page. As a result, hundreds of caring people called, wanting to adopt the unlikely pair. But only one special person could be chosen.

After being nursed back to health, Milo and Otis began their new life in rural Victoria with Margaret, who, living alone after the loss of her husband, needed them as much as they needed her. Safe at last, and together forever!

Favel, Victoria

Farmer Jack

My son Jack is a little farmer, though only eleven years old. From an early age, he has had a passion for animals, something which we share. He also has aspergers (a form of autism), an intellectual disability and ADHD, so generally he is a very 'active' child.

Jack was interested in cattle and everything to do with agriculture. Fast forward a few years, and of course being the experienced cowboy that he is now, mustering cattle and cracking a whip (or two at the same time) wasn't quite enough for Jack. He voiced his desire to have what every true Aussie cowboy needs: a Kelpie. Living in suburbia, the idea of having a working dog seemed a bit cruel to me, so for a long time I managed to put him off the idea by telling him it wouldn't be fair to have such an active dog in our small backyard.

Early last year, Jack and I went to the Canberra Royal Show. We stayed a few nights in our swags, enjoying the atmosphere of being around the farm animals. When wandering around, we entered the animal farmyard nursery – a must if you love animals. There in a pen Jack spotted three Kelpie pups being cared for by a team of volunteers from Riverina and District Animal Rescue (RADAR). They were instructing the crowd about the joys of adopting a rescue dog. One look at a little fawn pup and both of our hearts just melted. He looked up at me, and my words of 'No Kelpie in a suburban backyard . . .' crept back into my head. But there was also an even stronger urge to have a happy Jack, who when focused on animals, copes so much better with everyday life. It didn't take long for me to say 'Yes, we want him,' to Jack's delight. His dream had come true.

Before we even left the nursery, the pup had been christened Dusty and it suited him to a T. A local photographer had set up a stand taking photos of children holding one of the farmyard nursery residents, and suddenly it was Dusty who became the star attraction. I'm sure there were dozens of children who had their photo taken with Dusty the Kelpie pup at Canberra Royal Show 2010 that day. Of course I had one taken of Jack with his new best friend, and you can see how happy he is by that smile on his face!

Once home, Dusty was introduced to the rest of the pack, and was rounding up the cats from day one. We overcame any concerns I had about a Kelpie in suburbia by finding a herding class for him to enjoy most Sundays. We have also travelled to Galong in New South Wales for Dusty to take part in weekend workshops at a sheep and cattle station. Of course it's Jack who takes Dusty into the ring – I'm just the photographer.

The bond between a boy and his dog is always special, but when the boy has a disability and the dog is a rescue from a life unknown, it certainly adds a whole new meaning. Jack gives unconditional love to Dusty, and vice versa. My son has a new purpose: a four-legged friend relies on him for food, love, comfort and learning. Dusty accepts Jack without any reservation. He doesn't care if he can't read or write properly – Dusty loves him because of all he does for him. Whether it be out in the field rounding up sheep, or curled up cuddling on the lounge together, this is a special friendship that will last many years. Jack says of his friend: 'One day I want to have a farm with cattle, I want to drive a ute and take Dusty with me, but he won't be sitting on the back, he will be in the front next to me.'

So how do you imagine I feel, to see my son who struggles in the academic world and in society in general, to be out in the country air, his Akubra hat on and his faithful working Kelpie, Dusty, by his side . . . Words can't explain it, and I don't know which takes over first, the huge smile on my face or the tears in my eyes.

Judy, New South Wales

A Guiding Spirit

One Sunday morning, my husband and I decided to have brunch at a café in the Rouse Hill Town Centre. This is something we like to do occasionally, followed by a browse of the shops. And we always pop into the RSPCA centre to look at the animals.

This particular morning we came upon Benji and Bam Bam. They had been surrendered by an elderly owner who had gone into a nursing home. They were obviously loved and due to one of the dog's blindness, the RSPCA was reluctant to separate the pair.

Benji had been blind since birth and his father, Bam Bam, had been his 'guide dog' all his life. When we discovered them, Benji was four years old and Bam Bam eight. Watching them in the pen at the RSPCA, Bam Bam was sitting on a trampoline and son Benji was barking in his face. Bam Bam looked like a parent who had a headache and needed a break! Wherever Bam went, Benji followed.

Like all the other mornings we had visited the RSPCA, we said goodbye and walked away. We already had a house full of pets: one ginger cat, Meggsie, one little black dog named Dax, about six parrots of various breeds and a friendly, egg-laying chicken named Maryanne.

But we were both unable to forget the doggy dad and his son, and worried about what would happen to the one left behind if something befell the other. How could we help protect them? We returned to the RSPCA to bring the duo home.

Initially, Bam Bam was very subdued and his son didn't stray far from his side. They got on with Dax famously, but Meggsie the cat, not so. There was often a lot of commotion due to our grandkids all wanting to look at Benji and ask a lot of questions about why he didn't have eyes. When this happened, Bam Bam looked very serious and would put himself between Benji and anyone else. He never got angry; he just looked out for Benji constantly.

Over the coming days and weeks, Benji would wander around the backyard discovering his new surroundings, learning where objects were by constantly bumping into them. Bam Bam would often watch him from the decking and every now and then, he would go to Benji's side to remind him he was not alone.

It's been a few months and Benji now knows where every blade of grass is. He jumps up onto the futon lounge on the decking where he spends a lot of his time and when it's feeding time, I put his dish down, tapping it until he finds it.

As for Bam Bam, he is experiencing his second childhood. This eight-year-old loves to play tug-of-war with his toys. He also loves to chase balls. When Bam Bam runs around playing with us, Benji can hear the excitement and barks happily. He has tried to join in but he couldn't get the idea of holding the ball in his mouth.

It's utter mayhem when the leashes come out for walking time. I sometimes take Benji and Bam Bam by themselves and it's sweet to watch them walking together, with Benji walking so close to his dad that they gently bump together.

Just recently, the council opened a leash-free dog park near where we live. Both Benji and Bam Bam get to run and run. Bam Bam was happy chasing his ball and son Benji was just happy to run freely without bumping into things. He loves rolling in the clover. The most exciting part was my grandson called out to me the other day that

Benji was running with the ball in his mouth. He didn't know where he was going, but he was finally part of the game.

We now have two close, quiet-natured dogs who have a new lease on life. They still sleep near each other, and eat out of the same bowl. Daddy Bam Bam plays like a pup and loves to cuddle up on the lounge in the evening while Benji is coming out of his shell and experiencing life more every day.

Our little boys have since become celebrities, too. Channel 9 heard about their story and featured them on the *Today* show. But like everything else the duo have experienced, they are taking fame firmly in their stride.

Benji and Bam Bam aren't the only rescue animals in our family, but they are a special little family unto themselves.

Robyn, New South Wales

Paddle Pop and Angus

Pic: *Herald Sun*

Paddle Pop, a Terrier mix, came to Animal Aid in Victoria as a result of the horrific Black Saturday Bushfires. Her condition was very poor: she was overweight and her skin was inflamed. She was a absolute mess. Luckily Susie Taylor, Animal Aid's Kennels Supervisor, could see the beauty within Paddle Pop, and as soon as she was well enough to leave the shelter, she adopted her. This is where a very special friendship began.

Angus, the resident bully boy of Susie's household, is a green-cheeked parakeet who barks like a dog and whistles at Susie's completely terrified other dogs. He seems to think he *is* a dog, in fact. But he has no time for Susie's canines, and lets them know in no uncertain terms.

And that's where part of the miracle of this new friendship lies.

From the very first day Paddle Pop arrived in Angus's domain, the feathered one had an unlikely change of heart towards the canine species. Angus was suddenly in love. In fact, he is quite besotted with Paddle Pop! The scruffy dog and parrot sleep together, share food – Angus even rides on his friend's back and preens her curly hair.

Susie says, 'I have always believed that Angus thinks he is a dog, and now that he has Paddle Pop as his sweetheart, I know that he does.'

Debra Boland, Animal Aid, Victoria

Two for One: Sticky the Cat-dog

We had just moved house and my old blind Boxer, Saky, was distraught. I had had to leave his best friend, another Boxer, behind, as the result of losing a custody battle. Saky howled every day for a week. She had only just had surgery to remove one of her eyes due to a glaucoma infection, and I was leaving her alone during the day when I went to work, which was torture for us both. I had to get her a new friend, and fast!

I decided a boisterous young puppy would be too challenging for Saky, but maybe a kitten would be perfect? It would be playful, but also have more independence than a puppy, so would give Saky time-out too when she needed it. I'd always been a 'dog person', so adopting a feline was a new experience for me. Little did I know I was really bringing another dog into our lives . . .

I spotted Sticky the kitten's profile on PetRescue and felt he might be the one. He was with Paws 'n' Hooves Animal Rescue and when I visited his carer's home, I was immediately submerged under a furry mass of playful kittens! Despite all the felines there to play with, Sticky only had eyes for me, following me everywhere. He secured his place in my heart after chasing me into the toilet and throwing himself onto my lap! I knew *he* had chosen me . . . not the other way around.

I brought the eight-week-old home and introduced him to my gentle giant, dear old Saky. I was worried that my huge 32-kilogram girl would inadvertently step on or blindly barrel over this tiny kitten, but after a few days I realised my fears were unfounded. On the contrary, Sticky sensed Saky's handicap and soon used it to his advantage! The kitten would sit on the couch and wait for Saky to amble past, at which point Sticky would quickly playfully swat Saky in the face and run away to hide. The old dog would give chase, trying to track the offending feline down by smell, only to receive another playful swat and the game would continue. Eventually, they would curl up together, exhausted and snoring. Who would have thought a tiny kitten would help give an old, blind dog such a new lease on life?

With Saky's doggy influence from such a young age, Sticky soon decided he wanted to be a dog too. He would jump into the shower with me, paddle around in the bath (aren't cats supposed to hate water?) and drink out of the toilet bowl. He claimed Saky's dog toys as his own and he would watch me throw balls to Saky to fetch. Sticky must have decided that a cat couldn't be a real dog unless he could play fetch too, and had to do something about it. One day I threw him a ball of screwed-up paper along the ground. Sticky picked it up, ran back to me and dropped it at my feet. I threw it again, and he brought it back once more. Sticky's game of fetch had just begun, and he wanted to play it for hours! He even got into the habit of sitting up on his haunches and wagging his tail while waiting for the ball of paper to be thrown. I was gobsmacked: I had a rescue dog living in a rescue cat's body!

Life after being rescued has been good to Sticky – even if he does have an identity crisis! – but even more wonderful for Saky. From the start, my old girl was besotted with the kitten, sticking her nose to the ground and following him everywhere. In a way, Sticky almost become Saky's seeing-eye cat! Saky soon realised she could charge along behind her small friend and (usually!) not smack into things – the kitten would guide her way. Within hours I was able to leave the house without Saky whimpering: she had a new friend to rely on.

Soon, Saky became less stiff and more agile. There's nothing like a friendly cat swipe in the face to get Saky out of bed in the morning for an early aerobic workout around the house. Sticky the cat-dog brings out the puppy in my old girl . . . And neither of us can imagine life without him!

In loving memory of Saky, who passed away soon after this piece was written.

Jo, New South Wales

Meant to Be

When my son Jai turned five, he started to ask why his sister had her own dog while he didn't have one. It was a fair question! Finally, a few months ago, I decided that it was time to bring another pup into our lives. I spent countless hours on the phone talking with the foster carers of many rescue dogs and finally located a small black puppy, just two months old and not too far from our home, that I thought Jai would love. I printed out a picture of the pup to show him and was waiting with it at the school gate that afternoon. Excited, I showed it to him and his friends. It was the cutest pup I'd ever seen and the kids as well as the other mums fell in love with the little one then and there. Everyone wanted her . . . except my son! His response was simply, 'No, Mum, that's not my dog.'

The entire way home my daughter and I tried to persuade Jai that the pup was the one for him, but to no avail. So later I sat him down in front of the computer and told him to look through the hundreds of dogs on PetRescue needing homes so he could show me the type of dog he wanted. That's how he found Leo.

He printed me a picture and handed it to me. 'Here he is, Mum – this is my dog.'

I nervously called the rescue group Domestic Animal Birth-Control Society (DABS) and arranged a meeting. I explained that the dog needed to get along with all the other animals in the family, had to be good with children, and eventually fit in with us all. I felt sick. I didn't want my baby to be disappointed. He was so sure Leo was 'his dog'.

The day arrived. When Leo first met my son, he rolled over on his back and asked for a tummy rub. He now sleeps at the end of Jai's bed and lets him carry him (rather awkwardly) around the house. We have had him for a few weeks now and every once in a while I see my son lean and whisper into Leo's ear, 'I knew you were my dog.'

Fiona, New South Wales

You've Got a Friend in Me...All Three!

Pic: Alex Cearns

It was fate that brought Max and me together. Not only was it my birthday, it was also the eve of the day I had planned to go see the puppy I had been looking at adopting. Something made me decide to first check if the local pound had a dog rehoming program, however. After a few clicks on the City of Stirling website, there he was – one of six Akita Whippet mix pups born at the pound, available for adoption the following day! It was love at first sight . . . the white and brindle pup with the cheekiest smile – tongue sticking out and all – had stolen my heart!

It is now two years since the day the gutsy, cheeky five-week-old version of Max – 'Maxi BonBon' – came into my life. He still makes me feel the same way as he did back then . . . puppy love having transformed into true love! Max has grown up to be a handsome boy, well-mannered and gentle enough to be around DJ BunBunz, my rescue bunny! But more of that later.

Max has such a great personality that I decided to create an online social networking profile for him due to demand from friends – cats, dogs and their owners – who we met during an online pet competition. Since the creation of Max's Facebook profile, he's made pals not only around Australia, but from all over the world, including the USA, the UK and Canada. Max also uses his online presence to help spread the word about rescue pets, and this has caught the attention of local media and the wider community. But even with Max's soaring popularity, he remains a down-to-earth and adorable dog. Our journey so far has been made up of laughter, tears, happiness, worries, surprises, frustration, attitude, chewed-off bits of reticulation, memories of a once beautiful yard, *lots* of love and . . . Sambuca!

At the seventh-month point of our journey, the unexpected addition to our pack arrived – a three-month-old black-and-tan mixed-breed puppy who was left homeless twice in his short life due to no fault of his own. Sambuca was originally sold through a pet shop as a Rottweiler Labrador mix and was given up the first time when he didn't grow up to look like one. His second owner had no time for him, and Sambuca ended up being left by them at a local dog-boarding facility. It was fortunate that the operators were kind and responsible people, and they were determined to find Sambuca a forever home.

Fate of course brought Sambuca (now affectionately known as Sammy 'SamSam') and I together. I just happened to be at the boarding facility for a once-off work-related visit when the operators told me about him. A shaky start to the young pup's life was starting to take its toll and he didn't deserve it. I agreed to take him home for the weekend, longer if things worked out with Max, or until we could find Sambuca a permanent home. (Back then, little did any of us know that we had already found such a home for Sambuca . . . right here with me!) The experience I'd already had with Max was such a positive one, that it was a major reason why I did not hesitate to consider giving Sambuca a chance at having a stable life.

Now, you may be wondering how two large rescue dogs and a bunny can live together. DJ BunBunz was rescued from a backyard breeder, and would you believe is the 'big brother' in the pack, with an attitude to match! Both Max and Sambuca have grown up with DJ, and a lot of effort has gone into socialising and supervising the three of them to minimise any predator-prey risks and to make sure that DJ is safe. Both Max and Sambuca know their boundaries and keep out of DJ's area, which is on top of Max's indoor crate. Under supervision, all three are able to 'hang out' together and watch TV, with their favourite show being *The Bondi Vet*, of course. Sometimes, DJ will even groom Max and Sambuca and vice-versa! DJ packs a huge personality in his tiny size, and loves living on the edge . . . never a dull moment in this household!

Life has been an adventure with them all, and will continue to be.

People often tell me that Max, Sambuca and DJ are such lucky pets: what a favour I've done them by giving them a second or even third chance in life. Nonsense, I say – these three have rewarded me a hundred-fold: they've taught me so much, including the true meaning of unconditional love, trust and loyalty. They aren't just my pets . . . they are my friends for life!

Juliet, Western Australia

Isis and Uno's Second Chance

Our family have always been dog people. Four years ago, however, after the loss of our last dog, Monte, we rescued a stray cat. It was a learning curve – we had no idea how different dogs and cats really were! We soon realised dogs are like dependent toddlers, always at your side, needing you. Cats are like independent teenagers who do what they want, when they want! But we soon bonded with our new cat Uno, and he really is a sweet, gentle boy.

It wasn't long before we knew we couldn't go on without a dog, but we were concerned about Uno's reaction if we were to adopt a canine. We took the plunge and began searching for dogs on Victorian Dog Rescue's website. That's where we found Isis. We were instantly intrigued because her biography said she got along well with cats. She also looked very unusual – while she is a Chihuahua mix and is very small, she has colouring of an Australian Cattle Dog!

When my parents and I met Isis for the first time, we knew she was 'the one'. But the first few weeks were really hard introducing Isis to Uno. We had to keep them in separate rooms. Our new canine wasn't too worried, but Uno was grumpy and unsure. We bribed him with plenty of prawns (every cat's dream!) while Isis got lots of Schmackos. After about four weeks, our patience was rewarded. Uno accepted Isis after a lot of excess pampering and our use of special introduction techniques we found on YouTube. Soon, as Uno and Isis passed each other in the hallway, they began to stop and sniff at each other with curiosity.

Uno quickly became fascinated by Isis's wagging tail, which waves side-to-side like a windscreen wiper. He would stop her tail with his paw so he could inspect it, and Isis would try to hide it between her legs, unsure of Uno's intentions. Now that Uno realises his friend's tail is not a mouse, he leaves it alone and she is free to wag it all the time. They sleep together on the couch now, or out in the sun, and give each other licks and kisses as greetings every day.

Both Uno and Isis have brought us a lot of joy. We feel honoured to be giving them both their second chance, and to watch them make the most of it, together.

Stacey, Victoria

Teddy and His Rooster

Our handsome dog Teddy came into our lives when Dad came across a gangly young Airedale Terrier German Shepherd mix roaming the Chadstone Shopping Centre car park. The hungry and homeless stray was wandering around, sniffing the rubbish bins and looking for scraps. Poor Teddy had no collar and no tags. In those days that meant there was little hope of finding his owner.

Dad's heart broke. Fortunately, with the help of our friend and soon-to-be accomplice, Dad's heart recovered very quickly. They had a plan! Dad had a young family at home . . . all it would take was persuading Mum – a cat person, however – into agreeing that the gangly dog should stay. That was when we kids jumped in and of course talked her into it, so stay he did!

In time Teddy calmed down, as young excitable dogs do, and became very protective. It was Teddy's territorial barking that saved our house, and that of our closest neighbours, from burglary when all the homes in the surrounding streets were 'done over'. But we particularly loved observing the way Teddy watched over our chooks: five girls and one rooster. The young rooster was very conscientious, too, ensuring 'his girls' were where they had to be and when they had to be there: in their coops at night and out again after laying in the morning. But the amazing thing was that Teddy was the rooster's back up. The two boys watched over their chooks together constantly and with endless enthusiasm. It was an unusual mateship.

Unfortunately, our summers can be harsh and the heat and humidity can catch people and animals unawares. One unbearably hot day our rooster got heatstroke. The other creatures had carefully conserved their energy by resting in the shade and drinking plenty of water, but for some reason the rooster just couldn't manage. Tragically, he died.

Teddy's reaction to the unexpected death of his friend is the extraordinary part of this story. Following the sad discovery of the rooster's body, Teddy carried his lifeless friend to the shaded annex of his kennel. The poor dog howled, paced and then sat grieving beside his friend's lifeless form. He'd let no one near. He was distraught.

Eventually Dad came home to the sad news and it was decided it was time to bury the rooster, particularly because of the heat. Teddy watched mournfully as Dad dug the hole. The rooster was laid to rest in the shady back corner of the garden, with a steel plate and heavy spare tyre placed over him, not to mark the spot but to keep the master digger, watching on, from trying to retrieve his beloved mate.

For two days Teddy sat on the tyre, howling mournfully. He'd come reluctantly for his dinner but we respectfully moved his water bowl closer to his friend's grave. The chooks carried on 'unmanaged' for a few days until eventually Teddy's heartache healed at least a little bit. He came back on duty but without the customary zeal or enthusiasm 'the boys' had had together.

Teddy had many madcap adventures in his lifetime, but the sincerity he showed to his fellow beings was always special. The rooster was always his favourite, though.

I imagine them both in heaven now, watching over 'their girls' together again, happy and content in each other's good company.

Karen, Victoria

Cheeky's Little Buddy

We were on a normal walk on a normal day when Buddy first found his Cheeky mate.

Our beautifully natured rescue poodle was attempting to pull in a different direction from me, and seemed quite anxious that I was going the opposite way. That's not like Buddy, I thought, giving in to him. Whimpering loudly, he pulled us towards what I thought was a small dirt mound, but to my horror, there we found a dead mother cat with a sole baby kitten trying to suckle from her.

The flea-ridden kitten, who looked about six weeks old, was in a pretty bedraggled state. How long had he and his mum been living out in the elements? I did what anyone would do – picked up the poor mite and brought him home, Buddy trotting anxiously at my side the whole way.

From the moment we got home Buddy would not leave his kitten's side. I found a bed for the little one and Buddy would attempt to get in with him, as though trying to keep him warm. Cheeky even attempted to suckle from Buddy and silly old Bud would lift his leg as though to say, 'Oh, okay . . .'

Buddy watched over that little kitten as though he was his guardian angel. He would nudge Cheeky toward his Whiskas milk, then clean Cheeky up after he had finished lapping. It was a precious sight to see not only a different species, but a male dog, care for another kind in this way. And the admiration is mutual: when I bath Buddy, Cheeky is there by the side of the bath tub, making sure Buddy is all right.

Recently I cared for an elderly cat called Blackie for a work colleague who was on holidays. Buddy must have realised that this twenty-year-old was fragile and lame as he didn't leave her side the entire two weeks she was with us. Buddy whimpered every time he watched Blackie hobble to the kitty litter, and would nudge her behind with his nose in an attempt to help her into the tray. Buddy is a true inspiration. I can't thank the Sydney Animal Shelter enough for saving Buddy, so he could save Cheeky, and continue to lighten all our lives.

Patricia, New South Wales

A Friend in Need

Even though we already had two beautiful rescue dogs, I couldn't help still looking at PetRescue, where so many other deserving dogs were waiting for their second chance.

One day I saw a little Chinese Crested girl that needed a home. Because our second rescue dog, Gizmo, with his beautiful nature, is a Chinese

Crested, I couldn't bear to think of another without a loving family.

I contacted the rescue group and discovered the little lady I saw on PetRescue had a brother, and they needed a very special home . . . together. Their names were Coco and Bruce. They had had a hard time of life and were very afraid of people. Undaunted, I pledged to give them both a loving forever home, and the day came to collect them.

When they were first let out of their transport crate, the two shot off and hid behind the couch. When it was time for dinner, we put their bowls out, walked away and watched. Coco and Bruce very slowly and warily came up and ate their dinner.

It didn't take long before Coco and Bruce realised they were safe and they were soon running crazily through the house just like our other two dogs.

Our 22-year-old daughter Cassandra suffers from mild autism. She's at home most days while we are at work. She has had trouble with people picking on her, or taking advantage of her kind nature. However, over the past eighteen months since Coco and Bruce entered our lives, these two little ones have made a huge difference to our daughter. During the day they sleep on her bed if she is there, or follow her around the house and garden as if she is the Pied Piper. The way they look at her with unconditional love and devotion melts my heart. They don't care if she talks differently or is clumsy – they simply love her for who she is.

Cassandra is equally aware of little Coco's needs: 'She is afraid of storms, but I look after her when she is frightened,' she says. As for Bruce: 'He follows me around everywhere which I like because I know that I am safe and never alone. He worries about me when I'm upset and always comes to see if I am all right.'

Cassandra tells me she's so glad we saved these two little dogs, because she doesn't know what she would do without them now. I can only agree.

Sarah, New South Wales

Noddy Saves the Day

To begin with there were two of them – two magnificent Great Danes, Georgia and Odin. Georgia had been around for a long time before Odin the gangly puppy came to join her, and as he grew they became best friends. Georgia was his protector and his comfort. But she became old and ill, and when she died, Odin's world fell to pieces.

For two months, Odin grieved. He stopped eating, so the weight dropped off him, he was constantly unhappy, he suffered such severe separation anxiety that it became impossible to leave him alone, and he lived with thick ropes of stress-induced drool hanging from his jowls. My friends Axel and Leslie, his owners, did everything they could to help him, but it gradually became evident that they were in danger of losing Odin too.

That was when they had a brilliant idea – it was obvious Odin needed a companion and that a puppy probably wouldn't do. Why not investigate adopting a Greyhound? Because we'd been friends for years, and I'm a foster carer for the Greyhound Adoption Program of South Australia, Axel and Leslie came to me to discuss their needs.

It seemed to me to be an obvious solution to introduce Odin to boisterous, laid back, happy-go-lucky Noddy, who I was fostering at the time. If anyone could cheer Odin up, Noddy could! We headed over.

It wasn't love at first sight. Odin was not impressed; he gave Noddy a thorough bum-sniffing and once-over. Noddy, a fairly big boy for a Greyhound, was so overawed by seeing a dog that towered over him he just stood there. Odin made no further overtures but slouched off to his verandah. There had been no growling, so we bravely set Noddy free so he could investigate the 2-acre back yard.

After a while, Odin decided he had better keep an eye on this interloper and got up and followed him. Gradually, the dogs began to relax and we saw a few tentative tail wags. Would our experiment work? Could Noddy save Odin? After about half an hour I left them to it. The arrangement was that I would not foster another dog until we were sure this was going to work out, so that there was a place for Noddy to return to if worse came to worst.

At the end of the weekend, I rang to find out how Odin was going. The family were still hopeful but unsure: Odin was growling at Noddy whenever he went near any of his possessions, but they were playing together occasionally and sleeping in the same room. Odin was beginning to eat a bit better too, so this was promising news.

It wasn't until ten days later that I got the call I hoped for: 'We are keeping Noddy – come and see them.'

Noddy greeted me enthusiastically, and Odin – a totally different Odin – barked at me to protect his new friend. In that fortnight he'd put on weight, stopped drooling, allowed the family to go out and leave him with Noddy, and rediscovered his joy in life.

About eight months later we had a fierce storm through our valley and received a worried phone call from my friends. One of their fences had blown down. Odin respected the old boundary but Noddy was keen to investigate: Could I look after Noddy until the weekend when they would set to work and repair the damage? Of course I was happy to help, and Noddy settled back into my home quite comfortably.

To my surprise my friends turned up again about midday on Saturday to collect Noddy. I remarked that they must have worked like slaves to finish the fence in that time. Their reply delighted me. 'No, we won't finish it before tomorrow evening, but Odin is unbearable. He's howled and cried for Noddy ever since we dropped him off. We've got the fence posts up and strung baling twine across them. It'll have to do – none of us, Odin particularly, can bear life without Noddy any longer!'

Jennie, South Australia

The Doofus and the Genius

Rufus fitted in from day one. A small male German Shepherd, he appealed to me from the moment I saw him at the pound. Friendly, affectionate, responsive: this perfect foster dog would be easy to rehome. He got on well with my other dogs and with everyone he met. Unfortunately, I lost my two remaining rescue dogs shortly after Rufus arrived and fortunately for him and me, I decided to keep him.

After Rufus, Grace the cat arrived and then I decided to foster a kitten with the idea of adopting a second cat. I ended up fostering not one but *four* kittens: Elmo, Oscar, Cookie Monster and Grover. These five-week-olds came to live in my spare bathroom. Each was the size of my hand, sickly and in need of medication twice a day. It was expected that not all would live. As I bonded with the kittens, I would allow Rufus to look at them over a barrier. At first little Grover hissed at the big dog while the other kittens just looked at him with interest, one even coming closer. Rufus was excited and curious about them. Once I was sure he could contain his enthusiasm, I allowed him to come into the bathroom with me. The kittens explored the hairy mound of German Shepherd, massaging him with their needle-sharp claws, sniffing him in awkward places and trying to work out if this was their new mother. For his part, Rufus would pick up each kitten and carefully clean them all over. While Grover was never really happy about this arrangement, the other tiny ones soon bonded with their 'foster dad'.

Grover and Elmo were rehomed in turn and I was left with just Cookie and Oscar. I had initially decided to keep Cookie, as she and I were strongly bonded, but Oscar and Rufus had other ideas. The boys were as one. They had mutual grooming sessions, chasing games, stalking of Rufus' fluffy tail and so on. I made the inevitable decision to rehome Cookie and keep Oscar – how could I part such friends? Anyway, I was falling for the little tuxedo with the big white whiskers myself.

Today, eighteen months on, Rufus and Einstein (the kitten formerly known as Oscar) are as closely bonded as two animals could be. The dog only has to walk past the cat for him to start purring. The cat seeks the dog out to massage and groom him, and the dog returns the affection by licking and 'flea-biting' the cat. If Rufus chases Einstein, the cat runs and rolls over on his back and surrenders to the big hairy one. Occasionally, while being groomed, Rufus will yelp and growl – a sharp kitty claw in an uncomfortable place – but Einstein is instantly forgiven. The cat licks inside the dogs' ears and the dog licks the cat all over. Quite often my bed is invaded by both dog and cat and I feel that I should perhaps leave them alone for some private time . . .

Rufus is three years old now; Einstein eighteen months. Rufus is working on his obedience titles, but Einstein can still play fetch better. Grace watches on, incredulous of it all. Everyone is content in their niche. None of them know yet . . . but they're getting a little German Shepherd sister in a couple of weeks!

Maya, Victoria

Floyd Comes to the Fore

Floyd always loved Max, but Max was mostly indifferent to Floyd. One day, an act of bravery changed all that.

We rescued Max from the pound around ten years ago. He was meant to be around four years old then, a black-and-grey Maltese Terrier mix and, for most of his life, he had the temperament of a grumpy old man. We loved him anyway, of course. He had some strange habits, though – one of which was to only drink water from our shower or fish pond. He never wanted to drink from a bowl.

As time went on, we decided Max might be rejuvenated by having a young playmate. That's when Floyd entered the picture. We found him, a fluffy white Shih Tzu mix, at another pound and fell in love with him immediately. His Albino colouring meant he had pink-rimmed eyes, so we named him after Pink Floyd. Floyd didn't seem like the sharpest knife in the drawer, though – he was a little dopey but exceptionally loving.

Much to Max's displeasure, Floyd instantly became his little 'white' shadow. He followed him everywhere, sometimes within millimetres of him; other times, he just pounced all over his big brother. Most of the time, Max was not impressed and would give me a look that said: 'Yeah, thanks very much for the playmate, Mum.' You can observe the two different relationships in the photograph above. Oh dear!

A little over a year ago, we went on holidays. We had a wonderful house-sitter who loved dogs and took great care of Max and Floyd. But, upon our return, our elderly neighbour Bert told us a story that still brings tears to my eyes.

Bert said that he and his wife were about to sit down for an early dinner when they could hear one of our dogs barking incessantly – definitely not normal for them. At first, they thought nothing of it. After dinner, they went outside and could still hear the barking. Bert's wife insisted he find out what was going on, and thank goodness she did.

Bert climbed up and peered over the fence. He could see Floyd running madly around our fish pond, barking desperately. In the pond, he could make out our Max paddling around, in distress, and obviously unable to pull himself out.

With the summer heat, and us not there to keep an eye on it, the pond's water level had drastically dropped. Max had, as usual, gone for a drink but the low level meant he had to reach down further. He'd clearly fallen in and couldn't pull himself out.

Bert hurried over to our house and was able to pull Max out with the aid of a broomstick. Would you believe Max 'thanked' him with a growl and a snap? At least he was on dry ground and saved!

Even though Max has now gone to Rainbow Bridge, that experience made me love him more for the strength and stamina he showed – he must have paddled around and around, increasingly tiring, for at least half an hour or more. It also made me love Floyd more and realise that he is not as silly as he looks. Without him calling for help, Max would surely have drowned.

But, the truly wonderful thing was that, after this accident, Max himself had a new regard for Floyd – his first regard, in fact! Floyd still pounced all over him and followed him everywhere, but Max didn't seem to mind as much any more. Floyd had proven himself not half as annoying as Max once thought!

Floyd has missed Max terribly since we bid him farewell. Fortunately we have friends who have a new canine friend. Bollo is a black Labrador mix and is just as playful and loving as Floyd. They get along famously and Floyd gets to be the little white shadow once again.

Tina, Western Australia

Soul Mates

Do you believe in soul mates – that there can be uniquely strong connections between particular individuals? Well, I have seen it between a little girl and a rescue dog.

The story starts one weekend when we received some new homeless animals to care for. There was nothing new about this, as we are foster carers for Dog Rescue Newcastle. We are used to taking dogs in, loving them, caring for them and then – with a great wrench – letting them go. Our sadness is short as we know the new family will love them dearly. Each time a pet moves on to a forever home, room is made in ours for another life to be saved.

That weekend we received a very matted and sick little guy named Pumba. He was in such bad shape that we couldn't even tell what breed he was. Fortunately his personality was so vibrant that we were absolutely confident he would find a good home with someone to love him. Little did we know!

My nine-year-old daughter Georgia took over care of Pumba, who after thorough grooming turned out to be a Maltese mix. Like other dogs she had cared for, Georgia gave him his medication and his meals. She brushed him, walked him, slept with him and carried him everywhere. Yet, despite this, I didn't feel that anything unusual was happening. My children understand we prepare rescue dogs for rehoming and that we can't keep them all.

The day eventually came that Pumba was to leave for his forever home. A kind woman called Avis was adopting him and Georgia was taking the day off school to say goodbye. Yet as Georgia cuddled and kissed him farewell, we could almost see her heart breaking. Avis too was upset, watching what Georgia was going through, but had looked forward to this day – she too needed a companion. When Avis and

Pumba went out to the car, Georgia ran inside and, face down on the lounge, sobbed her heart out.

I didn't know what to do. My daughter had never once hinted that she wanted to keep Pumba! She went on to have an asthma attack and had the week off school. She only slept intermittently, waking up crying during the night. I was beside myself with worry.

Poor Avis and Pumba weren't fairing any better. He simply wasn't settling in his new home. Avis cooked all his favourite foods but he wouldn't eat and had to be hand fed. She nursed him for hours on end. The situation got worse when the little dog saw kids walking past the house. Was one of them Georgia? He would run to the door and try to get out!

Avis rang me and asked how Georgia was coping. I had to be honest and say she wasn't. Avis understood completely, as she had recently lost a much-loved dog herself and was heartbroken. She couldn't keep Pumba and Georgia apart.

When I told Georgia that Pumba was coming home, she cried with relief. But she was instantly worried about Avis not having her own dog, so we searched for another little friend for her. The new rescue pup we found settled in with Avis immediately, and they love each other deeply.

The day that Georgia and Pumba were reunited is a story I love to share. The moment he saw my daughter he ran to her, jumping up and down. Georgia gave him some lunch she had saved especially for her little friend. In the car on the way home, he leapt onto her lap, lay on his back and stretched out his legs.

The little soul mates slept all the way home.

Eileen, New South Wales

The Odd Couple

The favourite thing for my rescue dog Fernando and I to do on a Saturday morning is to meet my friend Jackie and her dog Josh (who is also a rescue dog) at the local dog beach. Not only are Jackie and I best buddies, but so are our dogs Fernando and Josh!

It was love at first sight for this odd couple. Josh is a black Pointer (pictured above right) and much larger than my small Terrier mix, but this doesn't hinder their friendship at all. Josh is wonderful with Fernando, always keen to play and gentle when they do. Tug-of-war is their favourite game. If one dog 'wins' by the other letting go, the winner will make sure the loser can grab the toy in his mouth again, and off they go once more.

Fernando knows who I'm talking about when I say the word 'Josh!' and he responds by getting very excited. He starts crying with joy and jumps on my legs. When we get to the beach, Fernando races around to find Josh, and when they finally meet he kisses and licks Josh around his mouth. 'Hi, buddy!' Not only that, when we go to leave, Fernando desperately tries to get into Josh's car! I try not to take it personally.

I feel that Fernando looks up to Josh like a role model and a mentor. There seems to be some sort of understanding from one rescue dog to another – true acceptance and love. We have a lot to learn from these four-legged friends.

Julie, Victoria

The True Meaning of Mateship

My wife and I enjoy a perfect marriage; she lives in Yarraville and I live 65 kilometres away in Geelong. I've been there thirty years, and that's when my four-footed mate, Buzz, came into my life. At last, I had a constant, uncritical companion.

Buzz was a gift from my mate Pat. 'Here you are, Wal,' he said. 'He's the best of the litter and I want him to have a good home.' (Pat makes you feel *you* are doing *him* a favour – he wouldn't want you to know he cared.)

Buzz, despite his puppy escapades, was everything a man could wish for. At night, he would sit at my feet with his head on my knee – his expressive brown eyes never leaving my face. Although I'd worked with guide dogs all my life, I had never known such constant devotion.

Buzz and I were great mates for twelve years, until the moment came that every pet owner dreads: he was diagnosed with a terminal illness and it was my duty to end his life in the most humane way. After he died, I vowed I would never go through that trauma again or bond with another dog.

A decent time later, Pat came around again, bearing a cute, five-month-old cream Lab pup. 'You can see he has chocolate pigmentation, so he's no good for the show ring,' said Pat.

The new pup was just Pat's kind way to help me over the loss of Buzz – he's that kind of bloke. So I called this dog Jazz. Everyone loved his 'roll-over-and-tickle-my-tummy' tricks, but there was only ever one Buzz in my life and I didn't have the same deep bond with Jazz that I had with his predecessor.

We got along well for ten years, Jazz and me, and then Pat turned up with yet another pup in a box. 'Now, look, Pat,' I said. 'I deeply appreciate you keeping me supplied with dogs, but right now I need another puppy like a hole in the head.'

'Jazz is getting on, and he'll soon have to be replaced,' said Pat. 'Meanwhile, the old dog can teach the young dog new tricks. His name's Rocky, unless you want to change it.'

You can't argue with a pal like Pat. Rocky, at ten weeks of age, was a direct descendant from Buzz's breeding line. How could I say no?

The older dog's mentoring instincts immediately went to work on his new companion. He soon became young Rocky's protector. He would hackle up and attack any other dog that dared to threaten his little mate, no matter how big or vicious they happened to be.

One hot day, when Rocky was two years old, I took the dogs for a swim, and then a run on the grass to dry off. Noticing a rustle in the long grass, young Rocky poked his nose in. At the same time, Jazz and I saw the large snake. Impulsive Rocky, thinking the snake was a new playmate, went after it. But Jazz was faster. An 'unsuitable-for-show-rings' pigmented body placed itself between its young charge and the snake. I yelled at them both to come back, but Jazz knew what he had to do: keep Rocky away from danger. He snarled, growled and barked, circling for an opening. The snake reared to strike, but Jazz was swift. Sinking his canines into the snake's neck, he shook it violently, fighting the reptile to its death.

Shaking, I bundled the exhausted Jazz and Rocky into the car and rushed them to the vet, who assured me that neither the valiant Jazz nor the mischievous Rocky had been bitten. After that near miss, I felt much closer to both my dogs.

They settled down to a life of domestic bliss. Rocky would follow his saviour Jazz wherever he went and at night, Rocky would sleep at Jazz's feet on the floor. Sometimes, young Rocky would come to me for a pat, but he always returned to his beloved 'father'.

Tragedy struck again when Jazz turned fourteen and suffered a stroke.

Rocky and I kept vigil with him all night, fearing the worst when he refused food and would not be moved. Rocky kept nuzzling Jazz and whimpering, but there was no way I could assure him his 'dad' would pull through.

Next day, I took the old fella to the vet who advised what I expected, but did not want to hear. I arrived home, carrying only Jazz's lead and collar, to be greeted by a distraught Rocky looking for his mate. Where is he? his stricken eyes implored me.

Rocky was in a state of bewilderment for days and off his food – wandering from favourite place to place, searching for Jazz, until his coat became dull and lacklustre. Understanding his confusion, my sympathy went out to him, yet I could not seem to give him the love and affection he desperately needed. So I spared more time for Rocky, taking him with me whenever I could and allowing him inside the house more often.

Today he still goes whimpering to Jazz's chair, but he realises his foster dad is never coming home. I believe that fate had a hand in helping Jazz save Rocky from the snake that traumatic day. Perhaps Jazz knew I'd soon need him.

Rocky and I are now inseparable. He comes to me and sits with his jet-black head resting on my knee. I look into Rocky's bright-brown eyes, and I almost see my first old four-footed mate, his ancestor, Buzz, gazing back.

Wally, Victoria

Who's Rescuing Who?

*Any dog adopted from a rescue group is a lucky one:
they'll get a fresh shot at life with a loving family
who've been screened to ensure the fit is right.
But sometimes it is the pet's effect on the new owner
that is most profound – nothing short of life-saving.*

The Best Therapy

After living in central London for eight years, it was time for Dan and I to move back home. Our distant shoebox existence left us yearning for some space around us, a backyard, a vegie patch, more time with family . . . and a dog. At the top of the list was definitely a dog!

We arrived back in Melbourne and married eight weeks later. So much joy, and so much to look forward to within our families. We had the world at our feet.

But six months later, Dan's younger sister fell ill and died very suddenly. She was only thirty-two years old. It absolutely devastated his tight-knit family, and her fiancé, with whom she was soon to start a life. One moment there was hope and promise, the next, an awful, yawning, black void.

Returning home after her funeral, we had to go back to work and tried to carry on. While my job took me out into the world and into a busy office every day, Dan worked from home, and spent ten or so hours a day alone. And being winter in Melbourne, the days were very long, dark and cold.

I was worried about my husband, alone with only his thoughts. I figured he needed a buddy. So I started looking on PetRescue, and one day, I discovered Bonnie.

This scruffy, lanky pup was clearly in need of some love and affection. I phoned Animal Aid at Coldstream to enquire about her and was informed that she'd been adopted already, but that her brother, Clyde, was still available. I was disappointed that we'd missed out on Bonnie – there was something about her little face that spoke to me – but Dan suggested we head out to the shelter anyway, just 'for a look'. Looking back, thank goodness I didn't disagree.

We drove to Coldstream, and there, behind the counter with her brother, leaving puddles on the floor, was Bonnie. She hadn't been adopted after all! There was a mix-up, and she was still in need of a home. I could barely stop myself jumping over the counter to claim her.

She was a little stand-offish around us initially, but in no time, she was curled up, snug in my lap. That was it – love! So of course we adopted her there and then.

The hard part was that we had to wait two weeks before we could bring her home while she was desexed and microchipped. However, even just the first meeting with Bonnie had a positive effect on both of us. Planning for the arrival of our new family member put a bit of light back in our lives, and gave us something new and exciting to talk about.

Once home on that special day, Bonnie's bond with Dan was immediate. It was as though she knew she had a job to do: brighten his day! I think he loved having someone to care for while I was at work, and she, in turn, adored him. A wriggling, happy, inquisitive pup who would bark at power cords and growl at hats was the perfect antidote to grief and loneliness. He'd work and she'd put her head on his knee and stare at him until he responded, or she'd sleep and dream the dreams only dogs know about, or she'd nudge him, wanting to play or explore the world outside.

And, as anyone who has experienced loss knows, finding someone who will just listen without trying to fix things is priceless. Dan loved having this small creature by his side, getting to know her signals and building trust. She gave him a reason to get up every day, to get out for a walk, or call me at work with updates and photos.

In turn, this new addition was celebrated by our extended families. Dan's parents and siblings couldn't wait to meet Bonnie, and hear more about her adventures. She joined us on holidays and anniversaries, and made us smile. She does wild, mad donuts of joy in the backyard when her energy overflows, talks to us, 'dream-barks' and still growls at strange things – stacks of newspapers, hoses, balloons, the mosaic chair in Fitzroy . . .

I think it's fair to say not only did Bonnie help us through our grief, she was sent to do so. One thing is sure – we know she's the best thing we've brought into our lives.

Prue, Victoria

Unwrapping Lucy

After my four-year-old son Kye was diagnosed with autism, I geared myself up with a wealth of knowledge on how to best assist him. Hearing that animals can be therapeutic to the aged and people with special needs aroused my curiosity. Perhaps it was time to bring a dog into our lives?

Lucy was listed by Dog Rescue Newcastle as mature, placid, but with 'playful antics'. I also needed her to be good with children, and very patient. When we went to meet Lucy at her foster carer's home she ran straight to my boys and me, so the decision was made by her!

Kye laughs uncontrollably when Lucy jumps in the air. He looks into Lucy's eyes when he strokes her, which is a great milestone for Kye as autistic children tend to have trouble making eye contact. His speech has also developed, and it is easy to see the trust he has in his four-legged friend. Everything in Kye has improved since Lucy entered our lives.

Our rescue girl is like a Christmas present: we unwrap her personality every day. We discovered she loves balls, likes to swim, is protective, and never runs away when not on a leash. We may only have a few years left with Lucy because of her age, but she has been a delight, and she has done more for us than we could ever do for her.

Belinda, New South Wales

A Reason to Dry My Eyes

Most humans would say that it was me who saved little Cody when he became loveless for the second time in his short life. But I think you will agree it was him that pulled me back from the brink.

Cody's first terrible episode was at the age of nine weeks, being dumped to wander the streets. Fortunately he was found and taken in by a loving old lady. But when she was forced to go into hospital Cody faced despair again.

Meanwhile, my heart was becoming homeless too. It was Easter Saturday, the day I knew that my dog Flo and I would have to say the saddest of farewells to Freddy, the ten-year-old Maltese Bichon mix whom we had loved so much. Freddy had a serious tumour and was uncomfortable, so putting him to sleep was the kindest thing to do.

Flo, herself a Maltese Bichon mix three years younger than Fred, was very distressed and cried for her lost friend all day Easter Sunday. So the next morning I took her to the vet who gave her something to calm her, one tablet then and there, and said to give her another half tablet that evening.

I woke suddenly at 4.30 a.m. the next morning. Flo was not in her usual position on the pillow next to me, but had moved down the bed. Picking her up, I gave her a cuddle and put her back on the pillow. Then, she sighed and suddenly passed away! Just like that – no warning, no illness, except her grief for Freddy.

I had prepared myself to come out of Easter without Freddy but not Flo as well. I was a heartbroken mess, staying in bed and crying for days. Even my wonderful and attentive friends could not give me the solace I needed.

Three days later, my little Easter miracle beckoned me. The daughter of a friend was offered Cody when his owner, the old lady, went into hospital. Erica rang me to see if I would like him. Like him? I couldn't get there quickly enough!

They say dogs have a sixth sense and I really believe that. Cody knew I was in a bad place and needed support. Even though he had been an outside dog before, he did not leave my side. He snuggled up on the bed next to me and if I turned over he turned over too!

Cody is the life of the dog party each morning at the park. While I wonder how could anyone dump a beautiful puppy at only nine weeks old, I'm so glad they did, because I believe this little man saved my life.

Judy, Victoria

An Open Heart

When I lost my Border Collie Toiya to kidney disease, I thought I would never get over it. We had grown up together; I only had to look at her and she would know what I needed. It took only one week for the vet to make the diagnosis every owner dreads and within that same week, I lost my best friend after eleven-and-a-half years.

A month later, I never thought I could face adopting another dog but I missed four-legged company, especially when out walking. So I drove up to the local RSPCA for a look around, with no expectations – just wanting to see some doggy faces and perhaps reminisce a bit. Walking by one kennel, I was stopped by a beautiful six-month-old tan Kelpie mix named Keely. Her beauty and her interesting name both took me by surprise, and as a lover of working dogs, there was just something about her that made me stop and reconsider.

Over the next three weekends I returned to the shelter to see her.

I think she knew something special was happening as the second time I visited, I decided to put my hand through the fence and she put her paw in my hand and looked at me with these big, wide golden-brown eyes. Toiya used to do the same thing, and from that moment onwards there was no turning back – that day I brought Keely home.

Losing Toiya was the most devastating experience of my life but finding Keely got me through it. Her sensitive and gentle nature, her trust in me and her endless love and affection are incredible – I still can't believe someone could have given her away. Keely is now four years old and has a cheeky little Husky sister called Jade. We are a family that is rarely apart, with trips to the beach, the farm, walks in local parks, swims in the dam, endless ball games and lots of laughs.

Although I may have rescued Keely, she has truly saved me by teaching me a very important lesson: to keep an open heart. When losing a loved one, no one ever wants to go through that experience again, and it was tempting to close my heart off completely, to protect myself from future grief. Yet Keely has shown me that an open heart actually helps one heal from the past, because you have the ongoing love of another to help see you through.

Leo, New South Wales

Happy Birthday, Cleo

Truth be told, the photo on PetRescue didn't do her justice. The little dog who clambered out of her transport crate towards me was the prettiest girl I'd ever seen. I bent down towards Cleo and said, 'Happy birthday, little one. I don't know when your real birthday is, but this day is the first day of the rest of your life, so this is your birthday from now on.'

Only weeks before, I had lost my beloved dog, King, during his sixteenth year. The hole he left in my life was so large, I started to feel suicidal. I didn't care about life or living, I just wanted to die.

Around two weeks later, something drove me to visit PetRescue. I thought, okay, I'll check out the dogs online, but won't adopt one. However, as I started to look through page after page of beautiful 'fur kids', I couldn't tear myself away. I was halfway down the third page when I spotted her: a Maltese mix, with the saddest expression I'd ever seen. She wouldn't look at the camera, just over the shoulder of the person holding her, so all I got to see was the side of her head.

I can't remember even reading her description, but all it took was that picture, and Cleo had already dug deep into my soul. I tried to move forward through the website, but I couldn't focus on other dogs. All I could see was Cleo's sad face; all other pictures were blurry.

I acted quickly, emailing Andrea at Companions for Life. But that wasn't enough; I decided I'd also call the rescue group straight away. I needed to explain my dilemma: I have bilateral lymphoedema, I live in a unit and have no means of transport. Was there any way I could still meet Cleo?

Fortunately, Andrea wanted to help. When she said that her partner traveled once a week to Sydney, and he could bring Cleo down on one of those trips, I was elated. And when she arrived, I instantly knew she was the best medicine I could ever have.

From day one, without even trying, Cleo opened up my heart. She showed me how to love others by showing me so much love. Before Cleo, I didn't know how to love. I didn't know I *could* love. I didn't know how to receive love . . . and I certainly don't remember living. I feel like I forever owe gratitude to Companions for Life for saving Cleo, who in turn saved me.

About three years after I adopted Cleo, I developed cellulitis in my leg. The pain was excruciating, and every time I cried out in pain,

Cleo was by my side trying to cheer me up, or following me around the house whenever I paced the floor. Whenever I went down the steps, one step at a time, Cleo would be right next to me, watching me put my leg down, then smiling up at me excitedly as if to say, 'You can do it, Mummy, that's it, now the next one . . .' Once on the ground floor, she'd cheer for me, running around in circles and barking as if to say, 'You did it! I knew you could do it!' She was my perfect little nurse maid.

Four years later, I visited PetRescue again, but this time with Cleo on my lap, looking at the pictures with me. I explained to her that I was searching for a sister for her. Cleo liked other dogs and deserved a full-time playmate. We soon came across a beautiful ten-year-old Shih Tzu mix named Opal, who was with New South Wales Animal Rescue. She had a sister called Ruby, and when both dogs were brought to my house to meet Cleo, she did the choosing – Opal it was.

Cleo made the perfect selection, as we have a real gem in Opal. She uses body language to talk to me, and makes me laugh when I ask her something: she actually nods or shakes her head, depending on her answer!

I owe a great debt of gratitude to both Cleo and Opal's rescue groups for helping me find these two treasures. Because of this, I try to pay back in kind wherever possible, telling everyone I speak to that they must visit PetRescue for their next family member and definitely give the pet shop and backyard breeders a miss. On my Facebook page, I devote at least one day a week to spotlighting animals from PetRescue to give deserving dogs extra promotion. I want everyone to know what a joy rescue pets are. I don't know where I'd be without my two, or even if I'd still be alive.

Carol, New South Wales

Thank You, Oscar

It is hard to imagine such an exquisite little puppy as our Oscar beginning his life in the degradation and misery of a puppy factory, but that is indeed where our little one was born. Following his rescue, he was adopted by us at eight weeks of age from Pets Haven Animal Shelter in Victoria. We were very much hoping he would provide our seven-year-old dog, Pebbles, with a willing playmate.

Pebbles, also a Maltese mix like Oscar, is completely deaf, and as a result I taught her sign language from an early age. She had lost a lot of her confidence when she went deaf, but having Oscar in her life has utterly transformed her. Her puppy playfulness has returned: she lets him jump all over her; she is more active, youthful, and also displays quite a maternal side towards him. Pebbles likes to feel the touch of someone against her as security when sleeping, and Oscar appears to sense this. He loves to cuddle up against her and often goes in search of her when it's 'sleepy time'.

However, it isn't only Pebbles that Oscar has rescued. My husband and I were recovering from a personal tragedy at the time of his adoption. We had been trying for a child for a long time and had recently suffered from a painful miscarriage. Oscar brought me out of my depression, giving us so much joy from the minute we brought him home. His constant charm and innocent happiness was the remedy I needed to find myself again. We now have two 'children' in the family, and within a number of weeks of adopting Oscar, we fell pregnant again. Thank you, Oscar.

Angela, Victoria

Roxy Returns the Favour

As the sun began to rise, the time was drawing nearer for me to say my last goodbyes to Benson, my beautiful thirteen-year-old Golden Retriever. I had just spent the final hours with him as I sat waiting for the vet to arrive. At 10:30 a.m. came the knock on the door that I had been dreading. Benson was more than a dog, he was my work mate, but most of all he was my best friend. I didn't think it would be possible for me to love another dog again. In addition, my life was in turmoil. My business had become obsolete due to advances in technology, a neighbour had driven her car through my house, I had been ill for a long time – everything was going wrong. And now Benson was gone.

As the weeks passed, I became increasingly unhappy. Then, one day came the phone call that would change my life. It was my friend Ray; he owned a mobile dog-grooming business and had been Benson's 'hair stylist'. Apparently the RSPCA in Newcastle urgently needed a foster carer for a Golden Retriever and her six ten-day-old puppies. It was close to Christmas and foster carers were in short supply. Ray thought of me immediately as he knew that I had not been coping with my loss.

I was so excited at the thought of caring for this little family – it was just what I needed! But when I approached my partner at the time with the idea, he objected. I knew in myself that I really needed to do this and decided to ahead regardless.

Christmas had become a sad occasion for my family as it was the time of year my dad had passed away. I knew it was going to be even worse without Benson. While I waited for the RSPCA to arrive with my new charges, on the anniversary of my dad's death, I couldn't help but wonder if he'd sent them to me to help me through. When the car door opened, Roxy walked slowly over to me and placed her head into my lap, asking for a cuddle. I thought I was going to cry – she smelt, was thin and in shocking condition.

Roxy's story was this, I was told: she'd been surrendered, heavily pregnant, with her brother to RSPCA Yagoona. She was only two years old and it wasn't her first pregnancy. She'd been starved by her barbaric owner and weighed only 23 kilograms before the birth of her pups.

Roxy was frightened, lonely and her fur had begun to fall out – from stress, no doubt. While her brother found a lovely home with a good friend of an RSPCA volunteer, the future looked much bleaker for his sister. Since Roxy was so weak, the vets thought she or her pups would not make it through the birth. The decision was made to put Roxy to sleep, with her unborn puppies.

Now, here I like to think Roxy knew what fate lay before her and decided to save herself and her babies, because a miracle occurred. She went into labour before they could euthanase her, and she and her six puppies survived.

And so before me now stood this forlorn mother and her six sick puppies. Ray soon brought around a whelping box, and gave Roxy a lovely warm hydrobath. For the first two weeks, Roxy hid behind the lounge chairs in between feeding her puppies. I had to be patient with her.

As each day passed, Roxy and the little ones became stronger. Several friends came daily to help me with the pups. I had no idea the amount of work that was involved looking after youngsters! The day started at 6 a.m. and continued until ten at night, with washing, cleaning and giving the pups their medication. Due to her weak state, Roxy lost her milk at three weeks. Ray came to the rescue and helped teach the pups to lap milk from a dish.

In the third week of caring for my new little family I knew I wanted to keep Roxy and give her the forever home she deserved. This caused another rift with my partner. He did not support me and told me to find another dog. Roxy was not an attractive dog at that point in time, due to her health issues. I knew it was going to be impossible to find the right person, as she was still going to need months of ongoing care. If she went back to the shelter, she would surely be put to sleep.

The puppies, however, thrived, and soon all six found their forever homes, several through Golden Retriever Rescue. Prior to this, they needed desexing, and when the RSPCA van arrived to collect them, Roxy panicked and hid behind me. She thought they had come to take her away. I knew then that regardless of the consequences, I had to keep this special girl. My partner would just have to accept it.

Then, one day, five months later, after Roxy had grown strong enough to be desexed, she officially became mine, and me hers.

On the anniversary of the puppies' first birthday, we had a reunion in Sydney, and Roxy and her young ones came together, all remembering each other – and me. As I stood back and watched them play with pride, I realised the time was nigh for me to make some decisions about changing my life for the better. Roxy had shown me that anything was possible, even when you think all the odds are against you.

I had to concentrate on both mine and Roxy's confidence. Her physical health was fine but she was missing the company of other dogs. Ray introduced her to his three beautiful Golden Retrievers, and they took to each other from their first meeting. Ray then suggested we become members of the Newcastle Dog Club. Roxy took to obedience immediately. She passed every training level in record time.

Roxy seemed to understand I was very unhappy in my personal life, and she tried to find ways to make me laugh. We had become best friends. Roxy was helping me in similar ways to how I had helped her.

Ray had been the one who initially helped save Roxy, and I think she knew it had to be Ray to save me. He had been a good friend for over seven years. He'd been there at the time of Benson's death and at many other sad events in my life. He convinced me to become an obedience instructor at the local dog club to build my self esteem. But I did not know what else he had in mind for me at this time.

During our walks with Roxy, Ray helped me think about my future career path and my failing business. I made the decision to close it down and use the skills I had obtained from the dog club to purchase a dog-grooming franchise from Ray. There was just a small problem: my partner again decided that this was not to be and put his foot down. So instead, I began a new at-home dog-minding service but it ultimately wasn't what I desired: I wanted to be a dog groomer. Twelve months later, I got the courage to leave my partner and did just that.

But first, my training had to commence. Roxy and I spent many hours with Ray and his dogs and we became closer than ever. I was having the time of my life in my new job and I owed it all to Roxy. The day I got that phone call from Ray I thought I was saving Roxy. I had no idea that Roxy would end up saving me.

Ray and I groom dogs on a daily basis now, and many of them are rescue dogs like Roxy. We help with fundraising events for rescue groups, which allows us to promote how great it is to adopt a rescue to our customers.

You can probably guess that Roxy's journey eventually brought Ray and me together. We now live happily with Ray's three Goldies – Khardi, Kes and Kira – and a healthy and happy six-year-old Roxy, of course.

It has occurred to me, if Roxy had not gone through the earlier suffering and sadness in her life, we would never have met, and she would not have brought Ray and me together. Thank you, Roxy.

Jennifer, New South Wales

Tully Valentine

Pic: *Herald Sun*

It's always a shock to be told you have cancer. The shock is then followed by seemingly endless tests, and then, quickly, 'the Op'.

Arriving home was such a joy, but I became aware very quickly that I needed full-time care and companionship. This was a hard call for the family. However, one of my daughters, who volunteered for Victorian Dog Rescue, suggested I adopt an elderly dog they needed a home for – one who was unlikely to get much interest.

Tully arrived from Mildura Pound on a scorching-hot Valentine's Day. We christened him Tully Valentine. He burst out of his crate with his little Chihuahua-shaped head and strange Whippet-like curvy body. He was missing the top of one ear and sporting multiple breaks in his tail. The phrase 'Only a mother could love it,' sprang to mind.

Soon after getting him home, imagine our surprise when this scrawny old boy proudly revealed a well-honed trick: leaping up in the air, straight into the arms of whoever was closest. His other claim-to-fame is lap-sitting for hours on end. It is hard to prise him off me!

Perhaps Tully isn't the prettiest of dogs, but I think he has had the last laugh, being chosen to feature in a *Herald Sun* article for Victorian Dog Rescue's Winter Appeal. Needing to raise money for heat pads to help their dogs stay warm, they had an overwhelming response: Tully unexpectedly inspired donations into the many thousands.

Tully has been my loyal friend, and I know he's hastened my recovery. His warm little body helped mend my injured body and heart. And two years on, both of us look and feel 100 per cent better!

Rosemary, Victoria

The Important Things in Life

'Until one has loved an animal, a part of one's soul remains unawakened.' – Anatole France

Chester was returned to the backyard breeder with not so much as the collar around his neck. After only six months, his owners had decided he was too much trouble and not worth having to put fences up for, and they dumped him.

The gorgeous liver-coloured Spaniel with this traumatic beginning was to become our beloved Chester. He was such a boisterous and carefree character, a big, clumsy, furry thing, full of life, energy and fun. Our little girl was only about two when 'Chessie' arrived, and I was worried when he darted around at full speed and knocked her over on a few occasions in his clumsy manner. Soon, however, the two were best friends, helping each other dig holes in the garden. What a sight – my little girl with a spade, and Chessie with his paws, taking turns to scoop dirt out of the hole!

Chessie did all the usual puppy things over the next few months, like pulling washing off the line and chewing a few things here and there – like my new pair of jeans – but you couldn't stay mad at him for long. The only inkling of his traumatic beginnings was when it was time to go for a car ride. Chessie hated the car, whimpering and crying as though he thought he may be dumped once more. It took a long time for us to reassure him that he would always be with us, and would never in his life be unwanted again.

Over the next fourteen years, Chessie played a different role to each family member: a wrestling partner for my husband, a 'brother' for our daughter who was an only child, and for me, a constant companion who was by my side at every turn. On Saturday nights when everyone else was in bed, I would stay up to do the ironing and watch TV. Chester would always wait patiently for me to finish and retire to the couch with me while I had a cup of tea. It was our quiet time together when he would just lie with his head on my lap.

Chessie was vibrant and puppy-like for so long that I hardly noticed he was getting older. But when the call came from the vet with his test results, indicating he had kidney failure, we knew we would have to say goodbye to our faithful friend. The whole family camped in our bedroom with Chessie on his last night. And we all went to the vet together, and held him and reassured him, as he was put to sleep.

Chester enriched our lives so much when he was with us, but has continued to do so even after he passed on. In the days after he died, the house seemed so empty, and we felt lost. We didn't think we were ready to love another dog, but within a week, a beautiful little female rescue Spaniel named Kaia came into our lives by chance. I really believe that she was sent by Chessie to help us heal, because Kaia has brought love and life back to our home when we needed it most.

Today, our family is blessed with three 'second-chance' dogs – Kaia, Brock and Oscar – each with their own story, each changing and enhancing our lives in their own special way. And there isn't any doubt in my mind that I am the one who is really being rescued.

Loving Chester gave me so much joy, and losing Chester helped me define the important things in life: love, loyalty and caring. He even helped me find my path in the world, and today I am studying to be an animal naturopath. I want to use my knowledge to help heal animals, and give a little back to the four-legged friends who give us so much. I know that Chessie, 'my boy' – wherever he is – will be proud of me.

Diahan, Western Australia

My Tilly

I don't know what it was about her, but I needed her and she needed me.

At the age of forty-nine, I felt my life was in a shambles. I desperately missed my dog Muffy, who had passed away, and because I can't get around easily I realised I could look for a new friend on PetRescue without leaving home.

Day after day, I scanned the pictures of needy faces. I applied for a little dog called Maggie from one rescue group, and was relieved when I wasn't chosen. Something didn't feel right about her. Then I saw Tilly.

A Shih Tzu mix, her name was Lucy then, and gazing at her picture I felt I was looking in the mirror. I couldn't get to her fast enough! I rang PAWS Sydney about her, grabbed the GPS and asked my sister to drive me to her foster carer's.

When meeting her, my sister said, 'She's so ugly, only Linda could love that dog!', but Tilly has softly wormed her way into not only my heart but those of my children. When she jumps on me in the morning, I'm glad to wake up.

When she first arrived, Tilly and I clung to each other for comfort and security. She made me feel needed and loved again, but most of all she made me feel wanted. That had been missing from both our lives.

The love my rescue girl and I have for each other cannot be replaced; the joy, the total rapture you receive from that very special smile. That love was on PetRescue, and that smile was on my Tilly.

Linda, New South Wales

Our Hero Ollie

Rain clouds hung heavily in the sky on the close of a hot, humid 40-degree day. Jasmine, our four-year-old daughter, was about to fall into the comforting evening routine of dinner, bath, books and bed.

It started with only a few raindrops. Then a crack, lightning and the heaviest downpour Geelong had seen in over a hundred years. Our home was safe, but living on a steep hill, there was a torrent of water flowing past, with prolonged deafening noise outside and above.

That storm was a defining moment, as for Jasmine it forever changed the way she coped with rain, thunder and things out of the ordinary. She began to suffer terrible anxiety.

Fast forward three years, and we had been thinking about getting a dog for a while . . . a big one, a small one, an energetic one, a cute one . . . we just couldn't decide. We eventually thought something like a Labrador would be best – we were a family, after all.

We looked on Pets Haven's website and there were two dogs available that day: a Labrador and a Terrier mix (which looked more like a Border Collie to us). We drove for two hours to the shelter and were initially disappointed when we found the Labrador wasn't there. But Sooty, as Ollie was known then, was the Terrier mix. We took one look and decided instantly he was the dog for us. We promptly renamed him Ollie and cuddled and sang to him all the way home.

We soon discovered that Ollie had an odd assortment of things he was frightened of: plastic bags, things that go BANG, brooms, and eating in public. But we also saw he tried really hard not to be scared and to be sensible about the things that worry him. He knows he is safe here, and over time has learnt to laugh along with us at the silly things he used to run away from.

Ollie is our hero, but most importantly he is a perfect role model for Jasmine in dealing with her own fears. She watches him with his anxieties and realises that fear is only brought about by fear itself. She sees in turn that her fears don't amount to the doom she feels. And it's only because of Ollie that she has gained strength and insight into her own thinking. Now on rainy nights he sleeps on her bed and makes her feel safe. Likewise, when things go BANG, she sits with him and scratches his tummy. And they are both okay.

Ollie has lots of other beautiful qualities. He keeps us fit with his love of the beach and the river. He protects the chooks in our backyard. He warms the seat for you before you sit down. And best of all, he is there to greet us like a long lost friend every time we need it most.

Stephanie, Victoria

Millie, my Angel

Once upon a time there was a lady who was unwell. She suffered from chronic migraines which left her unable to do anything but lie in the darkness in her bed. She became very lonely as her husband would have to go to work and she would be left by herself, in so much pain.

The lady and her husband decided to move to somewhere quieter, to see if this would help. It would be the first time they lived in a house of their own, too, which meant they could adopt a dog! The lady had wanted that very much for a long time. She searched on PetRescue for an older dog in need. Soon, she came across a photo of Millie, being cared for by Rigby's Rescue in Victoria, and it was love at first sight. The photo of Millie was printed out and displayed on their fridge before they had even met her, such was the lady's excitement.

When the lady and her husband went to Millie's foster home and met her for the first time, straight away the lady realised how special this little dog was. Millie was eight years old and very fearful of people because of abuse she had suffered in her past. She would jump at the slightest sound and cower in the corner if you stepped too loudly. She was a dog that needed some extra special care, just like the lady herself did. The two of them made a perfect match, and off they went to start their lives together.

It didn't take Millie long to know she was safe. Soon, she wouldn't leave the lady's side and when the lady was in the dark and in pain, Millie would lie with her, no matter what. Millie took extra special care of the lady and loved her unconditionally, as the lady did her. The lady then became unwell with another severe illness and Millie once again would not leave her side. Millie was like her angel and she gave the lady hope and love when she felt like all was lost. Millie was such a blessing in the lady's life and continues to be this day. The lady and Millie would be lost without each other.

Thank you, my angel Millie.

Shakira, Victoria

Ted's Devotion

I started volunteering at the Doggie Rescue animal shelter shortly after the loss of our twelve-year-old Chihuahua mix, Bonnie. The work was rewarding and a welcome distraction. Every morning a sea of little dogs waiting patiently for homes greeted me expectantly. Sadly, I was not ready to adopt another dog.

One day, among the usual noisy, tail-wagging, furry things at the shelter I saw Bailey, an amber-coloured purebred German Spitz, barking for my attention. At some stage Bailey had broken his leg and possibly because of this, had been abandoned by his owners but thanks to his rescuers, was saved from death row.

Bailey made his way to my side as I began tackling piles of laundry and stayed to keep watch until it was time for me to go. From that day, we became instant friends, rendezvousing at the washing machine on my volunteer days. It became harder and harder for me to leave him behind at the end of each shift.

When my husband dropped by the shelter for a 'meet and greet', Bailey attempted to leap into the open boot of our car, despite his crooked leg that had never mended properly. It was obvious that he felt his wait was over. Neither my husband nor I could resist, so we immediately adopted him. He came home with us and was re-christened Ted.

Ted's introduction to the family immediately changed the mood of the house. Our other old dog, Toby, was pushed reluctantly into an Indian summer, and Ted impressed all with his adroit spinning tricks and dexterous 'shake'. But throughout he never left my side, as if he knew how soon I would need him.

And the time came, when, in December, I lost both my mother and my only sister in a matter of three months, with our old dog Toby following closely behind.

Christmas and New Year were difficult times to grieve, with the stark contrast of the festive season only serving to highlight my loss. I retreated from the world but Ted stayed with me, foregoing walks and sunshine to keep me company. My husband would try to take him out, but Ted would manage to escape his leash and run home to me.

Day after day, Ted quietly kept his vigil. After weeks of inertia, I realised I was letting him down, making him wait longer for his much-wished-for happy family life. Ted had already faced his own trials and deserved more in return for his loyalty to me.

I recuperated slowly and again became involved with the animal shelter, Ted was my inspiration. Without his unwavering devotion, my recovery would have taken much longer. Enough cannot be said about the animal companions who help us through our darkest times, nor can we explain the quiet magic that they weave.

Ted has been part of our family now for eight years. He still diligently supervises the laundry work at home. We gaze at each other over the washing powder and reminisce about the day we found one another.

During our time together, Ted has taught me to live one day at a time. He has proven his selfless loyalty and endless capacity for love. He is my champion, the friend who stood between me and my depression, and rescued me.

Lori, New South Wales

Just for Fun

There's no denying that dogs can display incredible skills – saving lives or providing therapy, for instance – but most of their tricks are more about entertaining themselves, and us. Our dogs' ability to make us laugh will always be top of the list of reasons we love them so much.

Dizzy for Izzy

Pic: Maikka Trupp

I logged on to PetRescue and there she was: 'Izzy, scruffy Terrier mix'. She was at the very top of my search results and only just listed – it had to be fate! There was no photo yet but she sounded perfect for me. What I didn't know at the time was the sad truth that Izzy was on her second-last day on death row at a Victorian regional pound. She was being housed in a pen that was obscured by a sheet of iron, so she was not visible to potential adopters. It was only because a volunteer rescuer bothered to look over the iron sheet that this little gem was discovered.

The wonderful woman who rescued Izzy is a doctor by profession and dog-rescuer by hobby. With each descriptive email I received from her, I fell more and more in love with Izzy:

> She is a real cutie in that scruffy, Orphan Annie way with beautiful eyes and cute pixie ears – she stopped my friend and me in our tracks (we were there for another dog but couldn't resist her). She is an exceptionally lovely dog. The vet loved her, as does everyone who has met her.

Only then did I see her photos – Izzy was simply adorable, my heart melted and the rest is history.

Izzy is certainly a conversation starter. People have remarked that she might just help me meet the man of my dreams, but after a recent incident at the dog park I beg to differ.

It was a hot day, so we headed to the park where Izzy could access the creek alongside and enjoy a swim. All went well until she spotted a man and his Miniature Pointer playing ball, and she made a beeline for them. Izzy just loves playing ball, and given her 'possible' Kelpie roots, she is hard to beat in a race. She scooped up the Pointer's ball and fast-tracked it through the high grass to the creek, where I knew she was planning to drop the ball and cheekily watch it float away. Meanwhile, on the other side of the park, I tried to give chase, all the while screaming, 'Izzzeeeeeeee . . . Come!' The ball was one of those expensive hi-bounce rubber numbers, and I was petrified it was already floating downstream. As I ran towards the owner, I couldn't help but notice he was good looking . . . Out of breath and red-faced, I apologised profusely and said, 'I think your ball may have gone forever.' With that, he bent down and picked up the ball, which was at the edge of the long grass and neither in Izzy's mouth nor the creek.

I thought things were looking up as I regained my composure, but Izzy had other ideas. She suddenly came bounding past the two of us with an almighty long poo half-hanging out her bottom. It appeared she had consumed a fair amount of grass and a brown clump measuring no less than 20 centimetres swung readily from side to side. The handsome man and I looked at it, then at each other and then back at the offending dog. Mortified, I just walked away and hoped to God Izzy would follow. She did. Gaining a bit of distance, I bent down with a bag over my hand and pulled while she squeezed. I could see the good-looking man watching us from afar . . . but wait, there's more! Izzy looked at me balefully as I went in for a second time and removed the remainder. I didn't bother looking at the man again . . . . All that was left to do was to scurry away, humiliated.

When the coast was clear, I returned to the park and sat dolefully in the shade as Izzy frolicked on her own, chasing bugs and birds and rolling in 'stuff'. She had certainly recovered from *her* embarrassment. Then, a new dog arrived with a young couple and before I knew it, Izzy had her blinkers on and tore across the park in no time to make their acquaintance. Normally she just plays with other dogs, so I wasn't too bothered. But this time she had other ideas . . .

With the momentum that only a sprint across the park can give a four-legged, Izzy ran closer and closer towards the couple, and leapt at the man like a long-lost love. Unfortunately, she collided with his privates.

The man buckled in half, clutching himself in pain. In fact, he had to reach up and lean on his girlfriend for support to even stand upright.

The day couldn't get any worse. I didn't even bother apologising. I piled Izzy into the car and went straight home.

It's been almost two years since that day and I can't imagine life without Izzy, so all is forgiven. She makes me smile; she makes me laugh. She is active, loving, affectionate and . . . humiliating. She loves chasing birds, empty toilet-roll holders and doing belly-whackers in muddy puddles. Everyone likes to guess what breed she is but Izzy prefers to remain mysterious. I am so incredibly grateful that Izzy's rescuer not only saved her life but also chose me to be her new best friend. She has self-appointed godparents and a pool of Izzy Fan Club members who love spending time with her. She is Miss Congeniality at the dog park and is now in a long-term stable relationship with Sam the Beagle . . . . Half her luck.

Shannon, Victoria

Grommet Does His Block

Grommet is the strangest dog you have ever met. We got him when I was eleven and he's an English Staffy. That isn't the strange bit, though. You see, he's in love with a thick wooden block. Yes, a block of wood.

Grommet rolls 'Block' around on the lawn, and it would seem as though Block is his best friend. One day, Dad was mowing the lawn and he bent to pick up Block, who was in the way. Grommet was quite taken aback by this affront and started barking at Dad! Dad slowly put Block down and Grommet raced up, collected Block and sprinted away. We haven't seen Block since. I wonder where he has hidden it? Every day, Grommet disappears behind the shed and doesn't come back until dusk. We suspect he's hanging out with his mate Block back there.

Lexie, New South Wales

Wayward Whiskey

I'd been volunteering at the Sydney Dogs & Cats Home for over a year when I noticed a golden Labrador in one of the cages and enquired about him. I was told by a staff member that he'd just been adopted and would be going to his new home that day.

About three weeks later I noticed the same Labrador being brought into the yard. That's odd, I thought, and found out he was back because the adopters had decided he was too boisterous. What's worse, this was the second home he'd been returned from in the space of a few short weeks. None of them wanted to put the time and effort into training the young fellow.

I decided that in spite of my husband's emphatic 'No more dogs!' I couldn't let this poor boy keep drifting from home to home, and that we'd adopt him. He looked like the colour of Baileys Irish Cream, and I just love Baileys, so we decided on the name Whiskey.

Whiskey was never a naughty dog; he didn't pull washing off the line or dig holes. He just loved life and wanted everyone to join in on having fun every day. I think that with my husband at home all the time Whiskey finally had the company he craved, and within about eighteen months he quietened down considerably.

Whiskey did have an obsession, however: swimming. I used to take him to the local dog park where he would be the first into the swimming hole and the last one out. If any other dogs wanted to join him then it was party time, and he would be in doggy heaven, barking non-stop and racing in and out of the water. He became known as the Ian Thorpe of Como.

One unforgettable day, when Whiskey was about twelve months old, I took him down to the river where we live. I removed his lead as I knew he would want to swim, and in he went. The only trouble that quickly emerged was that he wasn't going to come back! The Georges River branches off in one direction to Bonnet Bay and in the other to Botany Bay. I called after Whiskey – he was going out too far, but do you think he would take any notice? Not on your life! He'd seen the seagulls and was off after them – his genetic programming had kicked in. The birds were having a great game with him and every time he caught up to them they'd just take off again, further out into the river. By this time I was literally screaming at the top of my voice trying to get him to come back but with no luck.

Fortunately the rowing club houses their boats close by, so I ran to them for help, telling them I had a wayward dog in the water. They got one of their boats with a motor out and sailed off in hot pursuit of Whiskey, who was still swimming in the one direction – out to Botany Bay! When they reached him they cut the engine and steered him back with their paddles towards me. All went well until he was almost at the shore and suddenly spotted more birds in the other direction! He took off again at top speed, with the boat once more in hot pursuit. This time they managed to grab him and haul him aboard, and boy was I grateful.

A couple of years later, we had a visit from some relatives, and as it was a lovely day, we decided to walk down to the local park by the side of the Georges River. Lots of people were picnicking by the water and although Whiskey was not on his lead, I felt he would be okay as he was quite obedient when out walking. We were deep in conversation when all of a sudden we heard a mighty cheer go up from one of the groups at the picnic tables. Whiskey had jumped off a 2-metre-high wall and was again swimming out into the middle of the river after the birds! There would be no way of getting him back – I couldn't believe it was happening again. We needed a plan of action, and quickly.

My niece and I stayed in the park, along with most of the picnickers – who thought it was terrific entertainment – and my niece's daughter, Heidi, who was thirteen at the time, ran as fast as she could to the rowing club, about a half-kilometre around the other side of the bay. Luckily the rowers were just putting their boats away, and Heidi managed to persuade them to go out after the runaway (swimaway?) Whiskey. Several minutes later, and after a considerable amount of coaxing, they finally steered him towards the shore. Despite being dressed in her Sunday best, Heidi bravely waded into the water up to her neck and grabbed the devil. Needless to say, I've not taken him to the river since: his swimming has been confined to the local swimming hole, where even in the drought when there was only a very small amount of water left, Whiskey would still be the only dog trying to swim in a puddle of only 1 metre in diameter . . .

Over the past ten years, we've had a few dramas, but Whiskey always raises our spirits. In 1999 my husband Ian was diagnosed with Type II diabetes and had a very bad time with neuropathy. We'd lost our old dog Blackie the previous year, and Ian had tragically also lost his sister and two brothers to cancer a couple of years earlier. Then, a couple of years ago I was diagnosed with early breast cancer and had to have radiation treatment. Through all of this Whiskey has lifted our spirits and kept us going.

Whiskey, our darling boy, you've made our lives complete – I hope you know how much we love you.

Patricia, New South Wales

Eggnog the Excavator

As we built our dream home, my husband and I knew exactly what breed of dog we wanted: a Beagle, or maybe even two. We both loved their big brown eyes and gorgeous drooping ears and wanted nothing more than to come home to a loyal dog that wanted only to play with us.

I'd grown up with a Beagle, so knew that people can quickly fall in love with their gorgeous looks and fall just as quickly out of love. Passions can become strained when your yard starts looking like a minefield and you are running down the street chasing your pup after they have jumped the fence in search of that smell they simply couldn't resist.

I wanted to give a Beagle a second chance in a home that understood and tolerated all their quirks. My husband, however, wanted to choose our pup from a breeder, something he had never had the chance to do as a child. So, after much thought, we decided to go to a reputable breeder for our first pup and then adopt a second one a little later down the track so they could keep each other company and hopefully out of too much mischief!

That was the theory, anyway.

After having our little Lulu for just a few months, my husband came across Beagle Rescue Victoria (BRV) on the internet. We saw a little puppy called Eggnog who, quite surprisingly, was only a month or two older than our Lulu and was tan and white just like our girl.

Eggnog's story was heartbreaking: she was one of a litter of five pups rescued from a disgusting puppy factory. The wonderful Tam from Beagle Rescue hand-reared them from the age of three or four weeks and didn't think Eggnog would make it – she had never seen a dog so riddled with worms or fleas. But make it, she did.

We were overjoyed when our application to adopt Eggnog was

approved. She and Lulu are simply the best of friends. Wherever one goes, the other quickly follows. As they have grown up together we have had many 'Beagle moments' as we now fondly call them.

Knowing that Beagles like to dig, we crazily thought that having two dogs would mean they would be so entertained by one another that the new plants we had put in the backyard would go unnoticed. Novice mistake! Within twenty-four hours the pups had worked very effectively as a team and the daisy bush, along with half the soil from the garden, was rear-ended through their dog door. A feat they were very proud to show us!

Regularly we chased the pups out the back to retrieve a stolen sock, a destroyed shoe or a box of tissues before too much damage could be inflicted on the item. However, they are fantastic at working as a team, as my poor father discovered while babysitting the pups while my husband and I were on holiday. Having placed his breakfast on the dining table, Dad sent a message on his mobile to my mother and went about getting ready for work. When he returned he went to grab his phone from the coffee table – however, he discovered it was missing.

He retraced his steps, thinking he must have put it elsewhere. Then he realised the pups were very quiet and knew immediately that something was definitely afoot. As he walked outside he found one very naughty puppy munching on his mobile phone! He retrieved it quickly only to find that they had managed to video call a work colleague . . . He quickly called her back and went about explaining why she had seen a pair of big wet tongues on her screen and heard panting noises. While calling his colleague and reprimanding the ringleader, he walked back inside to find the other pup happily sitting on his seat at the table, finishing off his Weetbix!

Life without our Eggnog would certainly be less energetic for us, and a misery for her little sister Lulu. They are simply a perfect match and make our family whole.

With the arrival of our first child they have grown into their new roles of protectors and future playmates with ease. Both my husband and I know that they will always be an important part of our pack, and although at times we can be pushed to our limits with their Beagle antics, it is always nice to come home to their big brown eyes, dropping ears and loyal hearts, the trail of destruction from their day of play following behind them.

Jane, Victoria

Political Animal

I never knew that dogs had a political bias until I met Barney.

It was almost twenty years ago when we purchased two dogs from a breeder as puppies. The dogs both lived for seventeen years and were the loves of our lives, but after recently adopting two rescue dogs, one from Sydney Pet Rescue & Adoption and the other from Dog Rescue Newcastle, I will never buy puppies from a breeder again.

Barney and Cartier are like chalk and cheese: Barney is the clown, funny, naughty and silly, and sister Cartier is Miss Perfect: perfectly behaved, obedient and sweet. At nine years of age she's a great role model for Barney, who is only two, especially when it comes to socialising. She will get in between Barney and a dog he is scared of at the park so he can relax and move away. In return, Barney provides a lot of excitement and fun for Cart, running through the house to chase birds from the front to back gardens.

It was around federal election time last year that Barney most impressed us, however, with his political commentary. During the election campaign, whenever he saw Opposition Leader Tony Abbott on the TV, he would run up and growl and bark at the screen. Barney clearly wasn't going to vote Liberal. Today, if Mr Abbott flashes onto the TV, sometimes he can sneak by without incurring Barney's scorn, but if our boy is on the ball – look out! He will still jump up and tell him exactly what he thinks of him. Oh, and he isn't keen on Oprah or Johnny Depp either (would you believe?), but he relaxes if we put his lead on, and allow him to recover on the couch! Fortunately, we don't have to run the TV show by Barney before choosing the week's viewing, we just need to comfort him when it all gets too much!

There is not a day that goes by that this gorgeous, sensitive, quirky fool doesn't make us laugh, and Cart doesn't make us melt.

Jessica and Nicola, New South Wales

Bath Day

'You don't smell like an apple,' I told her, disgusted. She sat there staring at me, her whole body wagging, fur shiny-wet from my recent exertions and no sign of an apology. The vet had prescribed an oatmeal shampoo for itchy skin that would make her smell lovely – like an apple, in fact, I was assured. The instructions said it should be left on her skin for up to ten minutes and I should have known the instructions oversimplified the whole traumatic process. And, moreover, she still smelt like a dog while I, however, smelt vaguely of apple.

I called her Polly and adopted her from Pets Haven Animal Shelter whose proprietor had saved her from death at the hand of some potential murderer at a council pound. She was named Isabelle at the shelter but this really didn't suit – she's not that kind of dog at all. Polly, on the other hand, is the perfect name for this model of dogdom. She plays when it's play time, waits patiently until happy hour to come inside, and watches the news with a critical eye. She's jolly when it's time to be, lies quietly when it's not. She likes cuddles but doesn't jump up on your clothes, comes when she's called, doesn't grizzle or bark much, will eat anything on offer and is hysterically happy about going for walks.

She loves meeting people and acts up for them dreadfully, offering her paw and winning every heart. A real character, she learnt quickly that the sofa was out of bounds but the soft mat I invested in to protect the carpet was okay. So she dragged the mat up onto the sofa and settled down cosily, watching me out of the corner of her eye to check my reaction. Clever, eh? Better still, she didn't sulk when discovered it didn't work.

All of these pluses completely outweigh Polly's one hang-up. She hated being brushed at first and was very hesitant when confronted by a gate or a door, but neither of these little issues could even begin to approach her hatred of being washed.

My doggy experience before Polly was largely with working dogs and they are a completely different kettle of fish, as it were. They tend not to get patted much, are rarely cuddled and never invited into the house. You don't brush them, de-flea them and you don't have to worry about their weight because they just run it off. Moreover, if they need a bath you just throw them in the dam. But now I had a pet and realised what a vast difference it is.

When bathing day dawned I woke knowing I was probably in for a hard time. I looked for excuses to put it off but the weather was right – a hot day – and Polly needed her anti-itch. Besides, an apple fragrance would be preferable to her doggy odour. I donned shorts and a T-shirt and kept my feet bare because I might get a bit damp. Oh, I planned everything meticulously – I would be in complete control and nothing could go wrong. My victim would be tied to the clothes-line post in the drying yard outside the laundry. At the ready would be the shampoo, the bucket of water and jug for rinsing, an old cushion to save my knees, a towel to dry her off and a couple of treats for being a good girl.

What a joke! None of it worked.

She lay on her back, squirmed onto her side, pushed me away with her feet. I hoisted her to a standing position, she flopped back down again, I hoisted her up once more, her tail so far underneath her it nearly touched her nose; no chance for me to kneel on the cushion. At last I got some of the shampoo onto her back and started kneading it in. Well, she seemed to like that, and when the leash and the post accidentally parted company I decided to leave her untethered. Wrong move. When I moved to the laundry door and opened it a squeak to get a bucket of clean rinsing water, she was off. Polly and the leash streaked into the house, heavily apple-coated and sloshing wet. Racing to grab the leash, my bare feet slipped on the wet tiles and I fell flat on my back – seriously.

Some moments later when I found I could move, I looked up to see Polly staring at me from the end of the passage, between us, the carpet draggled with apple/oatmeal coating, soggy footprints twice the size of her feet and a snail trail of slosh from the leash. Despairing, I called to her enticingly, offered a treat, but she rightly oozed suspicion and made no move. I staggered to my feet and advanced towards her, ever so slowly, hoping she might not notice, but she backed away, trailing the leash. She was too cunning to get trapped in the ensuite and when I followed her into the kitchen through one door, she went out the other. We went round and round the dining table, round and round the sofa, the distance between us scarcely varying. I called her firmly, I yelled abuse at her. I gave up. Then she decided I'd inched my way too close and bent her knees to squirrel under the sofa. But she forgot the leash! I was able to pounce on it, happily accepting the reminder that I'd hurt my back. Now all I had to do was get the soap out of her – and quickly. At least half an hour had elapsed during our to-and-fro tango; would Polly's hair fall out, I agonised, because of the delay? Would my dog be forever bald?

My girl is definitely the escapee extraordinaire of the canine species, able to pull out of a collar tight enough to strangle her. So the rinsing process became a sort of badly choreographed dance of side-stepping and flailing arms while I fought to maintain the anti-escape position. Eventually I got her in a vice-like grip up against my body and, while her apple coating and wetness conveyed themselves from her to me, I managed to reach for the jug and pour the rinsing water all over us. I gave up on the idea of towelling her dry just as I had completely given up all hope of staying in control. I released her. It was over. I collapsed.

A moment passed. She came to me, sat down and offered her paw. She looked at me adoringly. She covered me in licks and snuggled winsomely against me, clearly declaring she was prepared to forgive me. Who's forgiving who? I thought peevishly. But I was left in no doubt whatsoever.

Most of the morning had gone. Most of the expensive apple-fragranced shampoo had seeped from the bottle, which had fallen on its side and the laundry floor was drowning in the last of the rinsing water, which had missed both of us. I was saturated and exhausted and hurt. The carpet would probably need professional treatment and my back might too. I smelt like apples, but the dog still smelt like a dog.

But what can you do when a creature has so much to offer, so much loving to give? You can only thank from the bottom of your heart the animal shelter that simply doesn't believe in euthanising healthy homeless animals. It would have been nothing short of tragic if Polly hadn't been given a second chance to be the dog she is.

Judith, Victoria

Wally's Waste

Wally was a farm dog, a Border Collie, in need. His owner had accidentally run him over and as a result Wally had a dodgy leg and couldn't work on the farm with the other dogs any more. He was tied up under a tree all day. I heard about his plight, and relayed this information to my son, Greg, who was looking for a dog at the time.

Greg drove out to the farm, saw Wally tied up under the tree and took him home that very day.

Not long after Wally arrived, Greg purchased a garbage truck. He cleverly named the truck and the business 'Wally's Waste'. Wally travelled with him every day. Each third weekend, it was my son's turn to jump off the truck and empty the bins in the main street of our home town, Wagga. Wally loved the drill – he would run with Greg to every bin, often finding an empty coke bottle nearby. Wally would pick up the bottle in his mouth and sprint down the street to the next bin to be emptied. Then Greg would kick the bottle for Wally to run after, and he'd drop it at the next bin, and so on. It was a great game.

This particular day, however, things didn't go to plan.

Sitting next to Greg in the truck one morning, on his normal domestic run, Wally shifted his position and accidentally trod on the control that releases the garbage. To my son's horror, the entire truckload of waste they were carrying emptied into the middle of a residential street!

Many residents ran outside to see what was going on. Luckily for Greg, when he explained what had happened, they had a good laugh. Once he'd regained his composure, Greg called a bobcat to collect the rubbish and dump it back into the truck.

From that day on, Greg would often notice children standing at their windows, watching him empty their bin and waving to Wally. Wally became quite the celebrity.

Wally was forgiven, and was a wonderful dog. The life he had with Greg sure beat being tied up to a tree.

Sadly, Wally recently passed away at the grand age of sixteen. Thanks for everything, Wally. You will never be forgotten.

Lyn, New South Wales

My Quirky Duo

My two quirky four-leggeds aren't the best-looking dogs in the world. Robbie has two sets of bottom teeth, and Delta's body is about twice the size of her head. They're not the most well-behaved of dogs either: they're actually quite cheeky.

But I wouldn't change them for anything.

When we adopted Robbie from the NSW Animal Welfare League some years ago, a tiny little dog that would fit into our Aussie bush hat, I didn't know he could give us so much joy. And when that timid, skinny little Delta dog, who was scared of people hitting her, arrived in our home that magical Christmas in 2007, I didn't know how much she would make me laugh.

We found Delta through a different organisation, Paws Lodge at Cessnock, but miraculously they are the same unusual cross breed, Shih Tzu mixed with Jack Russell. What's more, they are now like an old married couple. If they are apart, even for five minutes, they get very anxious.

Every day they make us laugh, whether it's Delta 'talking' to me – moving her mouth as though to speak but no sound coming out – or Robbie singing along to the sound of the telephone ringing. In fact,

Robbie has his own Facebook page and a song recorded about him! It's called 'Robbie, Don't Eat My Underwear'. You see, as the song relates, Robbie has a strange fetish for undies. He likes to eat them. I can't count the amount of times that I've gone outside and found my dismembered underwear on the lawn.

On PetRescue, every animal's listing asks the question, 'Is this your new best friend?' Undoubtedly, where my two rescue dogs are concerned, the answer is yes. As I stare into their chocolate-brown eyes and remember the good times we've had and how we've been through thick and thin together, I love my quirky, lovable, fantastic best friends. I couldn't wish for better dogs!

Maddy, New South Wales

Scooby, Tree-climber Extraordinaire

We Carmelite Nuns of Nedlands, WA, needed a good ratter around the property, and it occurred to us that a Jack Russell would be just the ticket. A few phone calls later to Jack Russell Rescue, and young Scooby became ours, and made himself part of the family – both human and canine – very quickly.

Scooby lived up to his breed's reputation and the rat population was promptly reduced. So what was a Jack Russell then left to do all day? Scooby had to search for new fields of conquest.

The lilac tree! 'What is the view like up there?' he must have thought. 'I can go where no dog has ever gone before!'

So while Scooby found himself nimbly climbing up the lilac tree, proudly surveying his kingdom, he clearly hadn't gone so far as to contemplate how he would get down again. Some time later, he started to get a bit worried and began to call for help with some embarrassed-sounding yips.

That's where I, Sister Joanne, had to come in. A Scooby rescue plan was launched.

The ladder was hastily found, leant against the tree and I bravely climbed up to retrieve the errant Jack Russell. We could just hear him thinking, 'Oh, how humiliating! I hope the other dogs aren't watching. *Please* leave a dog with just a bit of dignity!'

Unfortunately for us, the lilac tree was not the last or the highest tree Scooby has 'conquered', nor was it the last time he needed rescuing! He has now perfected the art of tree climbing, and has gained a reputation in our neighbourhood for this particular skill. He found he could get to the top of our 6-foot wall from some of the trees and run along barking at other dogs: he has fallen or jumped off a couple of times but finds his way back to the front door and waits to be let in. He has also been brought to the front by neighbours who have 'rescued' him from the wall – not that he needed it, but I guess it all adds to the fun.

Sister Joanne, Western Australia

Jasper's Disgrace

How can one look so cute and angelic, yet be so full of naughtiness?

Jasper was our black Labrador pup, adopted from Moorook Animal Shelter. We took her to puppy classes at the local vet. She was the tiny wild one in the class, scaring the other dogs and generally running amok. On one occasion, we were all sitting down in a circle, with our little dogs proudly at our feet. The vet nurse, who was running the class that night, was going around from dog to dog, greeting them in turn. We were unaware that Jasper had been watching this procession, coiling herself up like a spring, waiting for her big chance.

When the vet nurse got to our angelic Labrador, she squatted down to make her acquaintance. 'Hello, Jasper, how are —' With no warning, Jasper launched at her excitedly. In reflex, the nurse turned her head. Jasper grabbed and swallowed her earring, then sat back down, all in a split second. The nurse grabbed her ear and looked at the dog, then at us, then back at the dog, with a look of bewilderment on her face.

'I think . . . I think she just ate my earring . . .'

My wife and I turned ten shades of red, and apologised profusely.

We tried to suggest that the nurse had perhaps already lost the earring elsewhere, but in the pit of my stomach it was clear our Jasper had indeed taken her own souvenir from the visit.

We were all standing there with the entire class watching on, looking at this tiny, happy, black puppy who was wagging her tail and looking back at us as if to say, 'Right. What's next?'

Still somewhat in shock, the nurse explained she would have to take Jasper into another room and have her X-rayed to locate the missing jewellery. We agreed that whatever must be done was best, wondering how much this unexpected procedure was going to cost us.

The nurse whisked Jasper away, and my wife and I sat back down, dogless, in puppy class, like the naughty children that have to sit in the front row so the teacher can keep an eye on them.

Some back-up was required, so the class resumed with a new teacher. After a few minutes our favourite nurse stuck her head around the door and ushered us into an examination room to confirm what we all suspected. Jasper had indeed swallowed the earring.

She was going to need to be sedated and given something to induce vomiting. Failing that, she would have to be operated on. It would be too dangerous to let the earring pass through her system. Either way, the nurse tried hard to reassure us, Jasper would be very drowsy, but fine. Silently I was calculating the range of costs that might be due depending on the different methods of treatment. This puppy was gorgeous and sweet, but boy, she was a demonic black ball of insanity! We agreed to anything the nurse advised, apologising again. We seemed to be saying sorry a lot.

So we skulked back into class again, heads down. We sat there as the class continued, occasionally looking at each other, saying nothing, but thinking the same thing: 'Jasper . . . what have we got ourselves in for?'

About five minutes later the nurse came out with a sleepy, floppy puppy. Immediately I melted at how cute she was. I am too soft!

We were surprised at how quick and easy the procedure had seemed to be, not like our Jasper at all. The nurse explained that the earring had been retrieved when Jasper threw it up. She would be drowsy for the rest of the night, would need to be kept warm, with plenty of water, but she should bounce back the next day. And there was no charge for the service!

We thanked the nurse profusely for her kindness and generosity, apologised again, and scurried off to the car, our tails between our legs.

We took our little bundle of joy home, wrapped her up in a towel near the fire, with a bowl of water nearby. Within fifteen minutes, she woke up and hauled herself groggily out of the towel. Taking the towel with her on wobbly little legs, she dragged it across the floor, stepping in her water dish, spilling it as she pulled. Another ten minutes and she was running around, chewing the chair legs and yapping at her shadow. Drowsy? Our Jasper? You're going to have to do better than that!

Ben and Kyls, South Australia

Dusty, TV Critic

Adopting Dusty and Cindy from Seniors and Silky Rescue in New South Wales is the best thing we've ever done. If they're not bouncing around inside like mad things together they're outside chasing each other or the local lizard wildlife, or, currently, mice.

As for Dusty, he soon emerged as a laugh a minute. When not screaming around the house or yard at 200 kilometres an hour he is sitting with his eyes glued to the television. His favourite show? Cesar Millan, of course! When Cesar appears Dusty sits bolt upright and becomes totally engrossed, wags his tail vigorously and 'barks', talking to the animals he sees. If we stand between him and the TV to obstruct his view, he will lean to one side to try to keep watching.

In true rescue spirit, however, Dusty's favourite advertisement is the one for the RSPCA. We were all in the dining room having breakfast this morning when we heard the RSPCA jingle coming from the TV in the other room. Dusty jumped off and headed straight to the lounge and had a happy bark at the screen. His rescue mate Cindy also now joins in on the fun and as the bandaged animals move off the TV screen, she 'chases' them around the door and into the hallway only to find, to her dismay, they have magically disappeared!

Dusty loves his TV viewing so much, we've renamed him 'Mr Floppy', because when his favourite shows are on he just flops in front of the TV. We just hope he doesn't start getting addicted to something like *Days of our Lives* . . .

Ken and Chris, New South Wales

Team Bruce

Our first rendezvous with Bruce was in the McDonald's car park at Muswellbrook, where we met the pet transport company from Londonderry's Save our Strays (SOS). We had planned to welcome our new rescue dog with a Schmacko, but in my haste and excitement to meet him, I forgot to bring them, so McNuggets it was! He woofed them down in five-seconds flat and from that day on we haven't had a dull moment.

Bruce calls the pub we run home, and is a huge favourite among the patrons. Not many ex-death-row pound dogs can claim to be a team mascot with their name proudly emblazoned across twenty-five shirts, but our Bruce is one of them! The local touch football team are now known as 'Team Bruce'. Bruce does not go to games, however – mainly because he would chase everyone – but he does help cook the BBQ each Thursday night back at the pub after the game is over!

Last Easter, Bruce gave us our most memorable adventure. My husband and I had been to a wedding in Dubbo and Bruce stayed overnight at a very nice kennel called Pinecrest. In the morning we picked him up and he charged out the gate with much enthusiasm to see us. We were running early, so we decided to have breakfast by the banks of the Macquarie River. All was good until the food ran out, then Bruce decided that he would go for an 'explore'. He was gone for only a few seconds before we suddenly heard a loud *splash*. Bruce had fallen in the river!

Panic immediately set in for us as Bruce, being a Bulldog and built like a brick outhouse, is not a very good swimmer. I ran towards the river, only to suddenly slip in myself – the grass was very long and it was a very steep drop. Another splash! I looked over and to my relief saw Bruce had found a tree branch to cling to, near the edge. When he saw me flailing about also, however, he thought 'Safety in numbers!' and launched himself towards me. So there I was, fully clothed and still wearing the pearls from the wedding the night before, treading water with a 37-kilogram Bulldog trying to hold on to me!

My horrified husband Karsten stood on the riverbank, trying to assess how he would get us both out of the water as it was quite a steep drop. He threw Bruce's lead down and after a bit of heaving and hoeing from both of us, Bruce made it back on dry land. Karsten looked relieved, but 'What about me?' I cried. He replied, 'Swim up to that log and climb out that way!' Because I had lost my shoes in the water, Karsten threw down the only other pair I had with us to help me climb out, and they were my heels from the night before . . . you can imagine how I looked, clambering up the riverbank in high heels, dripping wet!

Once I had scrambled to safely, all I could do was laugh. Karsten was still white as a sheet, but began to see the funny side as time passed. Needless to say when we got back to the pub, there were no doggy Easter eggs for Bruce!

I can't thank PetRescue enough for helping me find a dog that has given us so much love, companionship, friendship and laughs. Go, Team Bruce!

Ellen, New South Wales

A Big Name for a Big Personality

I didn't mean to get so wrapped up in Mini's life, but somehow I did.

I had been thinking about getting a dog for a while. I had made the decision to adopt a rescue as I realised there were so many unwanted dogs needing homes. As with most things, I like to do my research online. I shop online, I self-diagnose online, you name it – if it's on there, I will find it . . . so the doggy search began online too.

It was through PetRescue I came across Shar Pei Rescue in Victoria. I'd always had a soft spot for these dogs, but believed they were out of my reach due to being a rare and expensive breed. But the group had a number of Shar Pei available. I suppose like with many other unfortunate dogs, the adorable cute wrinkly puppy grows up, needs training and attention, and the novelty of owning a Shar Pei simply wears off.

Mini – short for Maiphatlayde Mini Dee – was homeless as a result of a relationship breakdown. She'd been basically left with other dogs in a backyard and ignored. Her picture got me instantly: a fat, fluffy chocolate-coloured Shar Pei with her lavender tongue poking out at the camera – you could practically hear her panting! Well, that got me . . . I wanted to meet this little bear straight away.

I was fortunate to be approved by Shar Pei Rescue after going through the adoption application process, and when I first met Mini, she proceeded to climb up on a foot stool and offer me her paw . . . like the princess she is. With that I was smitten!

Mini, her royal highness, soon 'explained' to my partner and me that she expected to sleep on our bed, not outside our room, and several hours of snoring followed. If you haven't heard a Shar Pei snore, it has been likened to everything from a piglet snoring (on the low end of the scale) to a motorbike being started, to an old man breathing through a straw, to a strange swamp creature . . . Needless to say, the volume, pitch and variation of the sounds Mini can make are quite extraordinary.

Mini has a pretty full social calendar too; I'm fortunate enough to work in an office where I can bring her to work with me. She is an assistant office manager, guest greeter and company mascot. She's got her own Twitter account and has regular updates on Facebook too. But that's not all! Footage of her has gone global, with Mini appearing in our company's presentations, and even our overseas partners enquire after her. She is a mascot for 'Spinners' – Shane Warne's clothing line – and has thus made a number of media appearances, including morning TV, the news and current affairs. She's even managed to upstage Shane a couple of times! And not forgetting another very proud moment, when she shook her head and managed to cover a reporter in drool.

Mini has a pretty set routine in the office: she rides to work in the car with her snoz hanging out the window so she can look at all the people at the tram stop, she gets to work, plays hard to get with the receptionist, then she follows whoever is having their breakfast around, trying to charm a snack out of them. Next she rolls around on the floor making her 'happy noises', just to let everyone know she's arrived. She guards the photocopier – well, it might be perhaps because it has a nice warm breeze coming from inside it. Here she gets down to her real work: the art of being a lump. She sleeps, she naps, she dozes and slumbers, accompanying all with the characteristic Shar Pei symphony of snores, sighs, grunts and snorts.

Mini has plenty of other quirks: she chases plastic bags in the park, she can tell the difference between organic chicken necks and regular ones, rejecting the non-organic every time, she uses her paw to poke and prod you if she feels she's not getting enough of your attention, and thinks nothing of jumping up on the bed and sneezing in my face when she believes it's time to wake up. She has a penchant for smoked salmon, soft cheeses and Chinese mooncakes. She is drama queen: stubborn and headstrong, but I wouldn't have her any other way. Yes, Maiphatlayde Mini Dee is a pretty grandiose name, but then again, Mini has a pretty big personality.

Sai-Wai, Victoria

Not Quite Perfect

Ever noticed how three-legged dogs' smiles always seem to be the widest? It doesn't matter whether it's a missing leg, patchy fur or poor vision, there is no defeating the spirit of some battlers. These dogs are not quite perfect but they're perfect to us.

Holding onto Hope

It was by the side of a busy highway in Western Australia where a blind and emaciated Shar Pei mix was found dumped. Luckily for her, a passerby saved her from being killed in the traffic, and the terrified female was taken to the Animal Protection Society. There it was soon discovered she was pregnant, and suffering from mange. She was a pitiful sight – who could have treated her this way?

With no identification on her, her carers named this dog Hope, in the desire that she could have her sight restored, but it wasn't to be. The specialist decided she had probably been born blind, and is able to see shapes only. One eye is worse than the other, so she has a tendency to collide with things on that side if she is not careful.

I was a volunteer at the shelter when Hope was brought in. I had been without a dog for three years, and wasn't sure I wanted to have another one with all the responsibilities it brings. Being a foster carer to a dog in need was a good compromise, I thought, and Hope came home with me. She needed to have her puppies in a loving and warm environment, which I could provide. Two-and-a-half weeks later, she became a mum in my laundry to two little ones – a girl and a boy. Thankfully neither of them were blind. Hope was a fantastic mother in spite of her blindness and all she had been through. The little ones went off to good homes at eight weeks old.

It was when Hope's pups were born that I realised I couldn't say goodbye to her – we had quickly formed a strong bond. I was born with a hearing impairment and believe Hope could sense that I was challenged like her. From my own experience, I knew the most important thing was to give Hope the protection and care she needed with her disability, but to grant her independence too, so she could live as normally as possible – the same way my parents had nurtured me.

Fortunately, the shelter agreed Hope could stay, and once the pups were gone I really 'went to work' on building Hope up physically and emotionally. Thankfully, many generous people donated towards helping with Hope's medical costs. Her skin was still in a poor state from mange, and I also discovered she had an intolerance to the preservatives in commercial dog food. I changed her diet to a raw, natural one after many hours' research. I ordered herbal remedies from an animal naturopath to help her skin and to get her suppressed immune system firing again.

Because of what she'd been through, Hope was easily frightened of the world, so gradual training and socialisation was important. After two years, I am happy to report she is well on her way to becoming a confident dog; more dogs are becoming friends on her visits to the park, and Hope even has a boyfriend now! A close friend of mine has a male dog that Hope adores, and she chases after him when he runs after the ball at the park. He's easy for her to see, being a big white boy who shows up against the green and brown of the surrounds.

At the end of last year, Hope met my parents' dog for the first time, and they have become friends too. Together they make us laugh with their antics in the backyard. Hope has learnt to trust and love people, and is slowly understanding that children are another source of enjoyment.

I never had a rescue dog before Hope. I now know without a doubt I would always adopt another rescue pet in the future. If you take your time to give them the love they so need and deserve, they will become the most loyal and loving dog you could possibly hope for. Hope makes me laugh with her antics; she has filled my heart up again; and in turn given me hope for the years ahead.

Leisa, Western Australia

Max on Wheels

I was turning twenty-nine, and about to receive the best birthday present ever! My dog Max.

My fiancé at the time announced that he was going to get me a dog for my birthday. We'd just moved back to Darwin and I wasn't going to give him the chance to rethink the offer! We visited the RSPCA shelter a couple of times but there were only Rottweilers and Chihuahuas there, breeds I just didn't seem to have a connection with. The third time we went there were two Blue Heelers – one a bouncy puppy and the other an older boy who just sat watching us patiently from his enclosure. Well, not being one for youngsters of any kind, I chose the two-year-old male called Harry. We had a friend called Harry at the time and the name didn't really suit my new dog, so we went with the universally popular name Max.

Max quickly became my 'heart dog'. Even the obedience trainer commented on how strong our bond was after being together for only four months. Max went everywhere with me. He tolerated being dressed up for the Million Paws Walk, learnt to wave to kids at the Pet Expo, had his photo taken with Santa and flew to Adelaide with me for a wonderful holiday during a family reunion.

As everyone does, we also had our embarrassing moments. Once I was walking Max around the local high school when he stopped to do his business but was constipated for some reason. After straining for a time Max decided that I should help him. He waddled over, still in the squat position, pleading with me to do something. Usually there were never people around but of course today we had a small audience. I couldn't leave him in distress so I pressed while Max pushed and I pretended no one was watching. Max was briefly grateful and ran off to continue sniffing, leaving me to bag his poo in front of the onlookers!

Another day we were walking along the leash-free beach and Max was well ahead of me, as usual. A group of young men were sitting on the sand, enjoying a few beers while watching the sun set. Max, being a typical male dog, cocked his leg on most stationary objects and . . . you can guess what happened next: the back of one of the men was not spared! The poor fellow jumped up, exclaiming. Max continued on down the beach and I pretended he belonged to someone else!

Max protected me from everything, from grasshoppers to people. If we had parties at home I couldn't dance with anyone because Max would nip them. When I split up with my fiancé, Max put his paw across my shoulders as I lay weeping on the couch. Unfortunately his assertiveness and confidence also meant that if there was an aggressive dog around that wanted a fight, Max would be in it.

The last time we were attacked, an enormous dog stepped over its fence and grabbed Max right around the middle and shook him like a rope toy. It happened so fast I couldn't react. The owner grabbed his dog, but it was too late. Max was crying and his lung had collapsed. I rushed him back to the car and to our vet. Max recovered but he aged very quickly after that.

In 2007 my husband and I married in the Botanic Gardens. Weddings are meant to be mainly the bride's day, but Max also had centre-stage! He was my attendant and was so well behaved. Max is in most of the photos, and one I particularly love is of us walking down a garden path together. It's black and white and I'm looking at Max and he's looking back at me. My poor new husband doesn't get a look-in in that one!

Three months later Max started coughing and the vet diagnosed him with heart failure. He said that Max either had three months or three years left to live – it was hard to tell – and prescribed the medication he would need for the rest of his life. I was devastated and we walked slowly back to the car.

The medication helped Max's cough but it was also a diuretic, to remove any fluid from his lungs. The resulting uncontrolled incontinence distressed Max greatly, being such a neat and clean dog. An internet search found a body wrap for male dogs and I discovered the world of incontinence pads. Max no longer woke up in a puddle and all was well for nearly another year.

Then his back legs started to give up. Another internet search, and I found Max a set of dog wheels! Max genuinely believed in his capacity to do anything and didn't accept his failing body. Consequently, he mastered his new wheels straight away and after learning to make allowances for going around trees and poles, there was no stopping him. On his wheels he chased a cat down the driveway so fast I couldn't catch him, and he still tried to mount other dogs at the vet! One day we were walking along the footpath and the local ranger pulled up and tried to fine me for not having my dog on a lead! After chatting about Max and why he had wheels, he decided to let me off because my dog was disabled.

At this time, we often walked along the foreshore but it now took twice as long because so many people stopped me to ask about Max and his wheels. Many wanted to take his photo, too, and offer him their nibbles. One day Max spat out the dry biscuit he was offered and I jokingly said that he wanted something on top of it. The poor man then got out a better biscuit with something tasty on it, and of course Max ate it! It was like being with a celebrity. Everyone wanted to know about Max and his wheels.

I emailed a photo of Max to the NT News, thinking they might pick up the story for the *Sunday Territorian* which ran a weekly article called 'Me and My Ride'. Usually it was dedicated to owners and their hot cars, but within twenty-four hours I had done an interview with a journalist, and a photographer came to do a photoshoot with Max. That weekend my boy had a full-page spread devoted just to him and his celebrity status went through the roof! Not only would people walking by stop for a chat, but drivers would pull over in their cars and ask if he was the same dog they'd seen in the newspaper.

Of course, my furry boy could not live forever. Shortly after his thirteenth birthday his front legs started to fail also and he didn't want to go on walks any more. I couldn't leave him at home on his own and took him to doggy day care while I was at work. Sadly, there came a day when they wouldn't look after Max any more either, and I took time off work to be with him. Max couldn't sleep well and I lay on the floor in the lounge room to keep him company. Eventually the lack of sleep started to take its toll on us both and I just didn't know what Max needed any more. The vet said she had done everything she could and everyone around me said it was time to put him to sleep.

The weekend before that dreadful day I took Max to his favourite places and bought him his most-loved food – a pie with sauce. I didn't know what I was going to do without him. My husband drove while Max sat on my lap with his head out the window, savouring the fresh breeze on his face for one last time.

The vet let me have some private time to say goodbye and I told Max I loved him, having never said it before or since with such sincerity. The time came and I held my boy in my arms and stroked his head. When Max realised what was happening, he started to struggle and tried to get up. He wasn't ready. He didn't want to go yet. But the vet sedated Max and he crossed over Rainbow Bridge. I was more alone than I'd ever been.

I was so lost in the weeks that followed I volunteered to walk the shelter dogs at the RSPCA after work. Six weeks later I walked a black Labrador Kelpie mix who found herself back at the shelter for a third time, through no fault of her own. We were both looking for something that was missing in our lives and so the next day I adopted Wendy.

That weekend was the Blessing of the Animals service at a local church and I took Max's ashes along with Wendy and me to be blessed. We ended up on the ABC news that night. Max was still a celebrity!

I have some professional photos of Max up on the wall in the spare room at my house. The night of the service Wendy jumped up on the bed, stood on her hind legs and pointed with her nose to the portrait of Max as if to say 'I know, Max. It's okay.' I mentioned this to a good friend of mine, who is an animal communicator, and she said that Max and Wendy were related in a spiritual sense. Max was now free of the limitations of his old body and would be with me when I needed him.

Two-and-a-half years later, I still miss Max. My relationship with Wendy isn't the same but then, why would it be? I have helped her find her confidence and she has encouraged me to love unconditionally again and to take delight in small day-to-day miracles. She is cuddly, is always wherever I am and will never let me sleep through the alarm.

In Max's memory, I try to be a better person and volunteer at the RSPCA shelter whenever I can. Perhaps one day Max and I will meet again. Until then, thank you for your love and loyalty, Max, and for showing so many people that most of life's hurdles can be overcome if you just believe in yourself.

Christine, Northern Territory

Captain Sully, the Pirate Dog

Who would want a seven-year-old one-eyed dog with a dicky ticker? Us! After our last Cavalier King Charles Spaniel died a few years ago, we decided not to have another dog – our hearts were too broken, but our eight-year-old son had other ideas. He longed and pined for a dog to love again, so we started to look for a rescue Cavvy, but were 'pipped at the post' every time. They were popular pups!

Then I saw the pictures of Sully on the Australian Animal Protection Society's website (AAPS) and fell in love, but kept it quiet from the family so as not to disappoint anyone. I remember my heart beating with both excitement and fear as I submitted the application. When the phone rang the next day I was prepared for disappointment. The co-ordinator of the Keysborough shelter in Victoria explained Sully's special needs and, to my surprise, hesitantly enquired whether I still wanted to adopt him. The answer was a resounding yes!

Sully had been at the shelter for a long time. Although it seemed that no one wanted a seven-year-old one-eyed dog with a dicky ticker, Sully was obviously just waiting for the right family to come along. We will all have special needs at some time in our life – sometimes when we're very young, and sometimes just as we age. Each member of our own family has special needs in one form or another, so Sully's health issues were of little concern to us.

When I arrived home with Sully, our son Perry, after getting over his initial shock that we could keep him, noticed he only had one eye and exclaimed, 'He's a pirate dog!' It has been true love for these two ever since. Sully didn't take long to settle in with the family routine and now certainly lets us know he's miffed if we don't stick to it. He reminds Grandma when it's time to get the boys from school, and insists on going on every pick-up. He reminds us, Mum and Dad, when it is time for the boys to go to bed and he lets us know when he considers it our bedtime too. If we're late in his opinion, he lets us know by pacing around and then lying down half a metre away, looking balefully up at us. He is only completely happy when the entire 'pack' is at home and is ecstatic when the last person arrives home, no matter who it is, so he can keep an eye on us all.

Although Sully is considered to have special needs, he actually helps us with the needs of our children. Sully loves having long calming cuddles with our intense, active eight-year-old, and they adore each other. His past is a mystery, but inspires such interesting tales that assist Aramis with his literacy issues. Our imaginary stories of 'Captain Sully, the Pirate Dog' have also motivated me to write a children's story.

Many people remark what a lucky dog Sully is and that we were 'wonderful' for adopting him. But we are the lucky ones. Because of his age, we may only have him for a limited time, and yes, our hearts will be broken again when that day comes, but his needs are minimal in comparison to the love he both gives and engenders every day within our own special-needs family.

Monica, Victoria

Spoon-feeding Arlie

We were told our puppy was a Boxer mix so we named her Arlie, after boxing legend, Mohammad Ali. We found out soon after that she was all Staffy, however. It didn't matter. She was the most beautiful, loving, wonderful pet, but she had no table manners. When she ate you could actually hear her inhaling to gulp the food down quickly without chewing! Then she more often than not promptly threw everything up again. We found a particular sausage food that we mashed up into her bowl that she would have to lick off more slowly and this helped keep some food down. We couldn't give her bones or treats at all.

It was a mystery. What was wrong with our little Staffy?

At one point she was sick for days so I took her to the vet and after an X-ray was performed, there appeared to be a blockage. The vet operated that afternoon and the golf-ball-shaped problem turned out to just be a clump of the finely crushed gravel that our driveway was made out of. Our vet was confused as to what was causing Arlie's food problems until I mentioned in passing that whenever she was sick her throat seemed to get bigger (I had assumed it was swelling). Our vet immediately arranged for her to be seen by the specialist animal endoscopy centre. The results were devastating.

Arlie had a constriction in her oesophagus where it joined her stomach. Most dogs born with this died or were put to sleep at a very young age. Thankfully, Arlie's case was mild enough that she had been able to keep *some* food down and managed to survive. She needed surgery the next afternoon but it would cost thousands of dollars. She had a 30 per cent chance of dying, a 30 per cent chance of needing to be fed through a gastric tube straight to her stomach for the rest of her life, and about a 30 per cent chance of the operation being successful and Arlie having a normal life.

Our girl was only two years old, so we were not very impressed with those odds. We spoke to the specialist and said we wanted the weekend to think about it – his reply was the longer we left it the worse it would be, but we needed the time.

Once we understood the logistics of Arlie's problem, it made much more sense. The food would go down her throat but get stuck at the constriction, then sit in her oesophagus. This stretched the oesophagus and formed a sack so that when she would eat, the food would just go into the sack instead of her stomach.

My husband and I came up with a plan. It was worth a try. We bought a high-nutrition, low-volume dog food, soaked it in hot water for about half an hour and then blended it into a purée. We got Arlie to stand with her front paws on one of our outdoor chairs and we tried spoon-feeding her small amounts at a time. We worked out that if we held her throat as well, we could keep the sack collapsed so that the food couldn't go into it. Was it going to work?

Arlie ate and kept her food down all that weekend. We went back to our vet on Monday and, impressed, he agreed that if it was successful thus far, why not give it a try for a while and see what happened?

So we did. For the next ten years we soaked, blended, spoon-fed and cleaned up after Arlie when she ate something she wasn't supposed to. During that time my other dog, Kirra, passed away. We brought a new canine member to our family, Tallis. We moved twice. We had two children.

Arlie was there for all of it. And she was worth every minute of the twelve years we spent feeding her the only way that ensured she could survive. My mother first said that we wouldn't be able to keep it up once we had a baby, but by then, feeding Arlie this way was just part of life. It meant that we couldn't go away for the weekend and have anyone else feed the dogs while we were gone. It meant that any time I took the dogs anywhere we would also have to take the blender. It meant that we would have to be vigilant that Arlie didn't get anything else to eat or the next couple of days would be a real battle.

We were devastated when told that our Arlie had liver cancer and wouldn't survive. Taking her to the vet and holding her as she went to sleep forever was one of the hardest things I have had to do. I wouldn't wish it on anyone. But having Arlie as part of our family for twelve years was worth every tear and every minute spent spoon-feeding her.

Leanne, Queensland

What's Big, Hairy and Full of Smooches?

Q: What's big, hairy and full of smooches?
A: Roxy, our gorgeous PetRescue German Shepherd!
After finally managing to buy our own house, getting a dog was a top priority and I was hoping to find an adult German Shepherd in need of a loving home. My family have previously adopted German Shepherds from 'deprived backgrounds' and they have all been big, boofy, wonderful, entertaining, loving, loyal and intelligent companions. So each night I checked PetRescue, frequently

sniffling and shedding a tear over the keyboard, wanting to help all those lovely dogs.

This particular night, there were a few German Shepherds, but my attention kept returning to a very forlorn-looking girl by the name of Roxy. She was a long-haired Shepherd and was terribly skinny. I kept my eye on her for a while, and soon her photo changed to a nicer one, but there still didn't seem to be many 'hits' on Roxy's page. So I decided to ring the contact person at the Animal Welfare League of NSW.

Audrey was very helpful, providing a description of Roxy's personality and also advising that she had a deformed eye socket. She'd been thoroughly vet checked, however, and it did not appear to be causing any problems. Her 'deformity' didn't bother me – I know that nobody's perfect, so Roxy didn't have to be either!

We met Roxy that weekend, and although she seemed more interested in racing around the yard and sniffing the grass, we decided she was the one. She jumped into the back seat of the car like she'd known us for years and then fell asleep on the way home.

Roxy was almost skeletal, and we were informed she had probably never been fed properly in her life. With time, good food and exercise, however, she has filled out beautifully. She still greets each bone, walk and meal with the same exuberant degree of anticipation and delight as she did in the very beginning. Of course, now she knows the sounds associated with each event, and bounds out to her 'spot', sitting as still as a big excited dog possibly can (that is, with lots of quivering and tail bouncing). I love watching her eat, because she just relishes each mouthful, thoroughly and repeatedly checking the surrounding area for the next fifteen minutes or so just to ensure no morsels have been overlooked. We have strawberries growing in the backyard and on one occasion, while my partner was chatting to the neighbour over the fence, Roxy wandered down, nosed through the strawberry patch and delicately plucked a strawberry off and ate it. Now we know why there are never any for us!

Within all German Shepherds, no matter how soft and sooky, beats the heart of a protector, and Roxy is no exception. Her large barrel-like body generates a very impressive bark – especially when it reverberates between the house and the metal fence! She lets us know when there's anything or anyone unusual around and we certainly feel very secure. We have high side gates so fortunately any potential crooks will only hear her, which is just as well as she could never look ferocious – her funny deformed eye gives her a cute, quizzical expression, and as a friend commented, it looks like she's winking at you all the time! Hardly a convincing look for a wannabe guard dog . . .

Each morning Roxy pads down the hallway to our bedroom and greets us with a cuddle and a good morning nudge from her velvet-soft nose; she then promptly heads back to her bed. At night, if we're up too late for her liking, she does a very loud, drawn out, exasperated groan from her spot in the lounge room, which clearly conveys 'Will you switch off that damn TV and go to bed?'

My partner had never had a dog in his life before Roxy, so it has been new territory for him. It has been wonderful to watch how close they have become. She really is 'his' girl. They adore each other and she fills a very special place in his heart. Perhaps their affinity is not so strange after all – the punchline for this story is that Martin has a dodgy eye himself. Martin jokes that between he and Roxy, they both have a full set!

Annette and Martin, New South Wales

Our Little Battler

Some look to sports people for heroes; some to rock stars or Hollywood actors. But I look no further than our little battler, Hooch.

Back in 1998, my husband and I were fortunate enough to rescue a three-year-old Staffy mix that was no longer wanted by his family. He was malnourished – virtually starving – and his name was Hooch. On top of that, Hooch had tragically been beaten as a pup, sending him blind. But despite all this, this brave, friendly dog came into our lives, wagging his tail and just happy to be alive.

Watching him wolf down his first dinner with us, brought a tear to my eye as it proved just how badly he had been treated. At that point we made a promise to love him for the rest of his life.

We became 'guide people' for Hooch. We were his eyes, but with trust and increased confidence, he became independent and was excellent at navigating around on his own. It was amazing to watch – you would never know he was blind at times. We even taught him to sit and wait for his food. He trusted us with all his heart and he was our best pal. He came everywhere with us, out in the bush or just for a run around the farm.

But as if his puppy life wasn't bad enough, in 2002 came the worst day of our lives: the vet found a tumour on his prostate. Surgery was the only answer to save our boy's life, we were told, and the vet promptly removed a tumour the size of a rockmelon! However, Hooch pulled through with flying colours. But not long after that, he inexplicably suffered a stroke. This little battler had so much determination to stay with us, however, and he got better again.

The odds were stacked up against Hooch from day one, considering all that he had been through. But he taught us patience, courage, and how you can still have a normal, happy life despite a disability. Against all odds, Hooch made it to thirteen years of age, and although we miss him to pieces, we are glad and honoured to have had him in our life. RIP, our little battler, Hooch.

Renee, Victoria

The Price of Kindness

Pippin was in a terrible condition and I knew I had to get him out of there in a hurry. He'd been dumped six months earlier at a boarding kennel, and his owners were clearly not coming back. He had a collar that was too tight, leaving open sores on his neck, he was skin and bone, and his behaviour was manic. As for his coat, it was dull, lifeless, and covered with fleas and sores. An urgent vet appointment confirmed an irregular heart rhythm and dehydration. Several weeks later, Pippin required $5500 worth of spinal surgery, to rectify a painful injury to his spine, most likely caused by either blunt-force trauma (such as kicking) or being dropped when young. How had one little dog endured so much?

Recovery was slow, and to this day Pip walks a little funny, but is able to run and jump now like other dogs. His emotional scars are deeper, however; he is still afraid of strangers (which we are working on, and is further evidence he was abused) and he cannot tolerate shut doors. But he is the most loving little fellow and enjoys life now, running around the yard and playing with his toys. He even has a penchant for swimming!

Pippin has a 'brother', my elderly boy, Jackson, who I adopted from Cavalier King Charles Spaniel Rescue of Queensland. His history is unknown, but he too came to them in poor condition. Jack has a hearing

HELPING EACH OTHER TO HEAL

'I brought Riley into my home and we started the journey towards his recovery. As he lay with his head on my lap, I promised him that no one would ever hurt him again. He just looked up at me as if to say, "Thank you so much."'

WHY CAN'T WE BE FRIENDS?

Above: Terrier-mix Paddle Pop takes on Angus, the bird who thinks he's a dog – and loses. Pic: Courtesy *Herald Sun*

Below: Adoptive Mum Donatella feeding her pups.

Top right: The real-life Milo and Otis, who happily found a home together.
Pic: Courtesy *Herald Sun*

Bottom right: Max and Sambuca hanging out with their rabbit pal, DJ BunBunz. Pic: Courtesy Alex Cearns

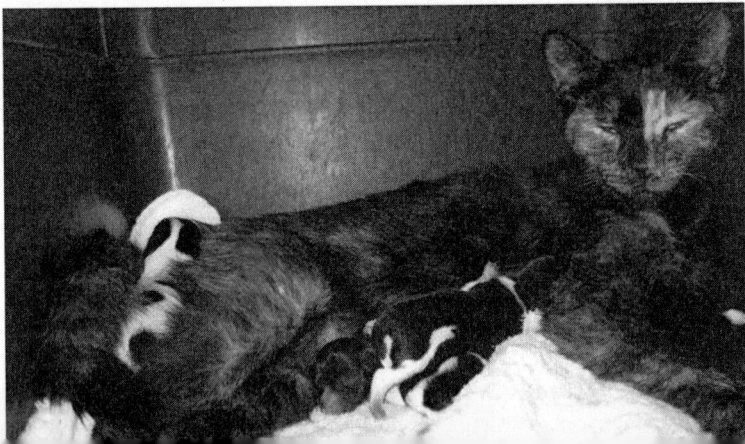

AGAINST ALL ODDS

Left: Sando, whose skull was riddled with shotgun pellets, now has a new home with a place for him by the fire and even his own doggy Driza-Bone jacket. Pic: Courtesy *Herald Sun*

Above: Barnaby the Wolfhound suffered agoraphobia as a result of being kept caged all his life. With lots of love from his new family, he is coming along in leaps and bounds at his country home. Pic: Courtesy *Herald Sun*

Right: Missy survived ill treatment in a puppy factory to become a support dog for her owner, who was battling breast cancer. Pic: Courtesy Katrucia Pet Photography

YOU CAN'T KEEP A GOOD DOG DOWN

Above: Izzy has a special ability to make her owner blush in their neighbour-hood dog park.

Below: Jasper the naughty black Lab liked the look of a vet nurse's earring so much that the pup nipped it off her ear and swallowed it.

Top right: Pub dog Bruce, rescued after being dumped, shares his luck as mascot of his local touch-footy team.

Bottom right: Scooby likes to survey his kingdom from a tall lilac tree but needs a bit of help to get down again.

KIDS AND CRITTERS

Above: Pumba the Maltese mix and nine-year-old fosterer Georgia both pined after they were separated, but happily were soon reunited.

Below: Rocket the Australian Cattle Dog mix acts as a third parent, sounding the alert whenever Tahlia cries, and guarding her when she's on the move.

Top right: Jasmine the stray stopped ten-month-old baby Bridget from crawling onto a busy road.

Bottom right: Eleven-year-old Jack and Dusty the Kelpie share a special bond.

Farmyard Nursery 2010

SUPERSTARS!

Above: Zumba has won many prizes for agility and has walked the red carpet at Movie World film premieres.

Left: JD, a Bull Terrier-Heeler mix, was subjected to medical experiments before he was rehomed. His good looks and placid temperament saw him become hot property, and he featured in catalogues, newspapers and TV advertisements.

Top right: Mini the Shar Pei starlet has gone from abandoned to adored: now she's the mascot for Warnie's clothing line and has her own Twitter account.

Bottom right: Champion trial dogs Rusty and Denny are 'proud mongrels' who leave pedigree pets in their dust.

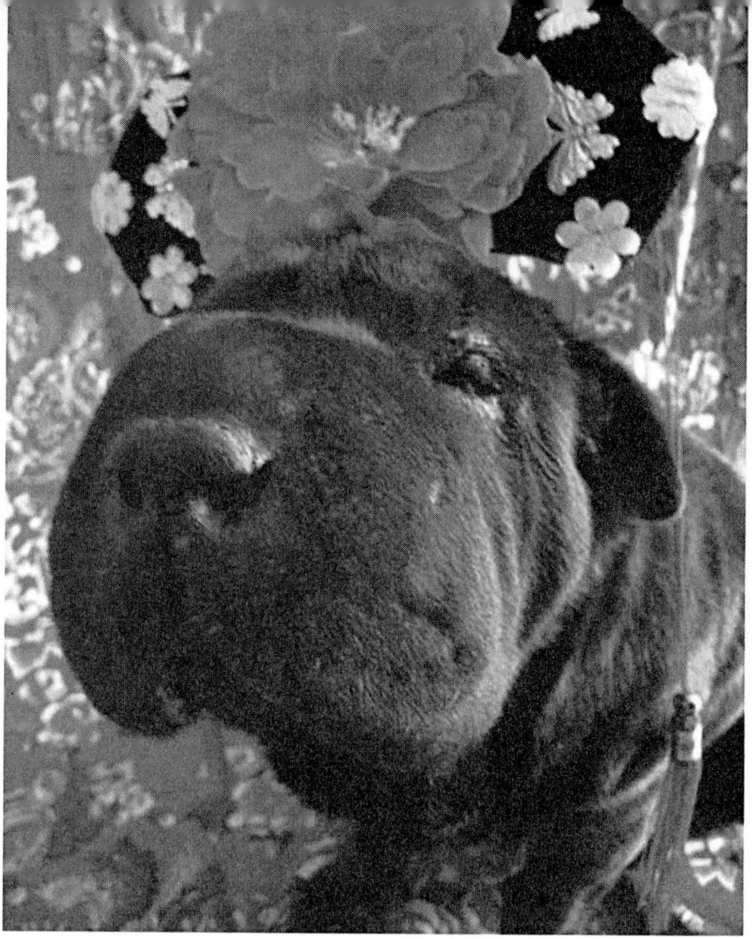

DOGS WITH JOBS

Above: Amber the Koolie, found abandoned at a truck stop, was marked out by a pound ranger for her exceptional intelligence and agility. She now serves her country in Afghanistan with the Explosives Detection Dogs Unit.

Top right: Gentle Wellington keeps the patients company as they undergo dialysis treatment.

Bottom right: Shadow, born without hip sockets as a result of puppy-factory inbreeding, does his bit as a doggy therapist at a dementia care facility.

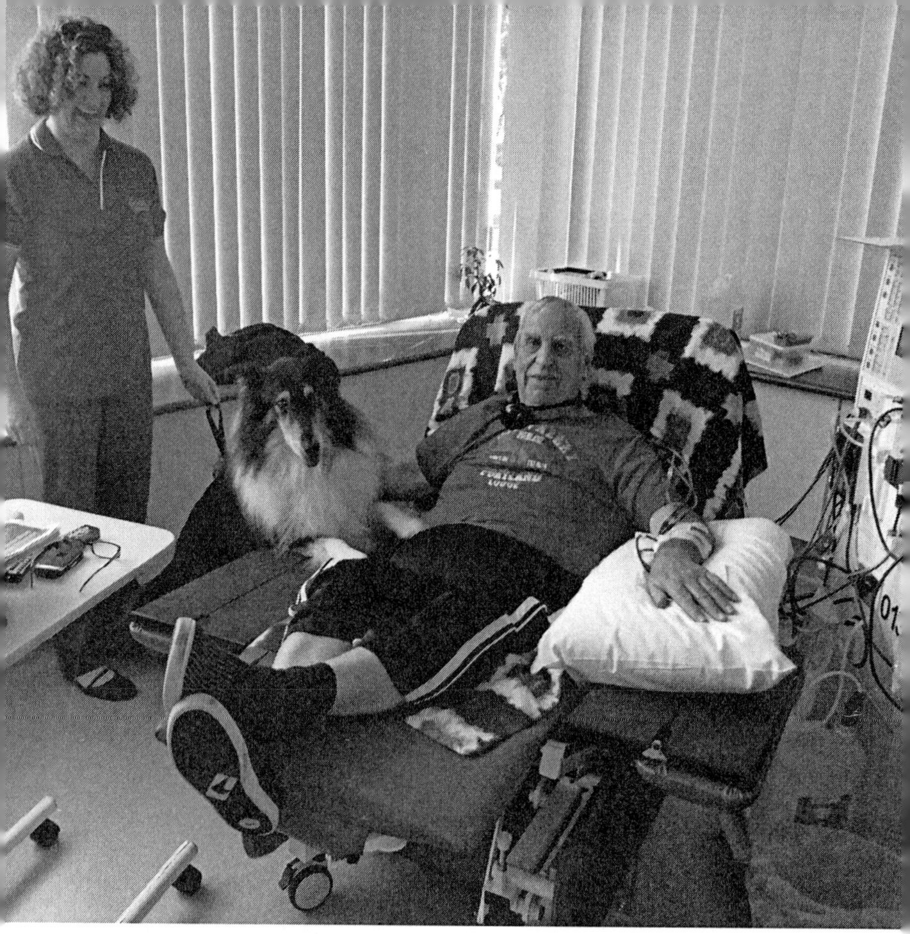

SILVER LININGS

Below: Princess was 'a dirty, smelly, matted mess' after being rescued from a puppy factory. Post rehabilitation and a haircut, she is happy and healthy with her pup.

Right: Kilmore resident Jetta the Kelpie-Lab mix was severely burnt in the Black Saturday bushfires. Her owners had lost their house and couldn't bear to lose Jetta too, and they and the vet hospital fought hard for her recovery. Miraculously, she pulled through, although her ordeal claimed one of her eyes. After two months at the vet's, Jetta returned home to her grateful family.
Pic: Courtesy *Herald Sun*

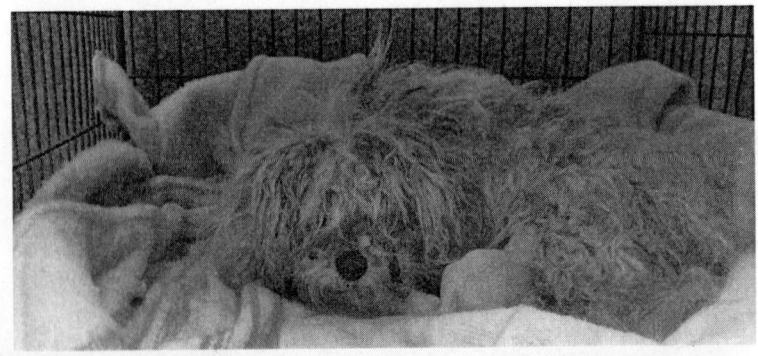

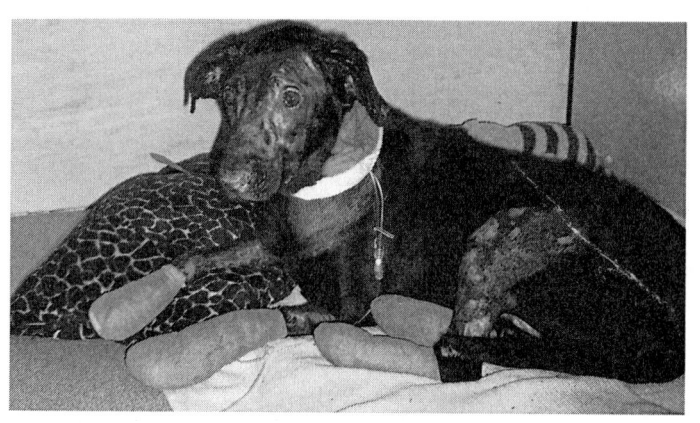

THE JOY OF SECOND CHANCES

'On a daily basis our rescue pets show us their capacity to love, to forgive, and to rise above circumstances that would have many of us two-leggeds utterly beaten. They remind us to find wonderment in the smallest things, and wake up every day with a smile,' Saskia Adams and Vickie Davy.

impediment, a cataract, and has just been diagnosed with syringomyelia, which is a terrible genetic condition where the skull cavity is too small for the brain. This is potentially life threatening for most dogs, and the usual treatment is surgery, which can be hit and miss. Luckily, Jack is on medication which is working well, although it is very expensive. He can live a mostly normal life.

These two dogs were most likely the product of puppy factories: especially probable in Jack's case, as no reputable breeder would continue to use genetically unsound animals. If fewer people supported this inhumane industry by refusing to buy the cute puppies in the pet-shop window – which almost always come from a puppy factory – the reduced demand would make this abhorrent industry less lucrative and attractive to their operators.

In addition to Pippin and Jack, I also had another Cavalier, whom I rescued directly from a puppy factory, who passed away at the age of three years from a genetic heart condition, mitral valve disease.

These loving little boys have changed my life forever. Because of them, and their suffering that I have witnessed, I am doing all I can to raise awareness about puppy factories and their associated cruelty by supporting the RSPCA campaign, Close Puppy Factories, and Oscar's Law, which also aims to ban pet shops from selling factory-farmed animals. Pippin and Jack do their bit to raise awareness too by wearing their 'I Want Oscar's Law!' bandanas when they go out and about. Jackson also has his own Facebook page, which he uses to raise awareness of factory farming of puppies, and diseases such as syringomyelia.

It saddens me that these beautiful animals suffer because some people feel money is more important than kindness. With a lot of love, care and expense, Pippin and Jack, despite their disabilities, are living fairly comfortable lives. But so many others born in puppy factories never will. Pippin and Jack want Oscar's Law, and so do I!

Vera, Queensland

Lovely Lily

The lily is a symbol of innocence, purity and beauty. This is why the dog you see in the picture is called Lily.

Lily was first owned by someone who used her as a backyard breeding dog. She had litter after litter of puppies. This person also left Lily behind when he moved out, and she was alone for a number of days without food or water. In addition to this, Lily was blind. Her plight was observed by a kind neighbour, who did their best to care for the abandoned dog, but eventually had to relinquish her to their local pound.

When I heard about her, I felt compelled to protect and care for Lily. However, in the days leading up to collecting her from the pound, I experienced some nervousness: Could I meet the needs of a blind dog? Would I be able to 'connect' without her being able to see me?

On the morning I was driving to pick up Lily, I called a friend of mine and broke down crying, explaining my concerns of not being able to properly provide for Lily, of not knowing how to relate to a dog with no sight. My friend reminded me of something important: 'Even though Lily cannot see you, she will feel your heart and know that she is safe.'

When I finally saw Lily and held her, I was more than sure that she felt every single beat of my heart and we immediately fell in love. Instead of taking Lily to our shelter, I drove her straight home and introduced her to my two children, to whom she immediately gave many kisses even though she couldn't see them. I was deeply moved. Lily maneuvered around my house as if she had lived there all her life.

Although Lily is blind, we had hoped there was a way she might see again. However, when we took her to an eye specialist, he said that Lily had glaucoma and her eyes were very badly damaged. No matter what they did, she could never regain her sight. He also explained that something needed to be done for Lily as soon as possible, as she was experiencing discomfort behind the eyes – similar to if we had a constant headache.

The disappointment was felt by everyone in the room. This amazing dog, who had forgiven humans for the life that had been thrust upon her, and who so desperately deserved to see, could not be helped?

The focus had to turn to what we *could* do for Lily. The specialist outlined two options, and we decided the second was the best: Lily needed to have her eyes removed, then sutured closed. The other option – giving Lily two prosthetic (non-seeing) eyes – had higher risks of injury attached.

But the worst news was yet to come. During the surgery, the vet found that Lily had advanced breast cancer. He called us to ask how we wanted him to proceed. There was no question – the vet was asked to attempt to remove the cancer and continue the surgery. However, we were informed that due to the prolonged length of the operation, Lily might die.

After six-and-a-half hours and the loss of much blood, a miracle happened: Lily made it through. She was remarkably lively after the operation, walking around the clinic (although slowly) and wagging her tail. That long, first night was the scariest and when we got the call the next morning to say she'd made it through, tears of joy were shed by us all.

If there is a purpose, a reason, to explain Lily's suffering, a way in which it can be of value, it is to bring awareness to the importance of desexing. It is widely known that leaving a female dog undesexed greatly increases their risk of mammary or breast cancer, and in male dogs, testicular cancer. This had nearly cost Lily her life.

Lily is now enjoying happy and fulfilling days with her loving family – both human and furry!

Trish Burke, Pets Haven Animal Shelter, Victoria

Sasha, the Three-legged Ambo

When Sasha was hit by a car, it turned out to be a lucky day for her.

She was only six months old when being walked along a busy street without a lead by her previous owners. At that age she was too young to have much road sense and ran out into traffic and was struck. Her left hind leg was badly broken in multiple places.

The owners took her to their local vet to be put down. They couldn't afford to treat Sasha. However, they could have brought her into the Lort Smith Animal Hospital in Melbourne where they would have been able to pay off Sasha's costs over time.

Sasha's local vet didn't want to put Sasha to sleep – her injuries weren't life-threatening, plus she was a young, healthy dog. This kind vet brought her into Lort Smith to see what could be done. Sasha was taken through to the kennels unit where she caught the eye of my then-partner, Animal Management Officer Emma, who instantly fell in love with her.

Despite being hurt and only on mild pain relief at that stage, Sasha was friendly and lively. Emma took great care of Sasha and later became her foster carer. The vet who brought her in also offered to help in any way he could, without charge. What a team!

We soon found that Sasha's leg sadly couldn't be saved, but following an emergency amputation she recovered well. Like most three-legged animals, Sasha nimbly adjusted to her new tripod arrangement, ever so grateful just to be alive.

Sasha wasn't quite out of the woods yet, however. She had a mild luxating patella on her unharmed hind leg that on a four-legged dog wouldn't require surgery, but with only one back leg remaining after

Sasha's amputation, the remaining back leg would need to be strong. She was given a couple of weeks to recover from the previous operation before she underwent patella surgery on the other leg.

After her surgery, Emma and I spent as much time as possible with her while she was confined in a small cage in which she needed to rest. It wasn't much fun for her, of course, and she needed lots of attention and hugs.

The little girl bounced back, yet again. She now lives at my house with a German Shepherd and a Jack Russell Chihuahua mix, with whom she is the best of friends. She spends hours each day running around the house on her three legs, playing with her housemates, her balls and her ropes. We have even purchased a life jacket for her to swim in during the warmer months!

Sasha is now the proud mascot of the Lort Smith Animal Ambulance, which I drive, and regularly comes out on runs with me to visit elderly pensioners and disabled people who have lost their pets. Sasha always brings lots of love and comfort to these people.

What wonderful teamwork combined to help save this special girl. And Sasha continues to repay us all in spades.

Carl, Lort Smith Animal Hospital, Victoria

Helping Millie See Again

Millie was left by her previous owner with a friend who never returned to collect her.

If that wasn't bad enough, Millie was nine years old and had cataracts which limited her sight to detecting only moving shadows and bright lights. In effect she was quite blind. This friend was physically handicapped himself and couldn't look after Millie, so she was surrendered to us at the New England Regional Companion Animals Shelter where her plight touched the hearts of our staff and volunteers. Millie had been a faithful companion for her entire life. Now, when she needed her human family most, she had been abandoned.

Millie would not normally have been made available for adoption because of her age and blindness, but she was quite fit for her age, her teeth were in excellent shape, her hips and elbows seemed fine. But most extraordinary of all was her zest for life. It was as if she was determined not to let all that had befallen her keep her down. Her message was not lost on me. We posted Millie onto our website, asking for a palliative care home.

Working in a shelter environment can be distressing for staff. Here, we encourage a policy whereby we sometimes permit ourselves to go a little above and beyond the norm to help an animal. It has to do with the reality that you cannot help every single homeless pet, but it's important for our sanity to have the ability to make a stand on behalf of one at times. I made this decision with Millie. She had been let down by others and I did not want to be another person to do so. And as events unfolded, it became very clear I wasn't the only one willing to go the extra mile.

After Millie's story was posted on our web page, a local supporter rang to offer to pay for Millie to have her cataracts removed! I was taken aback. I had no idea of what the cost would be, but with a little investigating, I found it would be in the range of $5500. No doubt it was out of the reach of the Good Samaritan and our shelter also. While I was explaining the situation over the telephone to the caller, someone who was adopting a dog at that time entered the office. Overhearing and seeing my disappointment, he also offered to donate some money to Millie's cause! Things were starting to look up.

As I thought it through, it dawned on me that there might be others who would be willing to help an abandoned blind dog who was not their own. The campaign to 'Help Millie See' had already begun.

Millie went to a local vet to have a health check and he found her heart, lungs, kidneys, and diabetes tests were all fine. A volunteer created a blog especially for Millie, and we began calling for people to help. Within ten days we were halfway to raising the $5500!

Next, the *Armidale Independent* local newspaper ran a front-page story on Millie's plight, and within another few days the target was reached. There were large donations, small donations, raffles and cake stalls. Everyone from café owners to buskers and small businesses pitched in. We even had offers from some donors to foot the entire bill, which blew us away, but we decided as a small country town, that we should achieve our goal collectively. Millie's misfortune was bringing people together. Millie was a local celebrity!

Most of us locals held our breath as Millie went in for her sight-saving surgery just one month ago. Dr Mark Billson, Specialist Veterinary Opthalmologist at Sydney Small Animal Specialist Hospital (SASH), was cautiously optimistic. I kept updating supporters about Millie's progress in her blog, and was delighted to be able to type the message after her surgery: 'I have just heard from Mark at SASH and the surgery went well . . . He believes that as a result, Millie should have good vision returned to her right eye and may have usable vision in her left eye as well!'

The rest, as they say, is history. Millie recovered steadily in the care of NSW Labrador Rescue over the last month and when I saw a picture of her leaving the hospital with her Elizabethan colour on, and clear brown eyes, I was very emotional. When we finally met up with Millie again, the difference in her appearance was incredible. We always knew she was a special dog, but being able to see into her clear eyes for the first time was truly remarkable. They do say, 'the eyes are the windows into the soul' – and Millie's eyes were beautiful.

The next wonderful chapter of Millie's story was to introduce her to her lucky new owners, Anna and Dave of Armidale, who were the very first couple to offer Millie a home, regardless of the outcome of her surgery. The list of people wanting to take Millie in before her surgery grew so large at one point that I had to stop adding people to the list! I could not have wished for a better home for Millie, but must admit I'm a little sad to see her go, having been such a large part of our shelter's life the last few months.

Millie's story doesn't end here, however: there is one final joy to share. So generous were the people of Armidale in donating to Millie's cause, we found ourselves in the fortunate position of having excess funds. We've thus arranged with the local RSPCA that this money will go towards other dogs and cats in need of veterinary intervention before they can find their forever homes. Elvis, a ten-week-old Heeler pup, is the first dog to be helped by the legacy of Millie's fund. He was saved from succumbing to the potentially deadly parvo virus after being dumped at a rest area outside town. He was found at dusk in the rain, sheltering in the long grass next to a garbage bin. He too will go to his forever home once he is well, as all homeless pets deserve.

I hope Armidale is very proud of what you did for Millie: I'm certainly proud of you.

Phill Evans,
New England Regional Companion Animals Shelter, New South Wales

The Three Amigos

Owning animals all my life, it just seemed normal to have at least one dog roaming around the house somewhere. When one eventually came to the end of his life, it was only then that I would adopt another dog. But over the years, dogs seemed to find me when they needed me.

First, it was Bob. I'd seen him at a shopping centre where I worked, and I would sit and talk to him and share my lunch. This continued for many years and whenever Bob saw me he would let out an excited squeal. He was very thin; his coat was falling out and his owners really didn't want him.

I was working late one night when Bob was brought into my shop. The owners asked if I wanted him. I didn't hesitate – I handed over $50 and Bob was suddenly mine, after all these years.

Once the vet had taken care of his neglect, Bob began to thrive. Wherever I was, he was no more than a few feet from me. Our first walk, however, was a disaster. He took *me* for a walk – dragging me on my hands and knees to tackle a tiny dog that wanted to kill him. I had no idea how to handle him so it was decided we would attend dog training, where Bob wanted to do nothing more than bark. He was cured of this by our second lesson, and soon Sunday – training day – became Bob's favourite day. At the end of our classes, a trophy was handed to the 'highest scoring' dog. To my great pride, it was Bob's name that was called out. He'd come a long way!

I had Bob for only three years when we found a cancerous lump on him. He eventually needed to be put to sleep. I was devastated and found it difficult to do anything. I ached all over and didn't want to speak to anyone. No one seemed to understand I had just lost my best friend.

By apparent chance, a friend had seen a Heeler who looked just like Bob in the local newspaper, needing a home at the animal shelter. Not only was there a striking resemblance, his name was Bob too!

Of course I had to go and meet him. Bob the Second took one look at me and jumped up and licked my face. That was the decider – Bob the Second was coming home with me.

I managed to trace my new dog's previous owners – the reason for him being surrendered? Because he wouldn't chase a ball for the children, plus they couldn't walk him because he was too strong. His owner before that family was an elderly lady, so I can imagine how that turned out. So mine was Bob's third home, and he was only three years old. I also soon had it confirmed that Bob would indeed chase anything that moved – cats, other dogs – but never a ball! His logic seemed to be that if he brought the ball back to me, I'd only throw it away again, so why bother?

One day, I noticed Bob the Second was having trouble getting around and had fallen down the back steps. The vet confirmed that Bob was going blind and there was nothing we could do to prevent it.

Soon after, we were joined by a Heeler pup called Ben. Born deaf, Ben had been taken to my vet after he was found wandering the streets. We took him home 'for a night' and that was now five years ago. I had never owned a deaf dog before, and was worried that we could not cope with him. But to our surprise his disability was no challenge to him at all. He was easy to train with hand signals, and was among the top of his class in obedience school!

I definitely had my hands full with Bob the Second and Ben at this time, both with their different disabilities, so imagine my concern when I spotted a terribly frightened and neglected-looking Stumpy Tail Cattle Dog in my backyard. He had a collar around his neck with a rope attached, so it was obvious he had escaped from somewhere. And he had jumped a 6-foot fence to get into our garden!

Going outside with our family dinner of chicken, I managed to tempt the starving dog over to me. On his collar was a phone number, but whenever I called I only got a busy signal, and this continued for several days.

Putting the dog on a lead, I was dragged up and down the streets placing 'Found' signs on lampposts and in shop windows. I also phoned local vets, all to no avail. It remained a mystery where he had come from.

I eventually had to phone the ranger and watch the stray dog go off to the local shelter, with my name on him as an interested party. I told them I would find him a home for him if he wasn't claimed.

I visited the shelter on a daily basis only to be told the homeless dog had not been claimed. Things were starting to look pretty grim for him. It was unlikely he'd pass a temperament test and be rehomed if his owners didn't come forward.

On the seventh day I phoned and was thrilled to hear the dog had been claimed! I phoned all my friends to share the good news. All my problems had been solved . . . or so I thought.

Imagine my astonishment on glancing into my backyard the following day and seeing the same dog back again! Not only back, but sitting, wagging his tail and waiting for his dinner!

In the meantime I had found out that he belonged two doors down from where we lived, his name was Anzac, and had been brought with his owners from interstate – hence the busy signal whenever I called the number on his collar; I hadn't known to add the Sydney area code first.

I returned him to his owners only to find him back again in less than a few minutes. And this continued. And continued. Every time I took him home, he was soon straight back. Anzac was clearly trying to tell me something!

Then, after a while, he didn't return. I had a feeling I should go and check if he was all right. And what did I find? Anzac was tied up on a short piece of rope with no food, water or shelter.

When I complained to the owner, he told me the dog could bloody well starve. Horrified, for the next week I returned to their yard to feed him, eventually explaining to the owner's mother that it was unfair to treat any animal that way, and no wonder he kept coming to my yard where he was free, happy and well-fed.

The next day I received a knock at my door. It was the dog's owner. He said unless I wanted him, he was taking him back to the animal shelter.

I didn't need another dog, but how could I send Anzac back to the shelter, knowing the likelihood he would be put to sleep?

I took him, but resolved to find him a home. I put signs up at dog training. I enrolled him in classes, too, but at first it was a complete disaster. He had never been on a lead, and Anzac's neck was so strong from pulling around a brick he'd been tethered to that I was dragged from one end of the oval to the next. He even bit the trainer, not once but twice!

It was soon obvious that no one wanted Anzac, and we had another problem: my family and I had become attached to him. We were resigned. So we got the necessary permit to keep a third dog and our neighbours kindly agreed also.

Up until this time, I'd had Anzac in a separate pen from my other dogs, blind Bob the Second and deaf Ben. Then one day I left the gate open by mistake and returned to find all three dogs happily playing together. The gate was never closed again.

The dogs bonded in no time, and were never far from each other, even sleeping all together. Anzac became Ben's ears and then Bob's eyes too.

The other wonderful development was that Anzac eventually turned out to be a great student at dog obedience. In addition to normal doggy skills, we taught him to roll over, say his prayers, walk backwards, bark on command and even push a pram! The list is never-ending.

Bob the Second and Ben have both sadly passed away now, and Anzac is mentoring another little deaf Heeler called Chance, whom he adores. Bob the First, Bob the Second, Ben and Anzac all got their 'second chance' – and now it is another Heeler's turn.

Judy, Victoria

With Love You Can Do Anything

Myron, our blind dog, is a celebrity. He has a Facebook site with 5000 friends, has been featured in international newspapers and magazines, and receives fan mail from all over the world for his courage and charity work. His videos on YouTube have gone viral, too. But things didn't look good for Myron when he started out, and they didn't get better for quite a while.

Myron's mother, probably a Border Collie Boxer mix, was dumped in Guildford, malnourished and pregnant. A kind family took her in and let her have her litter in their home, and she had eight beautiful puppies. Luckily, all the puppies were adopted just before the family had to send them to a shelter: I chose the little one with cross-eyes because I was afraid no one else would want him. But he was only six weeks old when we learnt that most of the puppies, including Myron, were blind, due to their mother's malnourishment. One by one the puppies were euthanased. But our encouraging vet believed that I could manage with a blind dog, and thankfully Myron was saved . . . but only to develop glaucoma a few months later! This time the vet said his eyes had to be removed, and to pay for the operation Terry, my generous husband, agreed to halt our home renovations at a time when we needed a new roof. So Terry, Myron and I lived under a green tarp for two years until we could afford to finish the job. Was Myron worth it? Of course! But he wasn't out of the woods yet.

Next he developed allergies. Soon he needed treating every three weeks with a special serum developed by Sydney University. But it works, thank goodness, and keeps him comfortable. As if that wasn't enough, Myron then developed epilepsy, which was almost too much for us to bear at first. But Myron has such a joy for life, we just had to do everything we could to keep him going. He now needs to take twelve pills each day to control his seizures, but he is such a happy boy; despite his blindness, he has learnt to fetch tennis balls and Frisbees, has a repertoire of wonderful tricks (which include impersonating a frog!), and loves his community service work. He has become a great four-legged fundraiser for the RSPCA and the cystic fibrosis cause.

Myron also brings incredible happiness to the elderly and the disabled people he visits. They seem to relate so well to him because, like them, he doesn't have just one disability to deal with – he needs to take loads of different pills every day too! These people love and admire that

Myron is still so happy, despite his health issues. And through his work, he's made some famous friends he likes to show off about too – he's had his picture taken with Kamahl, John Paul Young, Laine Beachly, Ita Buttrose, Ray Martin and Metallica, to name just a few of his mates.

I think Myron has inspired a following because he helps people understand that no matter what problems or illnesses you have to cope with, you can have joy in your life too. Myron teaches us that true happiness comes from helping others, no matter how bad your own situation might be. With love you can do anything. And we love you, Myron.

Raquel, New South Wales

The Dog No One Would Want

Sando was going to be a real challenge. When found roaming the bush outside Mildura, he was a bag of bones and barely alive.

When I first saw the Staffy Mastiff mix in the small rural pound, he looked tough and a bit scary. But as I watched, I soon saw this was a big, timid boy who was too shy to bully his way to the front of the pen when people came to see the dogs for adoption. He kept to himself, played quietly and, to further his troubles, he had a bung eye. Even the ranger said, 'That one won't find a home. No one would want him.'

Apart from his eye, at that stage there was little else indicating the terrible treatment Sando had suffered at the hands of his previous owner.

I had just started my own rescue group, Rural Rescues. When time ran out for this dog with no chance, I could not help myself. I refused to let him slip through the cracks. He was coming home with me.

Our first stop was to have the vet check him over and his twisted eye inspected. But we weren't prepared for what the X-rays were about to reveal.

Sando's head was riddled with at least fifty shotgun pellets.

Someone had used him for target practice. Either that, or they had tried to kill him.

The vet X-rayed the rest of this poor dog's body. Further inspection found more pellets towards his rear end, and beneath his regrown fur is evidence of at least three gunshot wounds.

Appalled, the vet then tested him for lead poisoning, and Sando was just under the survivable level of toxicity. As for his eye, the news wasn't good and he had to have it removed. The surgery was successful, but I still worried we might never find a loving home for this quiet, affectionate dog who had been through such horror.

Weeks later, I received an enquiry from a lovely lady called Deb who was very upset after just losing her beloved dog. Several teary phone calls later, I discovered Deb had a much-loved little foal with one eye and Sando's story had therefore struck a chord with her. I was overwhelmed with hope for Sando. In fact, I was almost too scared to let myself believe he may have found a forever home. But he did.

This lovely family welcomed Sando into their lives and had everything ready for him when we arrived: his own Drizabone coat, his own couch – even his own fireplace to sit by while everyone else was outside on the farm working in the cold and the rain!

It was a dream come true.

This dog, who shouldn't have survived such violence, or ever forgiven humans for such abuse, is now enjoying giving and receiving so much love. Even better, he's soon to be big brother to another special-needs rescue dog, Gracie, who has had several tumours removed and is apparently another dog that 'no one would want'!

Elizabeth Linklater, Rural Rescues, Victoria

Superdog!

There are many dogs out there who have a special ability, a skill that sets them apart from the pack. Some have star quality and love an audience while others perform important therapeutic work. Either way, these are talented pooches who earn their treats.

Bailey's Mates

A Greyhound is a racing dog that just chases things, isn't it?

For many, the public image of a Greyhound is of a vicious, untrustworthy dog. This perception is actually very far from the truth. Greyhounds are friendly, gentle-natured creatures whose favourite activity is sleeping! They are extremely affectionate, and are among the most docile, least aggressive of all dog breeds. Moreover, they require far less exercise than you would expect. These attributes make them perfect for aged-care facilities seeking a pet to brighten the lives of their residents. So we at the Greyhound Adoption Program (GAP) of South Australia were delighted when the Gilbert Valley Senior Citizens Home said they were interested in adopting a Greyhound.

Right away, we knew that it was important we find the perfect hound for the task, as we hoped he would be our ambassador for further adoptions into aged-care facilities. Who might fit the bill?

Leary! A young male, he hadn't been very successful on the track but was going to be ideal for his new career move. He was calm, placid and quiet by nature, gentle and unhurried in his movements, delighted to give and receive any affection on offer, and young enough to be playful if given the opportunity.

Leary visited the Home three times in the lead-up to his adoption, to be sure we had made the right choice, and the staff and residents were delighted with everything about him – except his name. They decided he should be renamed 'Bailey', a change he took in his stride just as easily as he had adapted without fuss to all the other lifestyle adjustments created by his move from racing hound to house pet.

To make sure Bailey was perfect for the job, we introduced him to some of the different situations he would meet in the Home: taking him past residents using walking frames and asking him to stand still as groups of people assisting each other walked past him. The staff at the facility created a program to ensure Bailey's daily needs and his health were managed correctly by giving him a care plan similar to those for the residents, and through the voluntary help of a dog behavioural specialist and a local artist, we created a pictorial education tool for young visitors, called the Polite Paws Program, to make sure that Bailey was not overwhelmed or frightened by well-meaning approaches by children unfamiliar with good doggy manners.

Bailey is proving to be an amazing asset to the Home, although there have been a couple of teething problems. Warned of the dangers of allowing a Greyhound to become overweight, Bailey was banned from the residents' dining room and the kitchen, and kept away from rooms while the residents had morning and afternoon tea . . . but some of the staff were not proof against his winning smile! This was rectified by warnings and his weight now remains stable. The other problem proved to be a bit more challenging: after a couple of months in his new role Bailey became a bit restless and grumpy, and less responsive to the residents.

Leslie, the nurse coordinator, rang me for advice. I was puzzled and after a few questions, asked her to talk me through his day. It gradually dawned on me that the one thing that had not been written into Bailey's care plan was a specific routine of putting him to bed at night! He was napping through the day and night, but doing his job – accompanying staff on their rounds – twenty-four hours a day! With a designated six clear hours for sleeping and a quiet spot away from night-time activity to go to, the problem was solved and Bailey returned to his normal cheerful, placid self. He was just working too hard!

There are some delightful stories about Bailey's relationships with the residents. One lady who had to spend time in hospital, confused, believed she was there for good and kept saying to her family, 'I didn't say goodbye to Bailey,' and 'I want to go home and see Bailey.' When she returned to the Home, Bailey followed her to her room and stood quietly for a long time with his head in her lap as she cuddled and patted him, delighted to see him again.

On one occasion, one of the residents was very upset and crying. Bailey, hearing her distress, went in and nestled his head deep into her lap, cuddling up to her and comforting her. Another lady who was very fond of Bailey gradually deteriorated in health, and her four-legged friend took to spending extended periods in her room, his head resting gently on the side of her bed, easing her distress as she approached her passing. The staff are adamant that Bailey senses when residents need extra care and he stays in their rooms for a longer period or visits them a little more often.

For a couple of months before Bailey came to the Home, one of the residents had been quite severely depressed. She started to look forward to his visits, however, and by the time he moved in full-time she was smiling, and continues to improve. She now seeks him out as she moves around the facility. Another resident with dementia can be quite obstructive at times, but with the promise of a walk with Bailey, all her objections dissipate. If she knows Bailey is coming along, she is eager to join him on her daily stroll!

Bailey's presence in the Home has definitely brightened the atmosphere, both for the residents and the staff. He also provides a wonderful point of contact between the Home and the community. The townsfolk know Bailey and greet him when he is out and about, the school children want to stroke him, and everyone smiles to see him.

When talking about the success of this initiative to people, I regularly hear the reply, 'Oh yes, I know someone who does that, they take their dog to visit a nursing home.' However, we at GAP strongly argue that this is different, and as good as visiting programs are, the residents know the dogs are just that – visitors. However, the staff and residents of Gilbert Valley and the Pines have a sense of ownership of Bailey and Rosco. The two boys are *their* dogs and they have bonded with them as any owner bonds with their pet. Time and time again when I visit Gilbert Valley, the residents say to me, 'I *do* love this dog', 'Bailey is *so* important to us', and my favourite comment, from a confused but charmingly determined lady: 'Is Bailey yours or mine? No, he's mine, isn't he? He belongs here.'

Jennie Alcorn, Greyhound Adoption Program, South Australia

Dr Ella

It was my Terrier mix Ella who told me I was pregnant.

One day, when playing fetch and bringing the ball back and dropping it into my lap, she suddenly stopped. She started looking at and licking my belly. Ella is a smart dog, so I decided to get a pregnancy test and had confirmed what Ella already knew. Did I mention she was smart?

As my belly grew, Ella got increasingly protective of my bump. One day, she wanted to sit on my lap (though at this stage of the pregnancy, she didn't quite fit) and she kept on moving around until she was comfortable. My baby gave her a little kick, but Ella didn't mind. She just licked my belly and moved over, obviously saying 'Sorry – didn't mean to squash you!' I knew then that Ella and the little girl I was carrying were going to have a special relationship.

I was right – Ella and Sienna are crazy about each other. My daughter loves playing fetch with Ella, and screams with glee when Ella brings back her red ball. And when Sienna is old enough to understand, I will tell her the story about how Ella knew before anyone else, that she was on her way.

Sue, New South Wales

Rex the Wonder Dog

I have always loved dogs, and have rarely been without at least one in my life. When I was a child of around ten, we had a wonderful dog named Rex. Possibly a Kelpie mixed with German Shepherd, I have never met a dog like him before or since.

My dad worked on the council as a grader operator. One day at work, some of his workmates were encouraging a stray dog to perform tricks in exchange for food. The dog seemed remarkably talented. Dad was on his grader when one of his mates told the dog to go and shake hands with him. As if he understood every word, the dog jumped nimbly onto Dad's grader and sat there with his paw extended, ready to shake hands. He sat beside Dad on the grader for the rest of the day. He seemed to 'choose' Dad out of all the men to be with.

When Dad came home and told Mum about this remarkable dog, she said she had been thinking about getting one. The stray was being cared for by people who already had a dog and couldn't keep him. So that afternoon we went off to collect him in our little Morris Minor, Mum and Dad in the front, my brother, sister and me in the back, so excited about our new friend.

When we pulled up outside the house, we waited in the car while Dad approached the gate. The family's little Fox Terrier raced up to Dad quite aggressively, but the biggest surprise was when the stray dog, who we later named Rex, came out of nowhere and bowled the Foxie over to protect Dad! As we drove home, Rex sat proud and happy in the back with us kids, enjoying all the attention. But we had no idea yet of the magnificent and intelligent dog we had acquired.

It didn't take long for Rex to amaze us. Anything we kids were playing he would want to have a go at too. It was like he thought he was human. I had a scooter that he actually learnt to ride a little, by placing his front paws on the handle bars, and one back paw on the foot plate and with the other he actually tried to scoot along the ground as he'd seen us do (we had to help hold the scooter up, though). He managed a couple of pushes with his paw and it moved a little until he fell off. In addition, he could ably climb a tall ladder, higher than I was game to go, jump hurdles much better than me, and even had a try at jump rope once!

When Pop came to visit one day, we'd had a lot of rain the previous night, so the track was flooded. Dad gave Rex a rubber boot, pointed to Pop who was over a bridge at the other end of the track, and told him to take the boot to him. He did, and then came back for the other one, and took that to Pop too. On another occasion while visiting our neighbours to beg for cake or biscuits, which he did so well (who could resist that face?), Mr Paton gave Rex a note and told him to take it home to us. Rex followed the instructions to a T, and Dad replied on the note 'Yes, he brought it home!' and sent Rex straight back with it.

Rex seemed to understand everything we said, as was proven one rainy afternoon when Mum was about to feed the dogs – we had two at the time: Mac was also a handsome boy, but not quite as savvy as Rex! Mac's dish was up on the back lawn and Mum, not wanting to get wet, tried asking Rex if he could go and get the dish for her. Well, he was back in a flash, Mac's dish in mouth. What a dog!

We enjoyed this amazing canine for around six years, then one day Rex just disappeared. Possibly knowing his time had come, as animals sometimes do, we believe he went into the bush to die. He would have been around twelve years old. We missed him terribly. Looking back, as a child I had no idea of just how marvellous he really was, but now I know, not having met a dog like him since. Rex reminded me so much of *The Littlest Hobo*, a TV show I loved as a child about a dog who would come into people's lives for a short time, to help them in some way, and then move on to the next person in need. I now think that about Rex – our Wonder Dog!

Lynda, Victoria

Rusty and Denny go to Work

Rusty chose me and for that I'm very grateful. She's completely changed my life and now all I want to do with my spare time is go to sheepdog trials, but more about that later . . .

Rusty (left in picture) decided I was 'the one' for her at Animal Aid's shelter in Coldstream. She and her Kelpie litter mates were in the very first pen we passed. They were found dumped in a box in the Toolangi Forest, on the fringes of outer Melbourne. The pups were cuddled up in a basket and as I walked up to their pen, a little red-and-white head popped up and the pup jumped out of the basket to greet me.

I remember noting the interest of the little female and as I walked away, she turned and hopped back into the basket. We looked at the other dogs there that day, but I didn't really connect with any of them. I did, however, see several people walk past the puppies' pen and noticed the little one who had run towards me stayed in her basket as they stopped to look. But when I walked back past, the little pup again jumped up and came running as fast as she could to the front of the pen to see me.

'That's the one,' I said to my partner, Heather, and so my rescued-working-dog journey had begun.

Heather and I went to see a sheepdog demonstration at Federation Square in the city. I loved it and the gentleman conducting the demonstration suggested we go to the National Trials at Koroit, later that month, which we did. That was when I decided that this scene was definitely for me and, better yet, Rusty. We went to a few more trials until we found a trainer that suited both of us. It just so happened to be Paul Macphail, who runs a very successful working-dog education program and Rusty and I launched into sheepdog work with great enthusiasm.

I soon decided that I wanted to get another dog to keep Rusty company during the day while we were at work, so I started telephoning Animal Aid every weekend to see what new puppies or dogs had arrived. When I was told that a nine-week-old Kelpie pup had come in, I could barely contain my excitement. Without telling Heather there was a specific pup I wanted to look at, I convinced her that we should go down and 'just have a look'. Sadly, my cover did not last very long as the lady in reception recognised my voice and said that I was 'the bloke coming for a look at the Kelpie pup'.

I was forgiven, however, and Denny came into our lives and our trialling work started to get serious. She was a natural and with just a little bit of training – a few months' worth – she was ready to compete nearly straight away and is probably a better trial dog than Rusty now.

During our first year in the trial scene both dogs did rather well, having a few wins against quality opposition at the Encourage level. We stumbled across Australian National Kennel Club (ANKC) Herding, in which my team now competes at the highest level, all the while continuing in yard dog trials as well. Rusty and Denny have both achieved great things in ANKC Herding, with many wins to their name. I always proudly tell the other entrants that my dogs came from Animal Aid and some of the looks on their faces are priceless, particularly when my 'pound mongrels' have beaten their much more expensive pedigree dogs.

From all of this you might think that Rusty and Denny's talents are only as trial dogs, but they are just as good at doing regular farm-type work too. Parks Victoria organised for Rusty and Denny to help catch an abandoned sheep at Warrandyte, after a chance meeting at Lilydale Lake one night with a ranger. They have also managed to find a whole mob of sheep that had been running loose for two years in the hills near Strath Creek and work them all back to a yard.

Even now eight-year-old Rusty can amaze me. I had been contacted by a man out in Gruyere, a semi-rural area on the edge of Melbourne. Two of his sheep had escaped and we had a very rough idea of where they were, as they had been seen high on a ridge on the opposite side of the valley. The owner and I carefully drove up the track to the crest of the hill to assess the situation. I stood up on a gate and saw one sheep staring up at me from down the slope with a look as if to say, 'You're not meant to be here!' I quickly opened the back of the car and let the dogs go to work. Rusty spotted the sheep straight away and given that she has an ability to 'read my mind', took off in hot pursuit.

The sheep ran a bit further down the hill to join its friend. Once having successfully turned one sheep back up the hill to me, Rusty blocked its every attempt to escape. When it was caught and put in the back of the ute, it was time to find the other one. I knew it had gone through the fence and into the next paddock. I then noticed Rusty was nowhere to be seen. I had spotted her walking in the scrub and guessed she was just sniffing about where a mob of kangaroos had been when we drove in. I called for her to come several times but she did not appear. As my calling grew louder, I suddenly saw a sheep running across the paddock. Rusty knew we were looking for the other sheep and must have followed its scent through the scrub and up over the back of the hill where she turned it to bring it back to us. She might not be as good a trial dog as she once was, but her ability to figure out and finish a job is second to none.

To this day and for all time I will be proud to say that I gave these rescue dogs a forever home and despite them not having the best possible start to life, they had so much to give and myriad talents to share. There are many dogs in pounds and shelters all over Australia capable of achieving the sorts of things Rusty and Denny have, if someone would only give them a chance. Go on – you will never regret it!

Daniel, Victoria

Wellington's Work

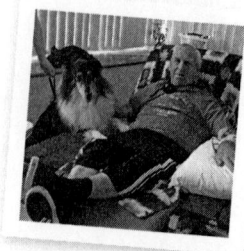

When I first heard about Wellington, he was in a shelter in Canberra and hadn't been adopted for the same reason most Collies aren't – they tend to shut down out of fear in a shelter situation. He was on death row when Victorian Collie Rescue found out about him and arranged to have him adopted out and put into foster care in Melbourne.

I grew up in the United States with Collies, and after a series of work visas that required me to bounce back and forth between the two countries, I had finally achieved Australian residency and was here to stay. That brought a sense of homesickness that could only be relieved by adopting a pet, much as I love my friends and family-in-law here.

It was love at first sight for me with Wellington and after spending some time just taking him for a quiet walk and giving him lots of pats and cuddles, my partner agreed he was the dog for us. A week later we were able to adopt Wellington and take him to his forever home – our home. At this point he had been in two different foster homes in the ACT and another in Victoria, so he didn't really know if he was coming or going, but he settled in very quickly, claiming the couch as his favourite space in the house.

We can't begin to imagine how this beautiful, gentle dog ended up in a shelter. From the first day in our home he has had impeccable manners. Wellington has never snatched food off a low table (just looks at it longingly and drools), never had a toilet incident inside the house and never chewed or otherwise destroyed a single shoe or piece of furniture. He does shed constantly, but that is just part of life with a Collie Rough.

When we first got him, our neighbours' children were terrified of dogs, but eventually they recognised Wellington's gentle nature and worked up the courage to come closer and pat him. Now he can't be out the front of the house without a child from somewhere in the neighbourhood throwing their arms around him in a bear hug. He loves any attention, and tolerates the kids with endless patience.

As Collies are actually working dogs, it is important for them to have a 'job' to do in one form or another. Our lovely boy was too old for most of the competitive doggy sports, and really too lazy to take an interest in the others. But when I learnt about DOGS Victoria's therapy dog program, I knew that Wellington would be the ideal candidate. He passed the temperament test with flying colours, even outdoing himself with good behaviour as though he knew how important it was to impress on this occasion!

The program coordinator found us an ideal situation – the nurses in the dialysis unit near where we live wanted a dog to come in and visit the patients. The patients are all different ages and from many varying backgrounds. The one thing they have in common is that three times a week they are hooked up to a dialysis machine for several hours. Any distraction from this tedious chore is a welcome one, and a big, furry distraction proved to be particularly welcomed, by both patients and staff!

Many of the patients don't ask or remember my name, but there is a resounding chorus of 'Hi, Wellington' and 'Hey, Wellie!' whenever we arrive at the hospital. It didn't take long either for several of the patients to begin setting aside a dry bickie or two on the day they knew Wellington was coming. One of the patients even began asking me about rescue dogs and how different organisations worked. As a result, he is now the proud owner of his own two gorgeous rescue dogs!

Although we don't know his background at all, it is clear that Wellington adores people and just wants to be patted and given attention. He is perfectly suited to therapy work and is always very gentle when taking food from the patients. He is just the right height to be patted while standing next to the patients' beds. And for those who want a more serious cuddle, he is happy to jump up on his hind legs and put his front paws on their lap.

It goes both ways, however. Wellington adores all the attention (and the bickies!) he receives on his visits and is visibly excited when he gets out of the car and realises we are at the hospital. I think he knows that he is making a real difference in people's lives.

And it has proven great karma for me. When I was in hospital myself recently, my husband was able to bring my therapy dog in to visit *me*. While he was there, almost every nurse on the floor popped in for a quick cuddle.

So, in the three short years we have had Wellington, he has turned our house into a home, helped children overcome their fear of dogs and brightened many days for scores of dialysis patients. He is truly an amazing rescue dog!

Karen, New South Wales

From Helpless Pup to Helper

Imagine if you can a small, dirty, grey bundle of mattered fur, lying on cold concrete in his own vomit and excrement. He is barely able to lift his head, while his soulful eyes look at you, waiting to see if you are going to help him. Just another helpless little mutt no one has bothered to reclaim, he lies in the local pound, dying.

There is a choice – the ranger can take him away and euthanase him, or he can be released to a rescue group and taken to the vet for treatment.

Dog Rescue Newcastle was at the pound that day to rescue homeless dogs. The ranger didn't think we would want to help this particular little pup, as he knew the vet fees required to give this boy a chance would be steep – at least $1000. He asked us if we'd like him euthanased. We decided that if there was *any* hope of saving this trembling pile of fur that no one wanted, we'd give him that chance.

We bundled him into the car, and off to the Warner's Bay vet we went. He was put straight on a drip, and immediately diagnosed with parvo, a virus that attacks many dogs and pups, and is often fatal. (Parvo is preventable with vaccines, and if everyone vaccinated their dogs we could eradicate parvo forever, just as was done with polio.) The little one was very, very sick. We called him Alex, so that if he died at least he'd have a name. Our volunteers Sue and Anne stayed with him, stroking him and cuddling him, so that he would know someone cared. He was on a drip for days, fighting for his life, but his little heart would not give in – and then one day, he turned the corner.

When strong enough, Alex went to a loving foster home, where he turned out to be a 'clean freak' – rushing around the house picking up toys and putting them away! Oh, and chewing a few things too, like most pups. He was an absolute delight to have around. Alex's bubbly personality and quick learning ability really stood out.

Then something even more wonderful happened. Alex was chosen to go to the Lions Hearing Dog Program in Adelaide. There, he will learn to be the ears of a deaf person, and to help enhance their life. The program's coordinator stays in touch with us, and when one of our rescue dogs fits their criteria, we give them a call.

Alex has come a long way – from helpless pup to helper. His new owner may never know the story of how courageously he fought for his life, or how much dedication it took, from strangers, to save him. But knowing Alex is safe and loved, and that this brave-hearted boy is helping someone every day, being their ears and comfort, is the best reward of all.

Anne Ward, Dog Rescue Newcastle, New South Wales

Zumba the Stunt Pup

Zumba was the last of a litter of Rhodesian Ridgeback pups who at five months had not sold. When I heard the owner was a retiring puppy farmer, I decided I should get her out of there as soon as possible. When we arrived, although a 'registered breeder', he had one Ridgeback, one Rottweiler (due to have puppies any day), one Golden Retriever and one Labrador that we could see. I didn't hesitate in removing Zumba.

Once we got home and settled in, I registered Zumba to do an obedience course and from there we went on to trick training, which put me in contact with the Pets for Therapy team. We regularly visited nursing homes for the elderly and performed in a themed show for the residents. Zumba's favourite partner in this was a miniature Poodle called Moet. They teamed up well doing a skit where Moet would jump over Zumba's back while she was in a drop and then Moet would continue with Zumba standing up, landing on and bouncing off her back. All the residents loved it. We even had a small tunnel really only meant for the little fluffy dogs but Zumba took one look at it and proceeded to crawl through after Moet, to everyone's delight.

Zumba also went on to learn agility and has won many titles and awards. She's even done a stint at Movie World when they premiered the movie *Cats and Dogs*! She teamed up with Wonder Woman and they walked down the red carpet to the theatre together.

Zumba was a great ambassador for the breed, and was known and loved by many across Australia. She has now passed on to Rainbow Bridge, but to me she was just the best dog you could ever be owned by (definitely not the other way around!)

After seeing what might have become of Zumba had I not adopted her, it inspired me to become the coordinator for Rhodesian Ridgeback Rescue in Queensland. I am passionate about the breed and, with the help of many other volunteers, have rescued and rehomed well over 300 dogs. Out of the six Rhodesians I have adopted, only one was an eight-week-old puppy (my first) – all the others were rehomes or rescues. These dogs still have so much to give, and despite any issues they may have, there is always the right home out there for these unwanted ones. It is just finding that forever family that can sometimes be the hard part. However, the joy I feel when I see a dog in their new home, getting their much-deserved second chance, makes it all worthwhile.

Ricki Smith, Rhodesian Ridgeback Rescue, Queensland

From Dog Number Four to Super Star

Pic: Phil England

Anyone watching the ease with which JD lapped up the attention of being a superstar would think he was born to it.

A Bull Terrier Heeler mix, JD had five glorious years in the spotlight – catalogues, newspapers, TV advertisements and shopping centre-appearances. Even people who were not dog lovers wanted to pat and cuddle him and became fans. In those years of fame and after his retirement, he had a wonderfully loving family. Life was good.

JD's early years, however, were wretched and unhappy, a common reality in the lives of actors. In fact, before he did a screen test, he was used for medical tests. Unloved, he was kept in a small yard. He was simply called Dog Number Four.

The medical research centre where JD first 'existed' (it could not be called living) was so secret that few people knew what really went on there. JD was left outside in a fenced, sandy area where the only shelter was a wooden structure with a tin roof. The only attention the poor dog received was when people in white coats – the medical scientists – came to get him for their experiments.

That all changed when a security guard was given a temporary new patrol route right past 'Number Four's' yard. For the guard there was something about Dog Number Four. He was always friendly and happy to see the man, he did not appear fearful and was so excited for attention that he was unable to bark; only high-pitched squeaks were made.

One day while on his patrol the man was shocked to see that JD was not in his yard. He made enquiries as to the dog's whereabouts and was told the animal's usefulness had ceased and that he was to be put to sleep, as was standard practice.

Fortunately the man was compelled to intervene, even though he already had a dog of his own. Would he be able to adopt him? Luckily for both the man and dog, the facility manager agreed to let the three-year-old be rehomed.

They went home together and the dog became JD. Despite his happy-go-lucky nature, JD had some demons leftover from his days at the facility. He didn't like people stepping near him when he was sleeping. He hated thunderstorms due to his days under the tin roof. He had no socialisation skills and was confused by other dogs. He didn't even know how to play with a ball. While gaining social skills took a little time, it was nearly two years for the psychological and medical issues to be resolved.

JD's rise to fame was accidental. The man's wife was a marketing manager and needed a dog for a photo shoot in a Christmas catalogue. No one knew how it would go, but from the minute JD stepped onto the set with his placid and loving nature, it was as if he had found his true vocation.

JD discovered that there was much waiting as people rushed around sorting out technical issues like lighting, make-up and getting the non-animal actors ready. Then there would be quiet for the part where JD had to play with a toy, or sit still with a human actor, engaging with him. A piece of a treat held aloft in his guardian's hand was sufficient to focus his attention for the correct angles for the cameras. What JD seemed to enjoy the most, though, was the human interaction. That seemed incredible after years of being alone, being put through medical experiments and even being referred to as a number.

JD showed there is hope, even in the darkest of hours, that every dog deserves a second chance in a loving home, and a real name.

Karl, Western Australia

Pawing it Forward

After twelve wonderful years of love and companionship from Indy, my Golden Retriever, she passed away. And although I always knew I would get another canine companion, I wondered if there could ever be another dog as generous and kind. Not only to me, but to the residents of the Pets As Therapy program in the dementia care facilities Indy and I visited, where she had given so much joy.

Something about Shadow's story on the website of Golden Retriever Rescue (GRR) really touched me. He had suffered incredible hardship: bred by an unscrupulous puppy farmer, and then dumped at Townsville RSPCA by his owner because he was limping. His owner was probably already aware that Shadow was born without hip sockets. This is not unusual when dogs are sourced from puppy factories and then on-sold through pet shops.

Thankfully, someone at the shelter saw something special in Shadow, and contacted GRR. That kind person knew that without GRR's help, and an operation, Shadow had no chance of a pain-free life.

Thanks to the generosity of Jetpets, Shadow flew to Sydney, where the angels of GRR fell for him – no doubt due to his cheeky personality and his love of cuddles! They decided to fund two operations and the titanium hip replacements that he needed, and give him six months of rehabilitation in foster care.

When he was ready to find a forever home, I registered an interest in adopting Shadow. GRR thought our family could be a good match, and arranged an introduction. As soon as we met Shadow and saw his beautiful nature and trusting eyes, we couldn't resist him. The minute he met my dad, Shadow nibbled his ear and cuddled him – which was amazing, as Shadow usually avoided men. A 'try out' was agreed to, and then we decided to adopt each other. He is an adored family member now, and loves his new role of protector.

We've had six months of joy with Shadow. He is a busy dog, and uses his new hips to the full, with lots of running, swimming, kayaking and meeting new friends. But he works too! He has taken whole-heartedly to his new job as a doggy therapist in the Pets As Therapy program.

Shadow's new best friends at the dementia care facility are Norm and Laurie. He gives them cuddles and kisses, and happy memories to his friends' eyes. And he's a terrible flirt, nibbling on people's ears when he gets the chance! The nurses always say that after Shadow has visited, everyone in the centre is calmer and happier.

When Shadow's wonderful story was featured in the newspaper, four families were inspired to adopt other unwanted dogs like Shadow. He gives so much love to the world, and he makes such a difference to so many people.

Paula, New South Wales

Special Seniors

Who says old dogs can't learn new tricks? Elderly dogs may move a little slower and need a bit more care than they used to, but they don't lack the spirit of their younger brothers and sisters. Being long in the tooth doesn't mean these dogs are short on love!

Little Alice of the Palace

It is nearly two years since Alice, a ten-year-old-plus Maltese girl came into Rescued With Love's care. She had been neglected, but her nature was loving. Her only immediate hurdle, it seemed, was a broken jaw from where her teeth had rotted through to her lower jaw.

Alice quickly became 'Alice of the Palace'. Then Al Pal, then Baby Pal, being the smallest and the gentlest of our doggy gang. All the other four-leggeds protected our little girl from the beginning, sensing something was special about her.

Two weeks after Alice arrived we were given the devastating news she had cancer in her bladder, a death sentence according to our vet because of the position it was in. She would have no more than a couple of weeks to live, maybe a month or two. We took her home and gave her the promise that in these final days she would have the time of her life.

As the days ticked by, Alice showed us she didn't know, or care, that she was terminally ill. She had very bad arthritis in her front leg, so she was carried up and down the stairs, and we brought her a doggy pram in which to joyfully ride around, covered in her pink blanket, looking out at the world around her.

Slowly the weeks ticked by: three months, six months, nine months, then a year, now nearly two! Defying all the odds, during this time she has endured three lots of surgery, and her jaw has now eroded so there is no bone in her mandible, so we help her eat. Yes, her tongue hangs out most of the time, but we consider that part of her charm. The tumour in her bladder is growing further into her stomach and not into her bladder, so each day we have her is a blessing.

Alice has taught all of our family and friends about embracing the quality of life that you have; about being special, and coping with those needs, whatever they might be. Despite having cancer, she is the happiest little soul, and continues to lead the charge to the breakfast bowls every morning, dancing playfully around our feet. Go, Baby Pal! We love you, honey.

Kae Norman, Rescued With Love, Victoria

The Rescue of Nanna and Aunty

Each morning before I am due to start my shift at 8 a.m., I sit quietly for a while, sipping my cup of tea and sift through several animal rescue websites. It's a ritual activity that has been the catalyst to my welcoming several dogs from pounds and rescue centres from all over Australia to my humble abode here in southern Tasmania. In fact, my current seven canines have all acquired their frequent flyer points this way.

Each rescue I remember with fondness, however none more so than that of Nanna and Aunty. Everything swiftly came together as if a magic spell had been cast to save these two old dogs, who were due to die that very day, and bring them almost 1700 kilometres to my doorstep in Tasmania.

The first indication that I was about to increase the pack came to me when I logged onto 'Sophie's Choice' website of pound dogs needing homes, and was immediately confronted with a large banner with the words 'Urgent: please save Nanna'. Above it was the face of a very old Red Heeler affectionately named Nanna by the pound volunteers.

They had fallen in love with her gentleness and the way she wobbled about on creaky old legs, wagging her tail like an old pump handle, greeting everything and everyone she could see.

Desperation overtook me to get her out.

While I sat trying to cobble together some sort of plan of how I, almost penniless until payday, was going to be able to fund another interstate rescue, I absent-mindedly browsed a few more pages, and it was then I saw Aunty. She could have been Nanna's sister: very old, and very much facing the same fate as Nanna on the same day, in the same pound, only a few pens along. Her red-rimmed eyes peered into the camera lens, and her splayed legs supported little more than a nest of fleas living on a bit of hide covering a few old bones.

It was going to be complicated without any money, but I knew I had to get her out of there too.

I rang the Hawkesbury Pound and spoke to the animal control officer. 'Is number 205 still there, and number 306? I will take them . . . how much would it be?'

'Just a moment.' The sound of footsteps retreated and after a while returned. 'Yes, they are here, and it will cost $50 each to get them out.'

'I will take them.' I knew I had nothing close to $100 in all my bank accounts put together, but somehow, I just felt 'the force' was going to be with me on this one.

'Where do you live?'

'Tasmania.'

Silence. 'I don't know how they will travel, they are very old and wobbly . . . One is about fourteen, and the other, I don't know, maybe around the same age . . .'

'It's a quick flight – are they healthy enough, do you think?'

Silence again. 'Yes, I suppose so.'

I raced out of work at morning tea and cashed in two lay-bys I forgot I had after finding the tattered receipts rummaging through my coinless, noteless purse. This netted $60.

The Nanna and Aunty juggernaut was now ready to roll!

A colleague suggested I call Jetpets, and I knew they supported PetRescue, however the quote I received from them, even with the rescue discount, would still cost over $700. I could never raise that amount of money in time, plus the costs of cage hire, and then there was the mandatory hydatid treatment required for every Tasmanian-bound dog. Not only does it need to be administered, but also certified by a JP or a vet!

Hurdles of all kinds began to boggle my mind. I logged onto the web again. Maybe if I go direct to the 'pilot', so to speak . . . Virgin Blue: they do 'things for good causes', don't they? And they are in cohorts with Toll Air Freight . . . Because the dogs were in Sydney it seemed to make sense to ring a Toll transport group there. There were several depots: I just needed to pick one.

The fellow on the phone from Toll advised me the dogs could be freighted for around $470, which was brilliant, but I still had no money and they had to be at the depot by 3.30 p.m. the next day.

'Okay . . . I'll call you back,' I replied. 'I just need to check on things,' meaning finances and back-to-drawing boards.

I heard muffled voices in the background.

'Oh, are you still there? Look, the big boss has just walked up, he's ah, he's saying we'll fly them for free.'

I was rendered speechless.

With that miracle granted, the next hurdle was how to get them from Hawkesbury to the depot, an hour's drive, and I knew absolutely no one in Sydney.

Feeling elated and anxious at the same time thinking about how I could make this work, I sat in the tea room once again, head in hands. Carmen, a colleague and fellow dog lover, approached my table and in general conversation I mentioned the plight of Nanna and Aunty.

'Oh,' she said, while unravelling the plastic around something scrumptious that I couldn't afford, 'my sister and her husband have an animal transport company. I'll give her a call if you like.'

'What! Where is it?'
'Sydney.'
'You're joking.'
'No.'

Again, I sat stunned while Carmen followed through with wording up her sister Narelle at animal transport. She passed the phone to me.

'Yes, we can pick them up and drop them off at Toll, we know the guys.'

'I need to have cages, too . . .'

'We have cages, just get the boys at the other end to return them.'

I was almost giggling hysterically by this point – everything was conspiring to help save these dogs! 'I need to get them treated for hydatids and it needs to be certified – do you know how we can do this?'

'I think . . . I think we may have a pack of tablets floating around here somewhere . . . .yes, we do. I'll administer them, but I don't think we'll have time to get anyone able to certify, so I don't know what you can do there. We'll be cutting time fine as it is.'

I rang the pound with the good news, well, at least mostly good news, but it was about to get even better.

'I have the transport organised for the dogs and I have the hydatids treatment to go, but I need it certified. Do you know anyone who can certify the administration of it?' I knew it would be a tall ask.

'Well . . .' the voice on the other end of the line said, 'I'm a JP . . . Does that help?'

At 5.30 p.m. the next evening, Nanna and Aunty arrived in good shape at Hobart Airport courtesy of Toll, Carmen, Narelle, the JP/animal control officer at Hawkesbury, and the volunteers who had first put the call out to save the old girls.

Eyes welling up with tears, I approached the trolley as they were wheeled out and I took stock of them. Nanna was the more animated of the two – she wagged her funny old tail a little and wobbled on her legs. I had been told she was profoundly deaf and a little blind, but more worrying was the larger ratio of bare skin to actual fur. It was red, itching and inflamed, and she had a very nasty sore that covered her side as if she had been bitten badly, enough to lift the skin. Her back legs knuckled over hocks so arthritic they barely held her upright. Each rib and hip joint was so prominent, shadows were cast. She let out a husky old holler followed by one of those 'dog smiles' that I think only dog people recognise. Hardly a tooth was left sitting in those old choppers.

Aunty's condition was even worse, and I could see she had been a mum at some time . . . probably more than once. She was wary, sick, had a bloated belly, and I actually wondered if I should put my hand in the cage to clip the lead. She was, by all standards, a poor, wretched old dog, abused and abandoned.

My other beautiful canines welcomed the old girls – Nanna was a little anxious with the attention, while Aunty immediately escaped to the dog yard and into a large pen, perhaps the only type of 'home' she had ever known.

Nanna, it turned out, was not only deaf and arthritic, but also suffered a heart murmur, cancerous sores and dreadful skin conditions that needed weeks of treatment. Her coat today is luxurious and there's quite a twinkle left in those soft old brown eyes yet. While she is on treatment for some of her other conditions, Nanna now totters around the paddock, and loves nothing more than a pat, her tucker and car rides.

Aunty's prognosis, however, wasn't as promising.

After six weeks her body weight had deteriorated further, and the vet diagnosed renal failure. She was sadly put to sleep in order to avoid further suffering.

We all felt honoured with Aunty's presence during her short stay with us. Rarely did she leave my side once she discovered a better life was to be had outside a cage. She would squeal with excitement at bushwalk times, chase her ball like a teenager and roll in the grass with a glee that only dogs seem to know. I could never guess just how sad a life this old dog had lived previously – only marvel that she was willing to trust again.

Just for that short time, Aunty came alive.

I will never forget her, and always give thanks that the universe helped bring these old girls to me, for the special time they had left.

Lea, Tasmania

Never Homeless Again

A sad and lonely Border Collie was found wandering the streets of Hervey Bay and impounded. Nobody cared enough to come looking for her. As a senior dog, her fate in most pounds would have been decidedly grim. But lucky for Maisie, and for me, Fraser Coast Dog Rescue decided she deserved to live.

When I first saw Maisie on PetRescue, I noticed she was in Maryborough, Queensland, and I was far away, in Melbourne. But I loved her photo and profile, and immediately knew we were made for each other. After lengthy conversations with her foster carer, we both agreed I would fly up, meet Maisie, and we'd spend some time getting to know her before we flew home together. I didn't want her to meet me as a stranger at Melbourne Airport.

We bonded quickly on my visit, and my new best friend and I flew home together.

Nine-year-old Maisie soon became a bit of a celebrity around town. Her interstate rehoming journey was featured in the local paper. I was so happy that she had a role promoting PetRescue and the adoption of homeless animals. Her story was also a reminder that older dogs should not be overlooked as potential great pets. One could even argue they deserve it *more so*, having given sometimes a decade or more of love and loyalty to their family, only to be betrayed in their twilight years.

Every dog and cat deserves to live out their senior days surrounded by love, security and comfort.

Maisie is my first rescue dog but she won't be my last. Adopting her has been such a rewarding experience. She is simply perfect – a gentle old soul that never fails to brighten my day. She has certainly filled a huge void in my life after my two Border Collies and both my parents passed away in recent times. Her endless love, trust and loyalty reminds me that whatever happens, we should always keep our hearts open and great things will come our way.

I would not part with my girl for anything, and I have promised her she will be loved, pampered and cared for by me until she takes her last breath. She will never be homeless again.

Lily, Victoria

Two Tiny Old Ladies

I looked into the box. Was it a dog? I am a veterinary nurse at the RSPCA. One day, one of our inspectors came in with a cardboard box containing an animal which at first glance appeared to be a very sick gremlin. The gremlin turned out to actually be a Chihuahua mix of about fifteen years of age, who had been abandoned in the backyard of an empty house. Weighing a mere 1.5 kilograms, severely dehydrated and struggling with a terrible infection in her uterus (sadly, she had never been desexed), she was barely clinging to life. We struggled to find a vein in her tiny body for IV fluids, and gave her antibiotics. We didn't expect her to survive the night.

But Elsa was a fighter. To all our surprise, she refused to give up. We spent a lot of time together in the pet hospital, and her eyes started following me around the ward. Her age and sickness deemed her not suitable for adoption to new owners, so when the vet suggested I take her home as a permanent foster dog, it was not a hard decision to make. However, I'd always been a 'cat person' – I'd never owned a dog before. Another nurse teased me that I still did not own a dog, as Elsa was smaller than your average cat!

So little Elsa came into our lives – a tiny dog with the heart of a lion.

A few months later, it was Fifi's turn. A longhaired Chihuahua, she'd been picked up as a stray. She was twelve at least, and in the early stages of renal disease. Fifi came home with me too, and Elsa and Fifi became the best of friends. My two old girls were so happy together. Elsa was the smart one, and Fifi (of very little brain) had the looks. They brought so much joy into all our lives.

Elsa stopped eating ten months later. She could no longer walk or stand, and I knew it was time to say goodbye. With tears running down my face, I quietly thanked her for all the joy she had brought us, and she passed away in my arms. She now sleeps in the backyard under the daisy bush.

Fifi and I miss our darling friend very much. Fifi follows me around like a shadow now, and I love her dearly. I hope she will be getting under my feet for a long time to come.

Irene, Victoria

Our Little Diva

I knew I had to meet this little lady. The ad said Diva was a gorgeous little Silky Terrier. She had been found at the Blacktown Pound, and was thought to be about six years old – so classified as a senior. I knew older dogs had a harder time finding new homes, and my dear mother-in-law Maria, also a senior, needed company: someone to love and fuss over, now that she was on her own.

Maria and husband Joao had been married in Portugal and migrated to Sydney in 1971 with their three children. At first Maria found it very hard in Australia, not speaking the language, but over the years she grew to feel that Sydney was her home. After retirement Maria and Joao enjoyed the life that they had worked so hard to build for themselves. Then, quite suddenly, Maria was alone: Joao passed away. My husband lived with her for a while, but then had to move on to start his new married life with me. Maria found it lonely in the house on her own, and felt unsafe. I knew she was down.

When the lovely Linda from Seniors and Silky Rescue brought Diva over to meet us, she was so cute I fell in love then and there. If my mother-in-law wasn't interested, I sure was! A two-week trial was arranged to see if Diva was a good match for Maria. She started life with Maria very quietly, sleeping a lot, but once the adoption papers were signed the real Diva emerged! She came out of her shell, grew in confidence every day and put on weight. We treated her like a diva – with lots of good Portuguese cooking and a life of luxury!

Since Diva became part of the family, Maria seems more her old self again. She says how safe she feels these days with Diva around, and how nice it is to have company and someone to chat to and watch TV with. Maria's life is much better now, sharing the days with her little friend.

Adopting a senior dog has many benefits compared to buying a 'designer' puppy from a pet shop. The seniors have been house-trained, don't need constant supervision, and don't tend to chew your shoes! They are loyal companions who deserve a second chance. Maria and Diva, two 'senior ladies', are so good for each other.

Jennifer, New South Wales

You're Never Too Old!

Just in case you're unsure, a dog is never too old to adopt!

With a move to a new house with a large backyard only a week away, we decided to get in touch with Melbourne Animal Rescue (MAR) to see if we could start fostering a dog. We finalised the formalities quickly, and three days before our move we got a call asking if we could foster a Staffy Red Heeler mix from Saturday, the day of our move! Both too excited about the idea of having a dog again to say the timing wasn't right, we said of course we would.

While unloading our furniture, Courtney arrived with Neli, a real cutie but for a nasty-looking and smelly tumour on her right front paw. She was surrendered to the group with twenty-four-hours' notice by her previous owner who was moving and couldn't take her for an undisclosed reason. If MAR couldn't help her, they would have Neli put down, they said. She was twelve years old. After more than a decade as a loving family pet, they suddenly didn't want her any more? Words failed me.

Being 'elderly', white and a little too small and placid for our liking, we thought Neli would make a great first foster dog, as we didn't expect to get very close to her. How wrong we were! The tumour was horrible, and apparently she'd lived with it for around seven years, untreated. Luckily our great vet removed it a week later, and over the next few weeks, Neli transformed: she lost weight, walked better, seemed to get fitter, happier and became more social with other dogs. She made us laugh time and time again when she would work herself under her bedding. Outside, one day, we couldn't see her and feared she'd run away, out the gate, but after a closer look it turned out she was curled up under her blanket!

After several weeks the inevitable question arose for us: Should we keep her? On the weekend the decision was due Neli gave me her first cuddle: while I was on my knees she walked onto them and tried to give me a kiss! She must have known what was hanging over her head and was trying to say, 'Let me stay . . .' So we did!

Nearly six months on, Neli is now thirteen, and we couldn't be happier with our decision. She is just gorgeous. She's been on bike rides in her brand-new doggy trailer and enjoys her trip in the car with a converted back seat tailored just for her! She loves the camping trips we take her on: playing in the mud, exploring the bush and sleeping in front of the camp fire. She is a crowd favourite just about everywhere we go. Neli has really come out of her shell and is so playful, no one would dream she's thirteen. Her character is just beautiful and gets stronger and cheekier by the day. We like to think she doesn't bark as such but she sure talks to us. Her head gestures and different tones of squeaks and barks tell us exactly what she wants . . . or she'll bring us her lead – another pretty clear sign!

After such a great experience with Neli, we decided to find her an 'elderly' friend and are currently trialling an eight-year-old Labrador called Ody through Luv-a-Lab.

We couldn't be happier with Neli and it seems like it was meant to be. Anyone hesitant about adopting an older dog should remember this: they might cost a bit more in vet bills, but how much will a chewed-up couch cost you, or your Italian leather shoes that a pup will make short work of? It's a tragedy older homeless dogs struggle to find a home. But what beats knowing you've given a dog the best 'golden years' they could have hoped for? We know Neli is probably happier and better off than she's ever been. In return, she provides us with lots of love, loyalty and laughter, and most importantly, has turned us into a family rather than a couple!

Maarten and Belinda, Victoria

Brodie's Story

Dumped, when he needed them most. At nine years old, and almost blind, they took him to the pound, turned away and left.

The reason they gave? 'The dog is too old.'

Luckily for the golden-coated Brodie, he was rescued by Hunter Animal Rescue. He was in a loving foster home for six months until I found him on the group's website and fell in love with him. I was looking for a dog who wouldn't mind being home alone all day while my husband and I worked and we thought a senior dog would be suitable. We were right!

We fell in love with Brodie instantly and his sight problem was not an issue to us or him. His greatest talent is world-class begging. He begs for food, walks or reassurance. If he is near me he will put up 'the begging paw' – always his right paw – and rests it on my leg. If I don't respond he will tap me, oh, so gently. If he doesn't know where I am in the house he will use the begging paw to ring his little bell that I've mounted on the door frame at his level. Who says you can't teach an old dog new tricks? He knows I will always come running when he rings his bell, day or night. Such a character!

Two years ago Brodie developed other eye problems which caused him to lose what little sight he had left. His eyes were watering and causing pain, so, since he was blind anyway, we decided to take our vet's advice and had them removed. Brodie has adapted extremely well – being blind doesn't stop him from enjoying life to the full.

We have also since adopted Snowflake, a Maltese mix from Dog Rescue Newcastle, and like all rescues, she has her own special story. My wonderful experience with Brodie and Snowflake has prompted me to become a volunteer with both Hunter Animal Rescue and Dog Rescue Newcastle. It's a great way to thank these tireless groups of volunteers for saving my Brodie and Snowflake – by helping them save more.

Terri, New South Wales

Touched by an Angel

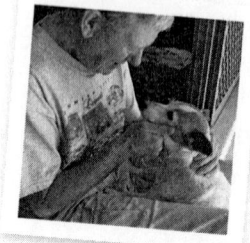

We are passionate dog lovers, my husband Tony and I, and over the years we have had quite a few dogs – Dobermans, Rottweilers, Labradors – but it was Angel, an elderly female Jack Russell, who changed our lives forever.

She caught my eye in the Sunday newspaper one day. Her profile said that after her owner died, Angel had to fend for herself, wandering around for weeks in search of shelter and food. This beautiful ten-year-old had a benign growth on her back but a malignant one in her ear, and she was going deaf. But her rescuers, the Fraser Coast Dog Rescue team, arranged the surgery and nursed her back to health. I emailed them to express my interest.

One of the amazing things was my husband had seen the same sad doggie story, and emailed the rescue group too without letting on to me! We got separate positive responses back and, as we share the same mailbox, realised that we were chasing after the same forever friend.

It was a wonderful revelation to us, as we had both thought (wrongly) that the other never wanted another dog. We had emigrated to Australia from South Africa and had to leave two precious dogs behind in foster care. It was fate that we had both felt this surge of compassion to rescue little Angel, and she was clearly meant for us.

My mother, who is getting older and lives with us, needed a companion, and Angel needed a good home for her twilight years. So after we were screened as suitable adoptive parents, Tony and I drove the 300 kilometres from Brisbane to Maryborough to meet her. The first thing Angel did was cover Tony's legs with kisses! (She licked everyone else she took a fancy to as well. My mother's nursing aide later wrote in her notes: 'Friendly little dog, likes licking legs'.)

Poor little Angel couldn't bark because of her hearing loss – she howled instead. And she howled the 300 kilometres home, too! Her greeting was always to howl. She would start calling for us from about 5 p.m. every night, her head peeping out through the slats of Mum's blinds in her room. When we got home from work she would run to the garage, wagging her tail madly, emitting her howl, until Tony bent down to rub his head against hers and say hello. The only time she would let out a proper bark was when she saw another dog – or a 4x4, for reasons we could never figure out!

Angel crept into our hearts and, despite the howling, we so looked forward to coming home after work to find this loving old girl, still frisky and full of life, waiting for us. Tony and Angel were inseparable – he called her his 'Poppet'. Although she started sleeping in my mother's bedroom, it wasn't long before this darling girl had persuaded us to make her a spot next to Tony's side of our bed. She slept on his T-shirts, too, in his laptop case, and started 'helping' him in his study when he worked at home. My mother used to say 'Angel came from hell to paradise', and we could only agree.

We had a wonderful fifteen months with Angel. We knew we wouldn't have her for very long, and it was sad when we saw her gradually slowing down, although she still loved her runs with Tony and walkies with me until the end. But one day, Angel had a seizure from a brain tumour, and we knew it was time to say goodbye. We have her ashes in a photo-frame box on a shelf in the family room. The inscription says: 'Our Angel "Poppet" – rescued from despair, your love changed our lives.'

Tony, Marcelle and Susie, Queensland

Lending a Hand

*It's a special class of person who will take in an unwanted
animal until it finds a permanent home. Sometimes the dogs
in foster care are traumatised or in poor health; other times
efforts to find them a new family have been all but exhausted.
Foster carers have saved a great many doggy lives – and just because
fostering is temporary, doesn't mean the benefits are.*

Fostering Fun

A hyperactive Kelpie who would howl on command. A Whippet mix who thought he was the boss of the world. An adorable Mastiff mix who wets himself every time he is excited or scared. A big, happy Shepherd with no teeth.

I have been lucky enough to have all of these dogs living at my home, and all in the past twelve months. I am a foster carer with Newcastle-based group Hunter Animal Rescue, and fostering is one of the most rewarding things I've ever done.

If you are recovering from the loss of a beloved animal, I recommend you try providing foster care until you are ready to adopt again. It was an easy decision for me. I had tragically lost my twelve-month-old Labrador to cancer and wasn't ready to take on another straight away. However, my house was so desperately quiet without a dog and I wanted to do more for animals in need.

To become a foster carer I first attended an orientation session and then my yard was inspected and approved as suitable. A tiny five-month-old Kelpie called Zulu was then delivered to my door. Zulu sat obediently in the backyard, looking at me as if butter wouldn't melt in her mouth. She was mostly black, with huge pointy ears that were almost as big as her. Unfortunately, coming straight from the pound, she was also skinny, dirty and flea-ridden. She was scared of men and unsure of her surroundings.

However, her true Kelpie colours soon began to show. Needing to be 'busy', she dug the deepest and narrowest holes you have ever seen and the outdoor furniture became her favourite chew toys. She constantly seemed like a coiled spring, ready to bounce off the walls at any moment.

After an hour-long walk, a twenty-minute game of fetch and a play with her tug-toys, she'd stop and look at me as if to say, 'So, what are we doing next?' Finding a home for an animal with so much energy was not going to be an easy task.

But one day a young couple came to see her. They told me there would be daily walks to the dog park and Zulu would be part of the family and allowed in the house. They sounded like a good match. However, what confirmed it for me was when the woman sat on the floor and Zulu crawled into her lap, looking like she had always belonged there. I could tell Zulu knew that this family was 'the one'.

Zacky, a four-year-old Shepherd, was next and looked like a tan-coloured wolf, with a big mane of dark fur around his neck. He had been abused and, probably due to anxious chewing, had ground all of his teeth down to little stumps. Zacky was terrified of men, sticks and belts, and had been living on the streets for a very long time.

I gave him more love and attention in a week than he had ever received in his entire life. And he appreciated every little thing I did! Simply giving him a slice of chicken followed by a big cuddle would absolutely make his day. Zacky is now living in a home where he gets to swim in a lake and is being fed three gourmet meals a day.

Trigger is my latest foster dog, a six-month-old Mastiff mix, with gorgeous eyes and a happy-go-lucky attitude. Even with his 'quirks', he brings me delight every single day and I know that he will find his forever home soon too.

Although it will be sad to see him go, and I will probably shed a tear or two, simply knowing that I have helped save yet another animal whose life was about to end will make me happy for years to come.

People always ask me how I am able to hand dogs over to their forever homes when they have been such a part of my life, sometimes for months. I reply that when I find each dog their perfect home it is easy, because there is always another animal on death row who needs me. And I will be there.

Jessie, New South Wales

Love at First Sight

I didn't believe in love at first sight until I met Maisie Moo.

I had been a foster carer for ACT Rescue & Foster (ARF) for roughly five years and always found it to be one of the most rewarding things I had ever done. However, plenty of people asked me if I'd become a 'foster failure' yet – when you adopt your foster dog – and I would proudly proclaim it hadn't happened to me. But everything was about to change.

I was looking at the pound pictures for Griffith, New South Wales, when I saw a dog that I couldn't get out of my head. It was a grainy picture of a small black young pup, looking over her shoulder at the camera. I continued on, looking at other death-row dogs but kept coming back to her picture. Eventually, I knew I had to save her.

My Staffy girl arrived with a volunteer driver on a warm Saturday afternoon. The minute she opened the crate I was in love with this smelly, unsure little pup who promptly rolled onto her back for a belly rub. My rational side was thinking I would get her bathed and cleaned up, and she would no doubt scrub up well and find a home quickly. The emotional side of me thought she was one of the most beautiful dogs I had ever seen. I had decided she would be called Maisie.

When I got Maisie home and she met our resident dogs Kenzie and Murdock, they got along beautifully – it was like Maisie had been with us for years. And once bathed, she looked beautiful.

As the weeks passed, I realised I was falling more and more in love with the cheeky young girl. I kept making 'jokes' to my husband about how he should let me keep Maisie as my Christmas present. Every time he asked what I wanted for Christmas, I would reply 'Maisie!' But my husband was the voice of reason. He would remind me of the myriad rational reasons why we should let her go to a forever home of her own.

Then, a few days before Christmas, a lovely couple that had adopted an ARF dog a couple of years earlier called and asked if they could meet Maisie and I had to reluctantly agree. They had a lovely large property at Yass, and ticked all the boxes. They arrived on Christmas Eve and unsurprisingly fell in love with my girl immediately. Thus it was with a heavy heart that I had to bid her farewell. I watched while they loaded her up in the car, and my heart started aching. As they started to drive away I wanted to run after the car and shout, 'No! I've made a mistake – you have to bring her back!' I cried all that day and some of the night too. I was devastated.

The next day I rang Maisie's new home and asked how she was settling in. I secretly hoped they would say, 'Oh, she doesn't get on with the cat, we will have to bring her back.' Unfortunately for me she was getting on wonderfully with all their animals! I had never been so gutted to hear of one of my foster dogs settling in so well.

During one of my numerous subsequent talks to friends about how much I wished I'd kept Maisie, a wise lady said to me 'If you love someone, set them free. If they come back, they're yours, if they don't, they never were.' Remembering that saying was the only thing that kept me going. My husband, seeing my distress and feeling guilty, kept telling me, 'If Maisie comes back, we can keep her.'

There wasn't a day that went by that I didn't think about Maisie Moo, but life had to go on. I was still fostering but had no connection with another dog like I'd had with Maisie.

Then, one day, I received a phone call from Maisie's owner. She said Maisie might have to come back. She had been visiting the neighbouring property to play with their dogs, and the owners were worried that another farmer may think she was a threat to their livestock and could get shot.

My heart leapt at hearing those words, but I suddenly turned into a nervous wreck. The worries started setting in: If she comes back, will I feel the same? Will she fit in with us again? I was so anxious, I sent my husband to collect Maisie with our dogs to ensure they still got on.

When I heard the door open, my Maisie Moo came running straight in towards me for a hug. Every feeling I had for her was still there and more. Much to my joy, she slotted right back into my dog pack like she had never been away.

Maisie Moo is now in her forever home here and is utterly cherished. In the meantime, I've developed a chronic back problem that I've had to have surgery for and another lot ahead soon. I'm in pain all the time and it can become quite depressing. But I can always rely on Maisie to lie with me on the sofa. Stroking her perfect soft belly makes me feel happier, and when I am feeling low, Maisie lifts my spirits. Maisie is back, where she is meant to be.

Beverley, Australian Capital Territory

Waiting for You

The reason is plain: I like animals better than children, so I decided to become an animal foster parent. Helping homeless pets is a great way to give back to the community now that I'm retired. Amber, a very pretty but timid Maltese Shih Tzu mix, had clearly had a lot of litters during her short life. She had been dumped at the pound, probably from a puppy factory where she had become too old for breeding. Perhaps she was lucky? Many retired mums on puppy factories are simply killed on the property and don't make it to the pound.

Amber arrived late in the afternoon, very anxious. I had to go to work, nightshift, so I left her on the bed next to my husband Alan, and she didn't move all night. When I returned it looked quite funny to see this big man squeezed onto the edge of the bed and this little dog lying so close alongside him.

When Amber's profile went onto PetRescue, I received a call from a woman called Jane, who only months before had lost her doggy friend of twelve years in a vicious attack. They were at the park when, without warning, a large dog ran up and killed her little friend, right in front of her. Shattered, Jane and her husband had needed time to grieve. But now they needed the love and comfort of another little dog. Amber was the first dog they had looked at online. I was deeply moved hearing her story, and excited at the possibility that this was a great home for Amber. Being a puppy-factory dog, she really deserved to have some special years ahead.

A time was set for Jane and her husband to come and meet Amber on Saturday at midday. I told Amber the good news. She must have understood, because of what happened next.

Saturday came, and Alan and I were sitting at the table having lunch. It was roast chicken, and we all know how dogs love that! All the numerous foster dogs were sitting at our feet, waiting for tasty treats, when I realised Amber was missing. That was strange. I called her and she didn't come. That's when I got up, looked outside and saw her sitting quietly at the front gate. I was speechless – I had told her that her new family were coming at midday to meet her. She was waiting for them.

Jane and her husband arrived at the gate. I opened it and was even more astonished at what happened next. Amber stood on her hind legs, balancing, and walked straight into Jane's arms. Jane instantly picked her up and asked if this was Amber. 'Yes,' I stammered, stunned at what I had seen. This little dog knew Jane was her new mum. She clung to Jane as though she had known her forever, and as we completed the paperwork and Jane handed Amber to her husband, she struggled and cried to get back to Jane's arms. The three of them went off home, to many years of love.

I wouldn't have believed this story unless I had witnessed it. This is just one of many joys and miracles I have experienced being a foster carer, and I wouldn't miss fostering for anything.

Angie, Queensland

There is Always a Home

Luca and Bambi are a pair of Italian Greyhounds who came to our rescue group after their original owner passed away. The woman's son took on the two dogs for the short term but as he already had three of his own he just couldn't keep them.

So Luca and Bambi found their way to us, but none of us had had experience with this breed before. Boy, were we in for some fun times! These two delightful dogs leapt around the house, bouncing from one piece of furniture to the next. They yapped and screeched and when excited they could leap as high as your head.

Word got around that we had a pair of Italian Greyhounds, and many of our fellow rescuers assured us that we would never find someone willing to adopt them both – they would have to be separated. We didn't argue with them, for deep down we felt that the right person was out there – they just hadn't come along yet.

There would be more issues to focus our attention on. Luca had broken his leg while living with his previous owner and she had had it repaired at great expense. However, Luca was suddenly no longer bearing weight on it and seemed to have some pain in the joint. After consulting the vet, it was decided it was better to remove the leg.

During Luca's time in surgery and recovery we were contacted by a lady in Sydney called Michelle. Michelle's family had always had 'Iggys' as she called them and her daughter currently had two. Michelle knew *all* about the breed and their behaviour; she painted a vivid picture of these two dogs before I even opened my mouth! I knew that this was the right home for the pair.

Luca and Bambi were collected by Jetpets, courtesy of PetRescue, and flown up to Sydney into Michelle's waiting arms!

A week later, Michelle contacted us on Facebook, raving about her two new pooches. Pictures followed and it's quite evident that this is certainly a match made in heaven for both Michelle and the dogs. We continue to stay in touch, hearing all about the pair's adventures. This story proves there *is* a home out there for *all* our rescues.

Matt Aitken Animal Rescue, Victoria

It's a Dog-help-dog World

Sometimes the last chance a damaged dog has comes from the least-expected place: other rescued dogs.

When rescue organisations in Perth, Western Australia, have a difficult case, they turn to 'pack power' and call on my dogs Tia, Jake and Shadow to help out. You see, all my three rescues know only too well what it's like to be plucked from death row and what it takes to find a good home. Tia is a fourteen-year-old Red Heeler mix; Jake a seven-year-old Belgian Shepherd mix and Shadow a seven-year-old Mastiff mix. Together with my partner Karl and me, their guardians, they all bring different skills that combine to help rehabilitate physically damaged or fearful dogs.

Tia was rescued from the RSPCA in Darwin as an eight-week-old puppy. She is the pack matriarch and in charge of social etiquette in the house. She advises how, with a shake of the collar, to make the name tag and council rego tags sing out, as it communicates to us that it's time for them to go outside to check their 'wee mails'. Tia also uses a number of distraction techniques to ensure new dogs learn their proper place. If they get up on the sofa, a privilege she believes they have not yet earnt, she simply finds a toy she knows they love and makes a 'puppy bow' play towards the toy. Once the new dog has jumped off the sofa to steal the toy, Tia then ducks off and jumps on the sofa herself. No matter how young, big, strong or clever the new dogs think they are, they cannot outwit Ms Tia. We think that outwitting foster dogs is the secret that has kept Tia very spritely in her twilight years.

Jake was a handful to start with. Rescued at two years of age by K9 Rescue, he had poor socialisation skills and a desperation to run for miles to see other dogs. If on a lead, and another dog was in the distance, Jake would yodel, lunge and almost backflip to express his excitement and keenness to get to that dog. He wasn't aggressive towards them; he simply reached them and promptly turned and ran back to us! No one would have guessed that the very characteristics that made him annoying to his previous owners would actually prove useful in saving other dogs' lives. Given his high prey drive and ability to run for extended distances, it was obvious Jake would need a job. And as we fostered rescued dogs, it was the lifeline he needed! He has a great job now as a personal trainer and coach. He shows dogs how to play with toys and a range of balls. He is observant of their body language and slows down for disabled and elderly dogs when running, and provides encouragement when they lose interest by dropping the toy or ball tantalisingly close to them so they can 'win' it back. Even the most energetic of breeds he manages to tire to the point where they are calm enough to be trained by us in good canine citizen skills, pack socialisation and then affection and treats.

Shadow had a last-minute reprieve from death. Her owners, who had her from puppyhood, took her to the vet at the age of five to be put to sleep. The reason? She didn't fit in with their plans to travel around Australia in their caravan. Luckily, the vet refused, and called on Saving Animals From Euthanasia (SAFE) to rescue her. We fostered her and then she became our 'foster failure' in a great way, as we adopted her as our own. Like most Mastiffs, Shadow can put up with a lot, including boisterous and ill-mannered foster dogs that have yet to learn the art of life balance! Her stoic Zen-like presence has a calming effect as she mentors insecure and fearful dogs to find a more balanced place. She shows them there is a time for energetic play and excitement and a time for stretching out under a shady tree and meditating.

As for us two-leggeds, we feel blessed that rescuing Tia, Jake and Shadow has not only enriched our own lives with love, companionship and happiness, but over the years it has allowed many other rescue dogs to find respite with our pack. Having addressed the specific needs of each foster dog who temporarily lodges with us, the biggest reward is to see them go on to a new life that this special second chance has allowed. Fostering is fabulous!

Julia, Western Australia

A Little Dog with a Big Heart

Here is a picture I took of Hughie. For a little guy, he sure made a huge impact on us. Hughie died yesterday and he took a big chunk of our hearts with him.

Hughie was our foster dog and was brought into the house by my partner, Colette. What little we know about him is that he came from a pound and his immediate future was not looking too flash. The word had gone out through the usual channels and Colette put her hand up to take on the little bloke until he was able to get right and find a loving home.

We already have a rescue dog, Yota, so we know the deal. Yota is a beautiful young lady – an Australian Koolie – who came from the bush and had been mistreated. Today, she is strong, loves to run and goes 'Woo woo' when we take her to the park and her working-dog personality regains its natural place in the universe.

I have to say it feels pretty damn good to rescue an animal from an untimely end or a brutal existence at the hands of some uncaring bastard. I guess that's made it all the harder to lose Hughie. For a dog that weighed very little and had trouble standing upright, our Hughie had enough personality for ten big pooches. When Yota came near Hughie's food, the little bloke would let fly with a mouthful that made everyone within earshot freeze and take a step back – humans included.

Hughie was, as far as we knew, a mini Fox Terrier. It seems that plenty of attitude is hardwired into them. He had more than most. He also had more issues than most: a laundry list of physical difficulties. Nonetheless, we fell in love with him and we knew it would be easy enough for somebody else to do the same.

After a few initial tough days, Hughie seemed to be finding his feet and getting about better. He would follow Yota around the house, his little toenails tick-tick-ticking on the floorboards as he found his rhythm. Hughie was never a 4/4 sort of guy. His beat was irregular, like a jazz soloist flirting between time signatures. You could tell, though, that he had struggled to get this far. He was achingly thin. His legs were all out of whack. One obvious sign of neglect was that he had very hairy paws. Where normally the hair between a dog's paw pads would be worn away from walking, Hughie had a lot of fluff. Clearly, he hadn't been doing much walking. Maybe he had been in a cage all his life? He had rickets, a bone-softening disease that comes from lack of sunlight. He would seek out a warm patch in the garden and soak up the sun, as if he was trying to cure himself.

When I looked at Hughie, sometimes I would want to cry. But we thought we could fill that little body with our own hearts and pull him through. The plan was to foster him and prepare him for somebody else. The plan wasn't to lose him.

Hughie went quickly. On a Saturday night, he fell ill. Colette woke early and sat with him, cuddling him to make sure he was warm. We took him to the vet as early as possible and the diagnosis was serious. His breathing was irregular and crackly, indicating pneumonia. He needed urgent attention and some tests. How could this be happening so fast? We took him to a second clinic and then to an emergency vet. In what seemed like no time at all, we were faced with the worst possible outcome. To be told by the vet that he was in terrible shape and going quickly was a huge shock. To have to make the decision to let him go was achingly hard and something we will always remember. Even the vet was in tears. I had expected her to be detached and professional, but she was obviously affected by us, the situation, and the fading little life force in our arms.

I'm glad we were able to say goodbye and see our friend off. I'm also glad that we got to take him home and put him in the soil in our backyard. It keeps him close to our hearts and reminds us of who he was and what he meant.

Our pets give everything of themselves to us. They are never jealous or spiteful or arrogant or greedy or mean. They just want us to love them and to show how much they love us.

I believe that Hughie taught us a lot in the short time he was here. He was brave, happy and loving, in spite of everything he had been through. He was a real survivor and he now survives in our memories.

Hughie was special. And I think that the people who help animals are special. We were too late for Hughie, but rather than allowing ourselves to feel despair about his loss, Victorian Dog Rescue & Resource Group decided to honour Hughie's brave, short life with the establishment of a Special Dogs Fund in his memory, to help more little blokes like him.

Marcus, Victoria

Dogs Overcoming the Odds

Behind every goofy doggy grin is the ability to bounce back from extreme hardship. Dogs' innate resilience means that with the help of compassionate human friends, they can prevail over the rough luck fate has dealt them. These are stories of pups who got a second crack at the happiness they deserved.

Perfect Timing

Pic: Katrucia Pet Photography

On Christmas Eve 2008, my world changed. I was diagnosed with breast cancer, and subsequently spent all of 2009 in treatment. Surgeries, chemotherapy and radiotherapy were difficult and included many side effects. I was unable to work. Suddenly, I was spending most of my time at home by myself; sick, weak and frankly, lonely.

I had seen Missy's profile on PetRescue and found myself drawn to the little dog, returning to look at her many times. She was in care with NSW rescue group DABS, and had been rescued from a vile puppy factory where she had been constantly bred. As a result, Missy had a lot of physical issues to deal with, but even more psychological problems. She was worn down physically and mentally. Her exhaustion and the parallels with my own situation were not lost on me. Even after six months of loving foster care before we met, Missy was still only just recovering.

On Australia Day, 2010, just as I had finished the formal part of my treatment and was moving into recovery, I completed the adoption process and Missy and I began our lives together. The timing for us both was perfect.

I didn't get to see her at her worst, and I am glad I didn't. It was bad enough knowing that her infected skin and hairless belly was from being made to sit in her own waste all day. She was underweight and needed most of her teeth removed as they'd long since rotted away in her mouth, meaning she couldn't eat properly. She'd gone nearly deaf from years of untreated ear infections. And she was plagued by arthritis and dominated by fear. And yet she'd still been made to bear litter after litter of puppies, destined for purchasers too blinded by the cuteness of the pups in the pet-shop window to understand what their mother Missy had to endure to produce them.

The first week I had Missy at home, I worried that I may have made a mistake, however – perhaps she was always going to be terrified? However, by the end of the second week, I was starting to see potential and a gradual change in her demeanour. By the end of the first month, and with a lot of physical attention, I really began to see the amazing little mind, hidden beneath all the years of abuse, starting to enjoy her new-found freedom.

Watching Missy come back to life was an inspiration. Before we met, I was too sick to walk around the block and rarely got out of my pyjamas. In wanting to teach Missy to walk and interact with other people, I got myself out of the house and into the fresh air. When I started to emerge back into a normal life, Missy was my constant companion. She and I would walk to the shops, have our morning coffee and meet friends. At one point, Missy was coming with me to the gym, and would sit quietly watching me while I did some basic strength training. When I started going back to work for a few hours a day, Missy would come along and sit with me in my office. Having her calm energy in the workplace when I was trying to get back into the swing of things was of enormous benefit.

Missy gave me something to focus on other than myself, and got me thinking beyond the day-to-day rut of being a 'patient'. She kept me going and stopped me from collapsing in a heap so many times. Her trust in me and unconditional love made even the worst days bearable.

Having Missy in my life has also changed me from being someone who loved animals to someone who now passionately advocates for them. Especially the ones we as a society don't like to talk about, like Missy, who was mistreated and abused so her owners might profit. Since Missy became part of my family, I've discovered she has a pronounced heart murmur, as well as syringomyelia (a neurological condition). Both are illnesses that should have stopped her owners breeding from her. Luckily, I've become a dab hand at administering medication and Missy's symptoms are controlled with tablets.

Who knows how many thousands of dogs like Missy are out there suffering with these debilitating conditions because the puppy factory owners just don't care? The most hideous fact of all is that puppy factories are legal in this country, and yet few dog lovers even know of their existence. It is an evil industry and I support the passing of legislation like Oscar's Law, to stop these people from continuing their disgusting trade. More information about this campaign is at oscarslaw.org.

Missy and I make a great team. With her as my inspiration, I recently qualified to teach pet CPR and first aid, using Missy as my very helpful 'demo dog'. If we're ever in an emergency and Missy needs my assistance, I now know what to do!

People tell me all the time how lucky she is to have me, but I believe that I'm the lucky one to have found her when I needed her most. Missy has taught me to be resilient in the face of difficult odds. I'm a much more compassionate and accepting person than I once was, which is very much how she approaches the world. And also, she's taught me, by necessity, that none of us are too good to pick up dog poo!

Rachael, New South Wales

The Difference a Little Love Makes

What a difference a little love and determination can make!

We found Josh, a black-and-white Poodle, in very bad condition at the pound. His fur was so matted that he could hardly move. His back end was burnt and very painful. It took me twenty minutes to try and coerce him out of his cage with treats and soft talking, but in the end I simply gently scooped him up. His whole body went stiff and he just shook in my arms. All I know is he had the saddest eyes I had ever seen. He had clearly endured years of abuse and neglect.

Even though we didn't want his first few hours with us being a bad experience, we had no choice but to give his coat an intense groom. He was such a good boy considering his fear and condition. He stood still with silent trust as three of us trimmed him back. It took about two hours to get most of the really bad mats off. We then gave him two baths and a good towel dry. It was very rewarding to see this extremely scared dog saved from the pound only hours before suddenly liven up and start rubbing his face and body all over the ground. He finally looked happy.

After a few days of settling in we took him off to the vet for his first visit – it would be one of many. The examination revealed his teeth needed urgent attention and that he had an unidentified lump on his rear end. The vet said that most lumps in that area are the beginnings of incurable cancers. I felt so sad to hear such news for a boy that had already struggled, to now face an even bigger battle to survive.

After the operation, the vet explained he had cleaned the few teeth he was able to save and removed the lump. There was great news – the lump was clear of cancer! But with one lot of good news, came another blow – while cleaning Josh's mouth, another more serious lump had been found in his jaw. We were off to a specialist.

Our fears were confirmed. The specialist explained to us that Josh had a cancer in his jaw and would need some of his jaw removed. If the operation was successful Josh would be able to live a healthy, normal life. The operation was quoted at about $5000 and as Halfway Home Animal Rescue is a small independent rescue charity, we just didn't have that kind of money. But if Josh didn't receive the operation, his jaw would eventually shatter.

We refused to give up. We decided, no matter what, Josh had to have the operation! It would mean Halfway Home would be struggling for funds for some time afterwards but we've always said that whatever dog or cat comes to us for care, they would receive the best we could provide.

After some thought, we decided to start a small appeal for Josh on our website where people could contribute to costs. As our site didn't receive much traffic, we knew it would take a long time and may be in vain, but a few generous supporters gave towards Josh and his operation. They were very much appreciated, but the fundraising was torturously slow.

Then, one of our foster carers, Natasha, called me and asked if we'd be interested in going to a major Melbourne newspaper with Josh's story. Of course we would! When Josh's plight appeared in the newspaper we couldn't believe the response. We received over 500 letters of support, 200 emails and in excess of the $5000 required for his operation within a week!

It kept getting better. On the last day of the appeal, we received a phone call from a highly respected Melbourne surgeon named Dr Charles Kuntz. He offered to do the surgery and any follow-up treatment for free! We were over the moon, knowing Josh was well and truly taken care of.

The newspaper did a follow-up story the next weekend and we were able to thank everyone who donated. Now that the surgery itself was also a gift, we asked if our donors wanted their funds returned, but everyone who donated happily agreed to have the unused funds put towards other dogs with similar needs. This allowed us to set up 'The Josh Cancer Fund' to help the next few dogs in our care that needed life-saving treatment too.

Josh's operation was a success and he recovered very well. To see how much he'd changed from that first day we met him until he found his new home was remarkable. He came into care terrified, but found comfort with us. He even fell in love with another foster dog named Ruby! We'd often find him curled up next to her. We're not sure if it was reciprocated, but we'd like to think so. She was an older lady so they made a lovely couple. He even ended up having a little skip in his step and it wasn't just because of the arthritis. He was genuinely happy. And probably for the first time in his life.

We found the most dedicated and loving home for Josh. Carol and Lee have gone above and beyond to provide the 'little man' with everything he could possibly need. They tell us that he gets so excited when they come home at night and it's dinnertime that he can literally bowl himself over. They've built up his muscles by walking him initially up the street and back to eventually making it around the block. Their other little dog Toby must always be with him, though, or Josh won't go!

Josh's sad eyes now shine with happiness and none of us could ask for anything better than that.

Jenaya Du Toit, Halfway Home Animal Rescue, Victoria

Pip, the Little Lion

Was he a dog or a little lion?

Our local pound regularly puts a flyer up in our pet-supply store to advertise the dogs they have available for adoption. On one flyer there was a picture of a little tan-coloured male Terrier mix with a ruffle around his neck that made him look like a small lion. I thought there was nothing I could do about him as I already had two dogs at home, plus a menagerie of other animals on the farm. I tried to convince myself that two dogs were really more than enough and I must stop thinking about him.

Yet every day I went to work, I saw the photo and it would tug at my heartstrings. It took me a couple of weeks before I couldn't bear it any longer – I rang the pound. They confirmed he was still there and should really have already been put to sleep by now. I took that as a sign he was waiting for me and told them not to do anything to him – I would be straight over!

As soon as I looked into the kennel run, the little lion won my heart. It turned out he, however, was in fact a she! She was not yet desexed or microchipped, so the arrangements were made and I was to come back in a couple of days to collect her.

The day my husband and I picked up our little lion, she looked sad and depressed, with stitches in her belly, sitting on the concrete floor of the pound kennel. We drove her to our store and picked out a soft round bed for her. Perhaps it was the first one she'd ever had, because as I laid her down in it, she let out a lengthy sigh. I guess it had been some time since she had felt anything soft or comforting. We drove home, placed her bed on the floor and watched over her. My sister came over too, and it would have been a strange sight for anyone coming into our house to see three adults lying on the floor around a little tan dog resting in a dog bed. We lay there for ages chatting and keeping her company and eventually chose a new name for her – Pip. After some hours, her little tail wagged a couple of times and I think she knew she was home.

Over the next few weeks, Pip recovered from her operation and got to know our other two dogs and cat. She was very unfit and delicate and I ended up carrying her some distance on our walks. Gradually she built up her strength and put on weight. She wanted to be with me all the time and loved getting out and about, walking on the farm. Now, she is fit and healthy and usually manages to keep up with my big dogs.

Pip is a quirky little odd ball. She makes funny snorting noises and has the strangest way of trotting. She has even, on one occasion, stowed away in our car to be sure she doesn't miss out on a family trip.

It was obvious, very early on, that Pip had been abused. Even to this day, on occasion she will flinch when you bend to pat her. She is still quite nervous and jumps at loud noises and has the occasional toileting accident, particularly if there is anything out of the ordinary happening around the house. We can't begin to imagine what she has been through in her past so we accept these little incidents without too much fuss.

When I see Pip lying on the floor, looking at me with what can only be described as huge brown puppy-dog eyes, she melts my heart. Her tail starts to wag until it is going at 100 revolutions per minute. It gives me the most wonderful feeling to know I indeed saved Pip's life and she is now so happy and loved. I really did not need another dog, but I am a great believer that animals come into your life when they are supposed to, for a reason. Giving an unwanted pet a second chance may have its challenges, but the rewards cannot be counted.

My rescue dog, Pip, has done nothing amazing, but the fact that I adopted her and saved her life gives me a feeling that is definitely amazing.

Tracey, New South Wales

Happily Ever After

I already have four much-loved Poodles, so I was not intending on adopting another dog. Then I met Princess.

Pets Haven, a Victorian animal shelter, rescued this ten-month-old little girl and her one newborn from a puppy factory and needed to place her in foster care. The tiny puppy, itself struggling to survive, was the sole remaining sibling of a litter of three and as a very young mother, Princess was not coping.

Asked to help, I took possession of what could only be described as a dirty, smelly, matted mess – you could hardly distinguish one end of Princess from the other. In the midst of this bundle of scruff was a small pure white explosion of fur. The puppy was so small and looked so incredibly out of place – he was less than forty-eight-hours old! I gasped when I saw them – could I actually help this pair?

When I got home I placed Princess's crate in my grooming room, away from my own dogs. Opening the crate, the terrified mother cowered in a corner, constantly growling, trying her utmost to protect her precious puppy. I had been warned that the vet had to noose and muzzle her so that she could be handled.

I let her be, but stayed close to the area so that I could make sure she was all right. After about half an hour she popped out of the crate and wandered around the room. I sat on the floor, speaking quietly and gently to her. Still, the look in her eyes showed raw fear and what could only be described as contempt for humans. I looked away and cried. My husband came in to see her, and he too welled up with tears.

I stayed with her for over an hour, offering her some food and water. She started to come closer to me but wouldn't let me touch her. After around three hours, I finally got to gently pat her on the back. She growled, but never tried to bite me. I picked up her tiny puppy and put him in a blanket on my lap. Her overwhelming protective instinct made her come up to me to see her pup. She then let me pat her a little more, and I very gently picked her up, putting her on my knee with the puppy. This was where our bond began. I had gained a small bit of her trust.

After a little while of sitting together, I got up and left Princess with her puppy while I went inside to come up with an action plan for this little family. I knew that the state she was in wasn't healthy for her or her baby. I decided that as hard as it may be, I was going to have to try and bathe her to get rid of the disgusting solid mat that was her coat.

I got out my clippers and put her on the grooming table. She was absolutely terrified. I decided not to tether or muzzle her, as I didn't want that to be her introduction to being handled by me. She only weighed around 3 kilograms, so how hard could it be? I soon found out. Very hard! She cried, growled, struggled and just wanted to desperately get away. I persevered, stopping whenever I thought she was getting too upset and spoke gently to her. Mostly I held her close. It took around forty-five minutes to get her coat off and when it did, it came off in one piece like a sheep's fleece.

I gave her a quick bath and dried her with a soft fluffy towel. Taking her outside into my backyard, I placed her on the lawn. I think it was the first time Princess had ever seen or stood on grass as she was quite tentative to move around on it. But then she realised her heavy coat was gone. She could move freely and her tail hair was no longer attached to her upper body, so it could move – more importantly, it could wag! I watched, overjoyed, as she ran around in circles, barking, in what was a 'thank you' dance.

The weeks passed, and Princess's rehabilitation continued. Her trust of me gradually increased, yet the world still contained many fears: one was that she wouldn't eat out of a bowl. To get her to eat, I had to sit on the floor and handfeed her. She was physically scared of a food bowl! Clearly, she had only ever had food thrown at her.

The little pup, now called Little Star, was growing quickly and was starting to move around more and more. Princess was a great mum, considering she was only a pup herself. I was starting to think about finding suitable people to adopt them both. Many applicants wanted to have Star, and I vetted every one until I found a suitable person. He left for his new forever home when he was ten weeks old, and once he had safely gone, Princess started to shine! She was more attentive, and began to follow me everywhere.

During this time, I started to let my dogs interact with Princess. Never being allowed to be a normal dog before, she had no idea about play, and constantly growled at them. However, my dogs understand there is something about her that requires a gentle patience. I watch Princess trying to copy the things they do, and I watch them trying to teach her . . . it's beautiful to see.

The biggest breakthrough was when she climbed into one of the dog beds with my boy Charlie. This was a great moment in her rehabilitation. Meanwhile, I was getting more and more attached to this little ragamuffin and she to me. I decided that I would adopt her myself; after all, I couldn't bear to betray the trust she had placed in me by sending her away, no matter how good a new family I could find for her.

Princess is now a fully-fledged member of the family. She still doesn't really know how to play with my other dogs, but she tries desperately. My girl Holly, who has an extremely dominant nature, teaches her so much. She shows her how to play, how to throw the toys around, even how to jump up on the couch. This has amazed me more than anything as Holly will growl and snap at the others if they annoy her enough, but with Princess she will give her a warning that what she's doing isn't right, and then go about the business of being mother and teacher to this little dog.

Princess still has a long way to go and displays many strange behaviours from the trauma she endured at the puppy factory, like constant tail-chasing, biting her own legs and fear of plastic bags. But with love and perseverance, her true self will continue to emerge. I sometimes look back on the past few months and realise how far she has come and how incredibly strong her will to survive must have been.

From the day I brought Princess home, thinking I had taken on more than I could handle, I have no regrets in allowing this beautiful little fur angel into my life. She is incredibly special, she is very much loved and she is safe. She is my little heartbeat.

And she now eats out of her very own bowl!

Yvonne, Victoria

When Anything is Possible

When I first got the call about a Dingo in distress, I have to admit that I had no idea of what I was taking on.

Banjo came to Chelonia, our Wildlife Rehabilitation & Release Shelter in Western Australia, with the worst case of mange that I have ever seen, and chronic cystitis. He was passing blood, urinating many, many times a day and crying in pain at each empty. I was shocked when I first met this poor creature, totally unrecognisable as a Dingo.

Dingoes are widely misunderstood in this country. There is much ignorance in the general community about them, and we do our best at Chelonia to try to dispel the myths and help this breed.

Banjo's story was sketchy, but he was roughly eight months old. He had been taken from the wild as a pup and had lived on a community for most of his short life. In this environment he lived pretty much as a free spirit, mainly fending for himself. But then he became sick.

Fortunately, that's where Derby Animal Welfare Group (DAWG) came into the picture. Banjo had been untouchable: the volunteer who had been feeding him had managed to get him to sniff her hand after some time, but even his owners were not able to catch him or handle him. He had to be dart-sedated by a vet to get him into care.

When he arrived, Banjo's face and feet were cracked and bleeding, and he was almost totally bald. His ears had been mutilated, and he was grossly undernourished. If it hadn't been for the food given to him by DAWG he would probably have been dead. He was a very sorry sight.

Within two days of being here he let me pat him; it was a moment which brought some dampness to my eyes. But the greatest challenge

I faced in my journey with this poor little fellow was socialising him. Right from day one, all of Banjo's food was delivered via my hand. After a while, while I was sitting on the floor of his pen feeding him, he would come and sit beside me but wouldn't look at me and I wasn't allowed to look at him. If I did, he would jump up and hide in his box. Eventually, after I had fed him, Banjo would let me touch him and give him gentle back and chest massages. Later, he also let me rub some soothing cream into his poor, rough, split skin. When I was treating him he would sit with his head bowed, his eyes shut, and he would tremble. This was the first time he had ever experienced true affection and it was clearly a deeply moving experience for him. He had definite 'no go' zones, though. I definitely wasn't allowed to touch his ears or his feet, and am still not allowed to touch his tail.

Banjo's eyes were dead and puss-filled when he arrived; now life has begun to return to them. Feeding him from my hand has helped us forge a strong and trusting bond. Now he sits at rigid attention while watching me prepare his food and enthusiastically scoffs it from his bowl when it is ready. His coat is very slowly growing back and although it is still very sparse, we can see that he has the hallmark badges of a Dingo: white feet, white chest, and a white tip to his tail.

Banjo is over a year old now and he and adoptive brother Djindi, an eighteen-month-old Alpine Dingo, play and romp together. They love playing tug-of-war and chasey. He thinks it is funny to chase the family cats that run in front of him, and gently kisses and nose-pushes the bolder ones who hold their ground when he approaches. A truly damp-eye moment was when he was first emerging from his pen to come inside the house. The resident kitten approached him at the door and as they touched noses Banjo took his poor, ratty little tail out from between his legs for the first time since arriving and wagged it. I was overcome with emotion, it was better than winning Lotto.

The experts all said that it was cruel to take Banjo away from his familiar territory and that he would never be socialised. In my opinion it would have been reprehensible to leave him in the state he was in. As for socialising, it took just four weeks to turn a basically wild animal who could not be touched by a human hand into a housetrained, proud Dingo living in a home and in harmony with many other domestic animals.

Banjo will never be a little Fido who rolls over in excitement for a tummy rub. He is very dignified and can only tolerate short bursts of touching, but he looks at me adoringly and I reciprocate. Banjo still has a long way to go; he is a work in progress, but also living proof that with a bit of love, anything is possible.

Lesley, Western Australia

Deck-chair Dog

It was 8 p.m. in Phuket, Thailand. I was in front of the resort where I was staying with my daughter. An employee was removing five deck chairs from the beach opposite. The young dog I had been feeding was, as usual, curled up under the end chair. Her shelter gone, she remained, uncovered. I crossed the road to give her a biscuit.

'Goodnight, Siam,' I whispered, stroking her.

Every morning the five deck chairs were set out on the beach, then removed as night fell. The dog appeared philosophical that her peaceful kennel disappeared every evening. The small cove was rocky and unpopular. Resort guests, myself included, preferred the pool. Apart from a couple of hopeful food sellers, Siam was the only regular inhabitant.

From the road above the cove I could see the sandy beach further down. A few people had stayed on the sand despite the darkening sky.

A small pack of street dogs was leaving the beach. They moved up to the curb, and stood patiently waiting for a gap in the fast traffic. They had wandered down to our cove yesterday. They sniffed Siam, then ignored her. They looked fit and healthy, although thin. Four of the group was wearing tick collars. All appeared desexed. They were mostly typical Thai community dogs: short, mainly brown, coats; black 'sunglasses' or muzzle masks; and tails that curled over their backs.

I knew from the first day I saw Siam she was different. She carried her tail like a flag. A thin black Labrador type, she lacked the air of confidence of the other dogs. She seemed to have no idea how to feed herself and although I had seen her approach the road she always retreated from the heavy traffic and went back to snooze under her deck chair. She was clearly ill, weak and hungry.

The following morning I saw she was further down the beach. I waved my fragrant bag of bacon and sausages, saved from the breakfast buffet. She came running; this was a milestone. When I'd first met Siam a week earlier and started feeding her, she was frail and wobbly. Judging by her small, shiny white teeth she was about six months old. Her reluctance to wander from the cove suggested she had been abandoned there. Perhaps she was waiting for a master who would never return.

From a distance she looked black, but up close black blended into deep chocolate-brown ruff. Now stronger on her bacon diet, she wagged her tail and demonstrated she was one of those dogs gifted with the ability to smile. I was distressed because I would be leaving Thailand shortly and was sure she would be hungry again, and eventually starve. As I flew out, I decided to search the internet for some kind of help.

Once home, I was at the computer before I unpacked. My first search attempt was 'Animal Welfare Phuket'. Instantly I discovered a huge no-kill animal shelter called the Soi Dog Foundation (SDF) on the north of the island. How I wished I'd known when I was there! Soon, after several email conversations with John Dalley who, with his wife Gill, runs the Foundation, I began to feel hopeful SDF could help Siam.

I sent John my photos of Siam along with descriptions of her, the beach and the deck chairs that were her day-time kennel. While John searched and scoured the beaches, I pinned her photo on my wall and remembered the feel of her soft silky ears. I thought about the way, when I sat beside her, she would go to sleep with her head on my lap. I was in love with the gentle affectionate dog I had named Siam.

I pondered if there was any way I could get her to Australia and through our brutal quarantine laws. It was worse than I'd realised. Thailand is not on our approved quarantine list. Siam would have to spend six months in a 'neutral' rabies-free country like Singapore and then more weeks in quarantine here. Hopeless!

Finally the email came: John had figured out which beach I had been describing. He got there in the afternoon only to be told by a *tuk tuk* driver that his very own dog catchers had been there in the morning and collected her. By the time he returned to the shelter, Siam had already been spayed and vaccinated! She knew she was special – she made herself at home and, remaining un-penned, she glued herself to John's side as he moved about the Foundation.

The next day John emailed that a volunteer vet was returning to America and she'd offered to take Siam. America requires only that a dog passes a rabies test in order to enter the country. Failing Thailand, a home in America would be wonderful for Siam!

As I put in a share of freight money, I knew this was a wonderful break for my Thai doggy friend. Gill, like her husband John, was a devoted worker for the dogs. She took Siam back to their house for a cuddly last night in Phuket.

Siam became an adoption speed record for the Soi Dog Foundation – on the beach on Tuesday and in America headed for a new home that Friday! John raced around getting a crate and a permit for her to fly. She went into her crate, curled up and dozed, as always a placid, agreeable dog.

I felt sad I wouldn't see Siam again; I remembered how gently she took meat from my hand, and her generous doggy smile. Yet I am thrilled she has the most wonderful loving home in San Francisco with another rescued Thai dog she adores. They play together and sleep on warm, soft beds. Deck chairs and damp sand are now just a doggy memory. She has a new first name, JaiDee, which in Thai means 'kind heart'. Siam remains as her middle name.

Rescuing the young Thai stray was a turning point for me. I have always donated to animal causes and I keep spoiled pets, but I have never given my actual time to animal welfare. I thought it would be upsetting and I wouldn't cope. After meeting Siam and learning about the wonderful work the Soi Dog volunteers do, I knew that I wanted to put more of myself into *doing*. I have started by becoming a volunteer at our local animal shelter in Melbourne.

My skin fits better now that animal welfare has moved from the periphery of my life to a central purpose. For this I thank the wonderful people at the Soi Dog Foundation and a young Thai dog called JaiDee Siam.

Diana, Victoria

Barnaby – Melbourne's Saddest Dog No More

Pic: Herald Sun

'Barnaby the Wolfhound is Melbourne's saddest dog,' the *Herald Sun* article announced on page three that morning. Of course, I had to read on. Little did I know at the time that after subsequent TV appearances, international attention and hundreds of adoption applications, Barnaby would end up as our beloved new family member.

His origins are unknown. Victorian Dog Rescue & Resource Group simply received a phone call from a caring pound ranger, asking if they would rescue a very timid Wolfhound due to be put to sleep. He had clearly spent his two years in a cage or cowering in a confined space, as his tail and paws showed damage caused by rubbing up constantly against a hard surface. Moreover, he seemed to have agoraphobia – fear of open spaces.

When the terrified Wolfhound went into the care of the rescue group, he was named Barnaby and foster carer Hollie took him in. She soon found the sad boy wouldn't leave his crate – it was like his security blanket. If she didn't force him to come out, he would have stayed in there all day and night.

Bit by bit, over the ensuing months, Barnaby started to gain some confidence, coming out of his crate in the evening to watch TV with his foster carers. But he'd always retreat back to his safe place when things got too much for him.

By the time Melbourne encountered Barnaby on the pages of its major daily newspaper, the group felt he was ready to be adopted into a kind and gentle home where his new people were willing to continue patient rehabilitation with him. But they never expected the avalanche of phone calls, letters and emails of worried readers, all wanting to help Barnaby or to thank the group for saving him. The *Herald Sun* office was also inundated, and on the day Barnaby's story 'broke', he featured on two nightly news programs! Barnaby was suddenly famous.

Deeply touched by his plight, my partner and I sent in an application for Barnaby also, having no idea at the time that we were up against hundreds of others. Our existing dog, Miss T, was getting older, and we felt she would like a quiet pal about the house.

It took some time for Victorian Dog Rescue to whittle down all the applicants to a handful of shortlisted new homes. When they rang and asked if they could bring Barnaby over for a meet and greet, we couldn't wait! But we were nervous, too: Would he be frightened, and retreat to his crate, which was going to come in the car with him? Or worse, would he try to run away?

We needn't have worried. Some people say that a rescue dog just knows when they are home; when they have found their new family. That seemed to be the case that winter's day when Barnaby came in to meet us and promptly lay down by our fire.

Our acreage on the Mornington Peninsula has proven to be the ideal setting for Barnaby to continue to grow in trust and confidence with the world again. He finally had room for long walks, and on the rare times he was left alone, his dignified sister-dog Miss T kept him company. And of course his crate sat in the living room for him to retreat into when he needed it. But it didn't take long at all for him to cease needing to retreat inside it at all, and it is no longer a fixture in our home.

Today, Barnaby lives a life running through the paddocks as free as the wind, his coat flowing in the breeze. He walks and runs beside us in country lanes and hops in with the sheep and sends them careering down the paddock. He then leaps over the fence again and up onto our decking and you can see him smile at his efforts. Another time you might be walking with him through the paddock and the sheep will gang up against him.

Likewise the chickens also let him know when he's in the way. As for people, he would sooner avoid them, but it must be the Irish in him which makes him love 'the little people' – our twin granddaughters – because he is always delighted when they come around. Although he's three times their size, he's as gentle as a lamb.

We often think about why Barnaby's story garnered such a huge public outpouring of compassion. It's as though he became a symbol of all the homeless animals who die lonely deaths in pounds and shelters, who have no one to grieve for them or give them a last pat or cuddle.

We're so glad Victorian Dog Rescue saved you, Barnaby. We're so glad a caring ranger rang and ask them to help, just in time. And thank you for letting us tell your story, and reach out to so many people who, next time they want a new companion, might just remember Melbourne's saddest dog and choose to save one of your kin at their local pound or shelter.

Some people said a traumatised dog like Barnaby could never be rehabilitated; it wasn't worth the effort; the damage had been done. They were wrong. Almost all dogs who end up in the pound are there through no fault of their own, and deserve a second chance. The most amazing thing of all, however, is that they are prepared to give *us* a second chance.

Margaret and Barry, Victoria

Part of the Family

Canines have been trusted companions to humans for aeons. In fact, archaeologists have found the remains of dogs buried alongside their masters in ancient cemeteries. Today, dogs are often thought of as an extra family member – integral to the life and wellbeing of a household.

Flower, Very Short Marketing Assistant

Pic: Ruthless Photos

I wasn't sure if she was a dog or an ewok when we first met, but until Flower became a member of my family I'd always considered myself a 'big dog' person – that's just what I was used to. What this little Terrier mix has taught me, however, is that companion animals are not about size or breed or even species – they're about personality. You bond with the furry members of your family because of who they are and how they interact with you, not what they look like (and often *despite* what they look like . . .)

I moved from Sydney to South Korea in late 2006 to take up a position with an offshore branch of an Australian investment bank. I didn't know much about Korea, so I decided that I would use my spare time to assist a local shelter or rescue group (having fostered dogs and cats for a number of organisations in Sydney). I could only find one English-language group, called Animal Rescue Korea, which was a very small group of volunteer expat English-language teachers. Not long after I made contact with them, a student of one of the teachers told her about a crazy old lady in the Daejeon countryside who had 250 dogs in her greenhouse and who needed some assistance. We thought we would visit and perhaps clean up, bathe dogs and see what else we could do to help.

Mrs Jung did indeed have 250 dogs in her greenhouse. Not only that, she also slept in a small corner of the greenhouse herself and somehow was caring for them as best she could on her $500-a-month pension. She was not a dog hoarder per se – she would never go out looking for dogs – but over the years residents of Daejeon learnt that if you found a stray dog your two options were either to take it to the local pound, where it would inevitably be killed, or you could take it to Mrs Jung who was a very kind soul and could never bring herself to say no to a dog in need.

The volunteers at Animal Rescue Korea began a foster and adoption drive among the expat community to reduce the number of animals with Mrs Jung, and within six months we had around 200 of her dogs either adopted by expats or placed into foster care. One of these dogs was Flower, who I first met very early on when visiting Mrs Jung's farm. I was taking random dogs for walks around the nearby countryside when I went to pick up Flower from her cage. Mrs Jung rushed towards me with her hands crossed in front of her face, which is the hand signal Koreans use to let non Korean-speakers know that they shouldn't do something. Upon closer inspection I could see that Flower had a huge hernia on her stomach that Mrs Jung was aware of, but couldn't afford to fix.

Naturally I took Flower home, arranged for a vet to surgically correct her hernia and added her to the growing list of Korean foster animals that were slowly but surely populating my apartment, together with the pets who had flown from Australia with me – my Golden Retriever, Bear, and my two cats, Oscar and Holly. The vet thought Flower was about five years old and, while her teeth weren't in great condition, other than her hernia she was in good health.

About two months after Flower came to live with me, she was still waiting for her forever home when Bear, my beautiful old Golden, passed away at the age of fifteen. While it wasn't unexpected at her age, it was quite devastating and it was Flower who I was surprised to find provided the most comfort to me during that time. She was such a gentle and even-tempered girl who got along with every single dog, cat or person who ever visited the apartment, that it wasn't too long before I had that 'lightbulb' moment and realised I didn't want to give her up for adoption. She was in fact already a member of my family – I just hadn't realised it yet.

Flower stayed with me for the last two years that I lived in Korea, mentoring my other foster pets, and she returned with me to Australia in mid-2009 when I decided to return to Sydney to do some full-time volunteer work in animal welfare. It's been two years now that I have been volunteering – initially with PetRescue and more recently with the Sydney Dogs and Cats Home. Flower has proven to be an invaluable marketing aid at any event I've attended on behalf of either group – people can't resist her big smile and Ewok ears and they invariably stop to pat her and ask what sort of dog she is. They're generally astonished to hear that she is a rescue from a shelter, which is a great way to start a conversation about the fantastic variety of pets who end up homeless, through no fault of their own, and need rescue.

While Flower had a tough start to life I reckon she has now landed fairly firmly on all four paws. She may have travelled a long way and had to overcome some language barriers (she is still more responsive to Korean commands than she is to English!) but I'm sure she is happy to have exchanged Korean winters of –20 Celsius for the Sydney climate. Most of all, she is loving her role as Very Short Marketing Assistant to companion-animal welfare causes.

Tim Vasudeva, Sydney Dogs and Cats Home, New South Wales

Oska's Life in Chapters

Chapter 1: How Oska chose me

It was April 1995. I'd rung my sister and asked her to come with me to adopt a dog. No, it wasn't one of those ill-conceived, spur-of-the-moment decisions that see so many pets end up in pounds. A pet is for life, this I understood. It was always part of my life plan.

I'd spent a long time imagining the pound scene and I didn't fancy the process of choosing one dog. I felt like it was a rejection of the others. So I took my sister's advice to 'Let the dog choose you' as we pushed back the gate that shielded the animal 'orphanage' from the busy highway.

The barking began as we walked along a pathway, flanked on one side by massive cages, each home to four to six dogs. It took a while to take it all in, but no time for the tears to form. We slowly made our way along the row, lumps threatening to close our throats.

About halfway down, a scruffy little whitish dog with one dicky ear sat at the back of the vast cage while the others rushed the fence. Mid-kerfuffle, the little dog got up without too much purpose and seemed resigned to joining the others. I stood stock-still and watched him for a while. There was something reserved and dignified about this one. I'm not sure how long I'd been holding my breath but a sigh slipped from my lips and he looked up and locked eyes with mine. My heart sang as this dejected little mutt's demeanour immediately changed. He whipped his tail from side to side as he suddenly pushed his way to the front. There, his gaze never leaving mine, he sat down very neatly, dropped his lower jaw to reveal a beaming smile, lifted a paw and placed it purposefully against the fence.

'Oh, look at that little fella!' my sister exclaimed. 'He's saying, "Pick me! Pick me!"'

I didn't bend down to greet him. I was fearful of an instant bond when I owed it to the other orphans to first at least acknowledge them.

As soon as we made to move along the row, the little 'pick me' dog threw his head back and howled and howled, stopping only to check I was still in sight. Children covered their ears and adults shook their heads, but on he went. And then it was out of my mouth: 'I'm taking that dog.'

Oska had made the decision that I was his new best friend, and I was determined to honour that call. I ran back the length of the cages, skidded around the bend and sat down in front of him. The noise stopped, never to be heard again. That was sixteen years of loving ago.

I'm not sure why Oska found himself in the pound. Back then, there was no information to be shared with adoptive parents. But time would give me clues. At first when I reached out to pat his head, he'd duck down. It became more and more apparent that this little dog had probably run away from his first home, egged on by a lasting fear of rolled-up newspapers, raised voices and hands too close to his head. I had to learn patience and to give him space. It was the least I could do.

Chapter 2: Rescue mutt or pedigree?
When I collected Oska I took him straight to the vet. I plonked my little rescue mutt on the stainless steel exam table. Then the misunderstanding started. To this day I can still hear the vet's laughter as it bounced off the tiled walls of his surgery.

Okay, Oska wasn't beautiful, he was dirty and matted, but I worried for his feelings. With each of the vet's raucous laughs, Oska's head dropped a little lower and his shoulders became more hunched. He looked humiliated and embarrassed. But the vet didn't seem to notice.

Being my first-ever visit to a veterinary surgery with my first-ever pet, I began to have doubts about my choice – the vet, not the dog. The little furry pup was already part of me.

As the vet worked my little bloke over, he and I chatted. I explained that I'd just collected him from the Sydney Dogs and Cats Home, having waited the required time to allow his owners to collect him or let him slip quietly from their lives. 'We're only here so I can get him a proper going over,' I said. Whatever the outcome of the examination, I'd wear it.

'Okay,' the vet said, placing a stethoscope onto my dog's chest. He then ran his hands up and down his furry form. 'I'm checking for any suspicious lumps and bumps,' he informed me as he worked his way up towards his face, a large hand pushing a floppy fringe away from Oska's black-as-coal eyes.

Finally the vet stopped and took three steps back. His eyes were wide but they never left the patient. My pup and I watched as the vet's face began to contort. His lips curled, then settled into a grin that I couldn't make any sense of. Then we realised he was stifling a hefty guffaw. With some trouble, he spoke. 'Do you know what breed this is?' He could barely get the sentence out for his merriment. He turned and ripped a tissue from its box and began dabbing at his eyes.

'Well, no, I was hoping you might be able to help me with that,' I replied, increasingly irritated. Clearly, I had picked what the vet saw as a dud.

'Ah, dear! You will *have* to excuse me, but this is *very* funny! What'd you pay for him again?'

'Fifty bucks,' I snapped. I nuzzled up against my new little 'brown, fawn and white Maltese mix' as his papers had declared, trying to shield him from further ridicule.

'Well, young lady, he isn't a Maltese mix. You've got yourself a bit of a pedigree here. He's a West Highland Terrier – only young, maybe four at the most. You do know there's a two-year waiting list and a $1200 price tag for a Westie?'

I looked down at Oska and back up at the vet.

'Fifty dollars! *Fif-ty dollars!* Oska, you've made my week!' The vet couldn't stop smiling. He took out a book and gently placed my now magical four-legged find on the lino floor. The pages displayed a stunning-looking animal – ultra-white, dignified, groomed and glossy – sitting beneath a big, blue headline: 'West Highland White Terrier'.

But the dog in the book didn't look anything like Oska, not in any light, nor from any angle. The vet reassured me. 'Take him home, give him a good bath and a bit of a tidy up and you'll see. He'll look pretty much like this picture. Promise!'

A bath later, a bit of a clip and a good brush, and my pound pup was, indeed, almost as handsome a hound as the book boy.

Chapter 3: The connection between Oska and me

When Oska hurt, I hurt. There was the time he caught his tail in the screen door; the time he had a big lump excised; the time he snapped his cruciate ligament. I hurt with him, each and every time.

And when I hurt – failed dates, work upsets, university stress and later, when I was desolate after my husband and I lost our baby, and all hope of a child – Oska was there. He didn't comfort me in that bouncy, over-excited, happy-go-lucky kind of way, but in a much more considered, measured, sincere fashion.

When I appeared sad or distressed, Oska would survey my mood from a distance. Then – his gaze never leaving me – he would waddle right up close and fix me with a stare to make sure what I was projecting was actually going on inside. From there, he'd take his cue. He would either decide that everything was fine and that he could go about his business, or he would see that a serious 'cheer up' distraction was called for, and he'd kick off his three-trick repertoire.

He had plenty of backyard in which to play and I hated saying goodbye to him each morning before work. Out he'd go and I would take a quick last look through the window to see what he was up to. He'd sit staring at the door for a few seconds, then spin around on his bottom to survey his kingdom. Then off he'd trot, tail wagging as soon as he'd found some new dirt to dig, a corner to rediscover or a mynah bird somewhere near the perimeter to chase.

As he first settled in, Oska brought me thank-you presents every day for two weeks. He left them dead-centre on the coir mat at the back door. The gifts ranged from garden treasures, such as newly planted petunias, to lizards large and small. There was even a mummified rat one day, bones he'd expertly exhumed and, though they were decidedly gross, they represented the best he had to offer. We were now a pack and I was his leader.

About a year after Oska came to live with me I had to give a forty-minute speech to eighty general managers from around Australia. Panic set in. I knew I'd have to practise in front of an audience but no one in my family seemed keen to help. I decided to wing it and deliver my speech to my three-seater couch. It wasn't until fifty minutes later that it hit me. Oska was on the couch and hadn't moved a muscle the whole time. He'd sat bolt upright, ears pricked and head moving quizzically this way and that. He was being my audience for me. I felt weirdly empowered. Needless to say, when the time came, my talk went better than I hoped. Every time I felt my confidence ebbing away, I visualised my little boy – his interest, his faith and his belief – and delivered the speech exactly as I had done in previous days to my special audience of one. Okay, he might have been wondering where his dinner was, and when was I finally going to shut up, but on that, I preferred not to dwell. At the end of my talk, I got a standing ovation.

Life with Oska had its scraps and scrapes. For instance, he came and went on his own terms. As soon as an opportunity presented itself, he'd be off. He always, but always, came home either on the half hour or on the hour but not before a search party had been dispatched. Then he'd romp home, wagging his tail, panting and exalted by another brief adventure. 'But I've had such fun! Don't be mad!' he seemed to say, trying to make us understand his occasional need to cut loose and be his own man.

Chapter 4: Oska's contribution to veterinary science

When I married and moved house, I finally settled on a new vet who took such joy in Oska and his 'predicaments' that he became his ongoing subject for post-graduate study for years. The vet helped Oska through all sorts of set-backs and advised me how to best care for my increasingly 'senior' dog. After a major check-up, I was invited to view Oska's full-body X-ray.

'But I can't read an X-ray,' I told the vet as he led me into the exam room.

'You'll be able to read this one!' he shot back. There, on the lightbox, was the strangest sight. He explained that inside Oska was a bone growing where it shouldn't be, lots of little spurs, holes and gaps where there should be a bone, and fusions in his spine. The vet continued, 'I really don't know how this dog is getting around at all. His is the oldest dog skeleton I have ever seen. We reckon he could be close to nineteen years old. He's amazing!'

I already knew *that*, but was trying to focus. 'And what's that big thing; that shadow here?' I asked, tracing its outline with my finger.

'Well, we thought we were in trouble there. We thought Oska had an enlarged heart. But on closer examination, we found your boy was simply just born with a big heart.'

As if I needed to be told.

Kathryn, New South Wales

Never Going Back

He just stood there, looking at us with his big eyes and massive ears. We took him home that day. He was a gypsy dog. We called him Django, after the gypsy musician.

How he ended up at the Lost Dogs Home, I'll never know. What I do know, is that he's never going back.

On the drive home he lay down in the back of the car, and when I turned to look at him, he had a worried expression in his eyes. He looked tired. As if he was used to going back and forth from pound to home.

Safely in our care, Django soon gained weight, was being walked twice daily, and had a massive permanent grin on his face to match his huge ears. He became every local dog's best friend. He learnt to sit, stay, hug, speak, lie down, roll over and press traffic-light buttons. He learnt to trust.

A year on, and he goes where I go. He needed someone the way I did. And I found a best friend for life.

Edith, Victoria

Online Love Affair

The internet gave me the man who is about to become my husband. So it followed that another of my important relationships was born online – at PetRescue.com.au, to be exact.

Our first dog, Thierry, was a pet-shop purchase. He was the first 'Jug' or a Jack Russell Pug mix we'd ever seen. Yes, we fell in love with him at first sight. I didn't know anything about puppy factories at the time. Now I've seen how many Jugs are flooding the market, I think it's quite likely he came from one of those awful places. Whatever the case, we knew we wanted our second dog to be a rescue pet.

We scoured PetRescue each day, looking for a suitable sibling for our first little furry child. We didn't have a particular breed in mind and that was just as well because the dog who would be our second child wasn't any particular breed! Roxy was listed as a four-month-old Pomeranian mix but we thought she looked more like a Pokemon than a dog.

Roxy was also listed as having a 'special friend' called Chopper, who would ideally be adopted along with her. This opened up a lot of thought and discussion. We didn't think we had room for two extra dogs (particularly not one that suited the name 'Chopper') so we almost let Roxy go. But there was something about her that kept at us, so we contacted the rescue group and arranged for a meeting.

It was no good going to see her without Thierry, since he was the one Roxy would have to get along with. So we bundled him into the back seat of the car and started the three-hour drive to Sydney, where Roxy was being fostered. Did I mention Thierry gets car sick? Four hours, two vomits and several pit stops later, we arrived.

The foster carer's house was so full of animals it could make Noah himself proud. The family were dedicated animal lovers and had several cats and dogs of their own, as well as Roxy and Chopper. Chopper turned out to be a feisty, white Terrier type who, like Roxy, was about the size of a small rabbit. Thierry wasted no time disgracing himself by urinating on the lovely family's curtains. Then, when Roxy and Chopper refused to leave the kiddie-pen they were sleeping in, Thierry barged through its open door and wolfed down their dinner.

Thierry was not making a good first impression, so we sent him into the backyard while we tried to win our new puppy's trust. Yes, it was clear from the second we walked in that we would be leaving with a new puppy. The problem now was: Which one? Roxy and Chopper were both adorable, and their foster mum raved about each of them. My boyfriend and I broached the idea of taking both, but decided in the end we wouldn't be able to manage three, and it wouldn't be fair to try.

The foster carer was kind to us as we struggled with the issue. She explained that it was ideal to keep them together but that this couldn't always happen. The dog who stayed with her would have no trouble finding a home, she assured us. The choice was made for us when the two pups joined Thierry in the backyard. Chopper wouldn't stop barking at him, but Roxy was quiet as a mouse. As beautiful as Chopper was we did have neighbours to consider. So we chose Roxy, and could see just how special she was when her foster mum shed tears for her as we left.

That was two years ago. Timid, quiet Roxy has grown from the size of a small rabbit to the size of a . . . well, a slightly larger rabbit. But her personality has grown exponentially. And as for not barking? That lasted about a month. Now she is quick to follow Thierry's lead when there is a knock on the door, a cat in the yard, a bird in a tree or the occasional shadow. She is also happy to voice her own opinion when we have forgotten her morning Dentastick!

Roxy and Thierry have become inseparable, after a bumpy start. They mouth-wrestle constantly – a game whose winner seems to be the one who can make the most ridiculous noises. They join forces to destroy any squeaky toys that dare infiltrate the house. And every now and then we catch them looking at us in a certain way as if they are telling each other, 'The second we work out how to open the food bin, we can run this joint. *Viva la resistance!*'

Then night rolls around, and they curl up into a multi-coloured ball on their mum and dad's bed, all thought of mischief forgotten – one small, but happy, family.

Kimberley, Australian Capital Territory

Our Doug

Doug arrived at the pound with no name except 'Dog'. His foster carers named him 'Doug' because it sounded similar. He is a friendly, self-contained two-year-old who is probably a mix of Tibetan Spaniel, Pomeranian and maybe even Corgi.

On a rainy Saturday morning we went to Save-A-Dog-Scheme in Glen Iris to meet him. He had not been walked that morning so he was a bundle of energy. We took him for a short stroll through the park and he was pulling in every direction because he has a fixation with birds. Fortunately he was so smiley it was really funny.

We were told his background was largely unknown and that he had spent the last three weeks in a foster home because he was distressed by the kennels and was barking a lot. Later, as we sat in the reception room, our eyes met. That was all I needed. Thanks to his wonderful foster carer he settled into our home quickly and especially loved his doggie door. All we heard the first day was flip, flap, flip, flap as he went in and out, in and out.

Doug was described to us as a 'family dog' and he truly is. We have two children, aged eight and five, and I remember one time my son accidentally caused the toilet to overflow and our carpet was flooded. Marcus was so upset, he sat crying, watching us mopping it up. Doug went over to him and put his head in my son's lap and Marcus gently patted him. Doug managed to comfort him, showing a side we had never seen before.

Water is a big part of our lives: we have a swimming pool and we live by the beach. Doug has responded to both with great enthusiasm. Just recently we walked him down to the beach at dusk. For the first time we let him off the lead and he raced around the sand: his ears were back; his tongue sideways; he was ploughing through the sand. Dougie then walked out in the shallow water with my husband. He then went deeper and deeper until his feet could not touch the bottom and he was swimming!

As I mentioned before Doug has a bird fetish and recently we discovered he has a bug fixation too! He loves to watch and chase the dragonflies and bugs that hang around the swimming pool. Several times he has fallen in and splashed his way to the edge where he manages to haul his skinny body up, his back legs kicking frantically. Once Doug hopped on the lilo and floated out to the middle of the pool. He looked very surprised!

Doug has fitted into our family perfectly, he loves to be a part of everything and he is. We have a camping trip planned soon at a dog-friendly park and I know we will have a great time.

Megan, Rohan, Amy and Marcus, Victoria

The Adventures of a Single Girl

It may sound like a cliché, but it really was love at first sight when I spotted Ivory on PetRescue. I knew exactly what I wanted: a small, happy, playful dog for 'companionship and fun times'. Here I was, a single twenty-something, living alone in my first home and far lonelier than I had expected. My beautiful new house did not need any new furniture, big-screen TVs or flashy fittings. It needed a pet: a happy face and wagging tail to greet me after a hard day in the office.

My search for love (of the four-legged kind) brought me to PetRescue. And there were plenty of adorable dogs to choose from, right across Australia. As I scrolled through the many profiles, I kept coming back to one dog in particular. 'Ivory' was a one-year-old Chihuahua mix with the biggest, bulging eyes I had ever seen. And boy, was she cute!

Something about Ivory grabbed my attention, and I watched the video footage of her over and over again. She looked cheeky and adorable, just what I had been searching for. I contacted the rescue group caring for Ivory, which was Saving Animals From Euthanasia (SAFE) in Broome, Western Australia.

I was advised by the very helpful staff that arrangements could be made for Ivory to be flown to me in South Australia. I did not need a lot of time to think about it. Within a few days I had finalised the adoption process and Ivory had been booked onto a Qantas flight to Adelaide.

Picking Ivory up from the airport, I felt like an expectant parent. I eagerly watched her plane touch down and thought 'This is it, now our adventure begins!'

As Ivory was brought out to me in the cargo-holding area I took one look at her and fell in love all over again. She was exactly like her pictures on PetRescue and just as cute as I had imagined! As to be expected, she was initially very timid, but with some gentle coaxing (and a few dog treats) she was out of her cage and running around my feet in no time.

Within a few days Ivory had well and truly settled into my home and it felt like she had been there with me from the start. When I said to Ivory, 'Make yourself at home' she barely hesitated and quickly found the ideal spots to spread out and relax. Of course they are on the couch and my bed, leaving me with little or no room. The perfect housemate!

Everyone who comes into contact with Ivory immediately falls in love with her. She has bonded well with other pets in our family, except Molly the grumpy eleven-year-old rescue rabbit who does not appreciate Ivory's game of chasing him around the yard, licking her lips like he's a future snack. Fair enough.

It has only been three months but life with Ivory has been wonderful. Some of our favourite times have been cruising in my car on the weekends like two best friends with her sitting high up on the front passenger seat. We love throwing the tennis ball around the backyard till we are worn out (usually that's me first), and we adore curling up on the couch watching our favourite shows.

What I love most about Ivory is her ability to make me laugh, even when all else seems hopeless. I melt into her big brown eyes with their long ginger lashes. Being welcomed home by her and her slobbery dog kisses is the best part of each day. I cannot remember life before Ivory. If anyone was rescued and given a second chance, it was well and truly me.

I tell all my single friends it really *is* possible to find love online. Perhaps not the sort you would expect. But genuinely blissful, crazy, fulfilling love all the same.

Alison, South Australia

The Secret

This is a story about love. This is a love that no human being can give another human being, I believe. It is a love that exists between a person and their dog: unconditional love.

I have had four dogs in my life, all rescue dogs from various organisations. With our first two dogs, I did not recognise this love. I was blind. But then we got Maxi.

A black-and-white Border Collie, about two years old, we adopted him impulsively on the way home from the Gold Coast, at the Animal Welfare League. But the timing was better than for our other rescue dogs: at least we had our own home, a good fence and more time.

At first, Maxi was just a dog to me. Albeit a very beautiful one. I found him quite aloof in the beginning, however, and that did not suit me. Weren't dogs supposed to be more loyal, more needy? He always kept his distance; did not come as soon as you called him and did not seem to want to be near you. He was more interested in the things beyond. But then I did some research on the Border Collie, a working dog that works at great distances. He was not a heel dog. I started to understand him. The more time I spent with Maxi, the more I started to like him. He was very intelligent and quick to learn. I started to see his loving eyes and, before I knew it, I was in love.

Maxi became everything to me and he came everywhere with us, from camping to bushwalking – you name it, the dog was there. We never went to a place where a dog was not welcome and we stopped doing certain things if Maxi couldn't join us.

Maxi became very loving in his own way. He would usually sit very quietly next to you and you would feel his weight, pushing against your body, leaning on you. He was so quiet and noble.

Six months before Maxi left us, another little dog entered our lives. This time it was not impulsively adopted but given to us by a neighbour, who was trying to get rid of him. The neighbour and his friends enjoyed pig hunting so we worried about the dog's fate if we said no. He was only six weeks old, and my husband and I were both fearful. We had never cared for such a young dog before, and we had heard so many horror stories about bringing up a puppy. But within a few hours we both fell in love with him. We called him Oscar.

Oscar was supposed to be a Border Collie too, but as he grew it became obvious that there was a little bit of Corgi in him. His legs have stayed short and stocky. He is a very different dog to Max, with a very different temperament. He needs to please. His eyes open with joy. When you call him, he does not just come to you, he *flies*. The whole dog seems to curl, his ears pinned back, little legs flaying in all directions, as he runs up. And is he a talker! He barks at you, willing you to understand him, and he cocks his head at you as you reply, trying very hard to understand, then barks at you if he doesn't.

In the six months Maxi and Oscar had together, the older dog reluctantly took Oscar under his wing. Oscar was a little dynamo, zooming around like there was no tomorrow. He had so much energy to burn, poor Max did not know what had hit him. He was very patient with him; however sometimes he cracked and nipped him when it all got too much. It was all done in a very gentlemanly fashion, of course.

Oscar revered Max as his mentor. He followed the older dog everywhere, watching and mimicking him. When Max used to bark up and down the fence at the cars, his little white shadow followed him. When it stormed and thundered, Max was outside chasing the thunder, his little white shadow joining him. When we went to the beach and Max chased the jet skis, his little white shadow told them off too.

When the time came to say farewell to Maxi, it was the hardest thing we'd ever endured. It was like saying goodbye to a child. It has been nearly a year now, but the scars are still raw. We miss him terribly.

I always admire young people who recognise the joy a dog can bring into their lives. I did not appreciate it until I was in my forties. I had always loved animals, forever stopping and taking wildlife off the road, trying to find owners for stray cats, etc. I only learnt later in life, though, what joy a dog could bring.

Sometimes when I now walk Oscar, people pass us by; they don't even see my friend next to me. Their faces are sour, they don't look happy. They are not aware of this special bond, this special love they too could have. But other times people pass who smile at my dog, sometimes even stop to ask me his name, or his breed. They want to touch him. Their faces are full of smiles. These people are special. These people are happy. They know a secret.

If you want to know this secret, have a close look into a dog's eyes. It may be a beautiful dog, it may be an ugly dog, it may be stray or an unkempt dog. If you open your heart and look closely into those eyes you will see trust, you will see devotion, you will see wisdom, you may even see a little helplessness, but above all, you will see love . . . unconditional love.

Christine, Queensland

When it's Just Meant to Be

~~

*Sometimes a dog is more than just a pet – they are a soul mate.
There are dogs who always seem to know when you've had
a bad day and others who display inexplicable intuition.
The connection between hound and human in
these stories runs deep.*

The Little Dog that Started a Movement

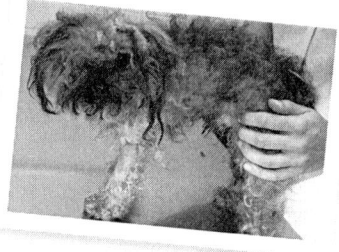

I have been rescuing hundreds of suffering dogs from puppy factories for nearly twenty years. All of these dogs have touched my soul, but none have changed my life like Oscar did.

In January 2010, I was called to investigate a puppy factory in central Victoria. The owners were overseas and had left a neighbour in charge, and he was horrified by what he saw.

The smell of a puppy factory is unforgettable: an overwhelming stench of urine and faeces. The simultaneous barking of hundreds of dogs creates a wall of sound that makes it hard to think, let alone converse. I first saw Oscar cowering in the corner of his steel-and-concrete pen. As I reached out to touch him, his tiny body felt rock-hard. It was like touching concrete – as though there was no dog within the mass of grey fur I picked up his trembling body and realised his entire coat was matted and rough. I held him close and he settled into my arms. He whimpered as I tried to examine him: the fur on his genital region was matted fast to the fur on the inside of one of his back legs. He had numerous wounds where the matting was pulling at his skin. He allowed me to check his mouth, and his teeth and gums were inflamed and red. I knew from experience that he also had an ear infection as the smell was vile.

The decision was easy. I simply couldn't leave this dog in this putrid shed. He needed a vet and I was taking him to one.

When the vet first opened Oscar's crate and peered in, she looked at me with shock and simply said, 'Oh my God.' She then started a thorough but gentle examination. Oscar's condition was so poor he needed a general anaesthetic to cut away the matted fur from his fragile skin. Once exposed, a number of painful grass-seed abscesses were visible that required draining. He was malnourished and severely underweight. His inflamed and rotting teeth and gums from years of an inadequate diet were causing him pain. Teeth needed to be removed, and his ears were debrided and flushed.

In the meantime, I rang all authorities, including the police, and reported this registered puppy factory that was breaching all standards of animal welfare and tried to get immediate assistance for the dogs that remained.

Oscar came home with me and required pain relief every few hours. We soon began to understand each other. I handfed him three times a day – Oscar did not know what a food bowl was. He must have only ever had food thrown on the ground. So much frightened him: a phone ringing, a door opening, a toilet flushing. Sounds that we don't even notice were terrifying for him, as all he'd known during his short life was a steel shed and the sound of other dogs barking. Dogs suffering, just like him.

Slowly, he stopped shying away from human hands as he learnt to trust me. He loved blankets and would spend much time burrowing deep and getting comfortable. Soon he was sleeping on my stomach and I didn't dare move in case I disturbed him. I couldn't bear to be away from him and he began to follow me all around the house. We were inseparable and I was unable to focus on anything but getting him well again. Oscar became my entire world.

It should have been a new beginning for Oscar. But a week later, the nightmare began.

The unthinkable happened. The police arrived at my door, accusing me of theft, of stealing Oscar, and demanded him back. They were going to return him to the puppy factory. My head spun. I begged, I pleaded with them. I told them if they returned Oscar to that place, he would die. He was so unwell still; he would never survive that shed again. I pleaded with every ounce of my being but no one was listening.

I started to panic. I could hardly breathe. I held Oscar tight as I begged. They prised him from my arms and took him away.

I remember weeping uncontrollably. No one could console me. Nothing my family did or said to me helped. I had failed this dog.

I got into the car and drove with no direction for hours. I had spent eighteen years of my life trying to close puppy factories and help dogs like Oscar – and I had failed. I was done.

I sat in an open field under a tree for hours until it was dark, trying to figure out a way of getting Oscar back. Nothing else mattered. I sat there sobbing for this tiny little dog and kept saying to myself, I wish there was a law I could use to help protect and free Oscar. And then I came to the realisation that although I had been trying to use existing animal welfare legislation to help these dogs, an adequate law to protect and free them didn't exist.

I founded the Oscar's Law campaign that day in January 2010. I vowed to change the laws, to protect and free all the Oscars hidden away from the public eye across Australia. To let all who have never heard of a puppy factory know and understand about these mass-breeding facilities. The dogs are usually kept in cages or pens their entire lives. They live in filth, sometimes without food or water. Many dogs go insane. What is most disturbing is that puppy factories are legal. Even puppy factories that are 'clean' and pass every council inspection still confine dogs for their entire lives.

Oscar's owners have never been charged with cruelty or neglect, and their puppy factory still operates. I think of Oscar every day. I don't even know if he is still alive. But he came into my life for a reason. I didn't rescue Oscar, but he rescued me. He changed my life's direction and his memory inspires me to do all I can to close down this industry that turns our best friends into breeding machines. No more.

I want Oscar's Law.

Debra Tranter, Oscar's Law, oscarslaw.org, Victoria

The Little Brown-and-white Dog

When my long-term relationship broke up three years ago, custody arrangements for our Mini Foxie, Oscar, and our Kelpie, Jeb, were heartbreakingly difficult. It wasn't fair to split up these good friends. My ex-partner had space, and I didn't know if I would have a suitable new home for the dogs, so I left my beloved pets behind – an unbelievably hard decision.

I settled into my new single life in a unit in Sydney with my cat Millie, but I felt empty not having a dog to kiss and cuddle and care for. I kept gazing at doggie rescue websites, but for a time I felt so guilty about 'dumping' my other dogs I couldn't let myself have a new one. But eventually I found myself driving out to the RSPCA, just to 'have a look'.

Every dog I saw while wandering along the rows of kennels I wanted to take home! There was only one row that I didn't get a good look of, deep in shadow because of the angle of the sun. I walked right by, focusing on two adorable little dogs further on. But waiting in the reception area with my number to be called so I could go and meet the two dogs, I became totally absorbed in watching the animal shows on the TV. I came out of my reverie when I noticed the centre was quieter, and then a RSPCA volunteer was telling me that the centre was closed, and that they had called my number an hour ago.

The dogs on my list were gone. But the volunteer must have seen the disappointment on my face, and offered to take me on another quick look.

We walked past the concrete kennels that had been in shadow earlier: the sun had moved, and was now shining on the dogs inside.

In one particular kennel, I saw a small brown-and-white dog through the mesh who had some sort of skin disorder, and the saddest eyes. I asked the volunteer to meet her, and as the small one slowly approached me I was shocked by the horrible condition of her skin. It was horrendous. Instantly, I knew this dog was coming home with me, so I asked what the skin disorder was so that I could have it properly treated.

The next shock was hearing that the poor girl didn't have a skin condition at all. She'd been purposely burned with boiling liquid.

The little one had been in hospital for a month recovering before being put up for adoption. But no one had wanted her – until now. I made a vow at that moment that this dog would never suffer cruelty again.

Gracie and I went home together. Her wounds healed, and so did mine. She still has a long bald patch down her back, however, and people ask me about it. When I tell them her story, they are horrified.

Time went by, a new partner came into my life, and Gracie, Millie and I moved in with him. Unfortunately, he gradually forgot that I was a 'mad animal lover' who wanted her fur kids to be comfortable, and that we had agreed Gracie could sleep inside. He tried to make a new rule of 'no dogs in the house'. Gracie looked very unhappy. I remembered my vow to her on the day we met at the RSPCA, and I packed up and left.

I returned to my unit with the park behind it that welcomed dogs. Gracie, Millie and I were a happy family again. I now have a new partner, who adores Gracie as much as I do. He is the one who named her 'the little brown-and-white dog'. Gracie is my best friend, and I love her. Yes, it was meant to be.

Jennifer, New South Wales

Finding Hope

In August 2009, I was parted from my beloved dog companion Sasha, a Border Collie Kelpie mix. Sasha had been my shadow for over fourteen years. I had been in a fortunate position where through my work as an actor, performer and director for the stage, Sasha had been able to accompany me to auditions and rehearsals, and would always bond in her own way with the entire cast. Sasha effectively found her place as 'Theatre Dog', and would delight in spending quality time with her Dad, doing what he loves best.

Many people who have dog companions in their lives might suggest their dog is special – well, in Sasha's case, she was *very* special: more human-like in many ways than canine. She possessed an extraordinary awareness and perception, and my communications with her both verbally and mentally would see her respond always with great enthusiasm. Sasha was always up for a new game or adventure, and sharing my journey with her was, in a word, blissful.

As I became aware Sasha was growing older, I pondered the thought of not having her in my life, and the pain in even contemplating the inevitable was more than I could bear. Without dwelling on her departure, when it came it came quickly and with a great shock. One morning I woke to find her trembling in the bathroom. I immediately took her to the vet, and countless tests over the following two weeks were carried out.

Leaving her at home to rest one day, as the flight of stairs at work proved to be too much for her weary body, I had a sudden urge to go home to see her. When I arrived I was greeted by her smiling face and wagging tail, however she did not move towards me. I coaxed her to her feet and called her, and saw that she had lost the use of her back legs. Directly to the vet we went, and Dr Alice ordered X-rays. The results several hours later were not good. Sasha had severe spinal problems in the centre of her back. Her vertebrae were being pushed into the spinal column by some unseen growth or tumour. Dr Alice medicated Sasha with Valium and said, 'Take her home and spend time with her.' There was nothing she could do.

Upon returning to the clinic the next day, I said my final farewells, and Sasha was put to rest. My heart was torn apart. I was in total disbelief that she had gone.

Some five days after Sasha's passing, I met with another dear friend and her mother for a coffee. My friend's mother handed me a page from the Sunday paper, and said, 'I know your heart is aching, and I know you have a lot of love to give . . . This may be too soon, but here is a page of rescue dogs needing homes. Just have a look if you feel up to it.' I glanced at the page and several dogs had been highlighted, all needing homes. One dog in particular caught my attention, a one-year-old female Border Collie.

When my friends drove me home and I got out of the car, one of them said, 'Don't forget the paper!' and handed me the page which I had left on the back seat.

A couple of hours later, I picked up the paper again, and looked at the pictures of the rescue dogs. Finally, I thought, I'll go online and just see . . .

Looking at the listings for Fraser Coast Dog Rescue, I clicked on the Border Collie who had featured in the paper, only to learn that she had already been adopted. There were no other dogs profiled that caught my attention. I guess in the back of my mind I was thinking that if I was ever to have another dog, then ideally it would be a Border Collie or mix, just like Sasha. As I sat gazing at the home page of PetRescue, I noticed in the top right-hand corner there was a search engine. I immediately found myself choosing 'Puppy, Female, Queensland'. I pressed search.

What came up next was a picture of the most adorable female Border Collie mix tri-colour puppy. Abandoned at three weeks old and weighing less than a kilogram, she'd been found and taken to Fraser Coast

Dog Rescue. Now seven weeks old, the group was seeking someone to build her confidence and give her lots of love. The name given beside her picture was Hope.

My heart wept tears of joy, and immediately, instinctively, I knew – I needed Hope and she needed me. Grabbing the phone, I dialled the number. While I waited for an answer, I said quietly to myself, don't get too excited, the puppy may have already found a new home . . .

I was about to hang up as it had rung for an extended period when a male voice at the other end finally answered. I spoke briefly about seeing Hope on PetRescue, and the man said, 'Just one moment, I will get Annette.' He went on to say they were just going out for a Sunday drive, when she'd heard the phone and said, 'We should answer that.'

Annette came to the phone, her voice warm and empathetic. I quickly gabbled my story, my sudden loss of Sasha, my friend giving me the paper, my coming online to learn the dog in the paper had been adopted, and me finding Hope through the search engine. I paused for breath, and asked Annette the most important question of all: 'Has Hope been adopted?'

There was a slight pause before Annette responded; she left me with the hair on the back of my neck standing on end. She replied, 'No, Ian, Hope is still here. We've had many calls enquiring about her from all over the state; we even had someone ring from the Northern Territory. I've said no to them all, and have just actually had my husband ask me, "Why are you saying no to these callers?" I told Ron that there was a special person for Hope, and I will know them when they call, and now I know, because I am talking to you.'

Tears flowed down my face as I heard Annette's words, for it confirmed what I felt instinctively too. Hope and I were meant to be together.

I arranged to travel with a friend to Maryborough the following morning to meet Hope. On the journey, I found myself quietly talking to Sasha, saying I hope she understood Hope was not a replacement for her . . . It was more that my heart needed to share the enormous amount of love that I still had for Sasha, which I could no longer share on earth. I concluded by expressing in my thoughts that I hoped she understood and endorsed me bringing Hope into my life and to give me a sign if she could.

When we pulled up in Maryborough, Annette was in the front garden with Hope. My friend and I opened the gate and entered the yard. From the other end of the garden, Hope ran to greet us. When she was a metre or so away, she leapt in the air and into my lap. She then proceeded to lick me like a long-lost friend. I wept openly, and Annette had tears welling in her eyes too. It was like a reunion . . . It is difficult to explain, and in many ways beyond words, but it was like we had met before.

When it came time to leave with my new companion, Anne walked us to the gate saying, 'I've put a puppy collar on Hope – not sure how I came to have it, but it's new and fits beautifully, so please keep it as a gift.'

As I held Hope in my arms, I looked down at the collar and stared in disbelief. I found myself starting to shake. 'What is it, Ian?' Annette asked. The collar around Hope's neck was black leather with little silver bone motifs. In my hand I carried Sasha's favourite lead – which matched Hope's collar . . . black leather with little silver bone motifs! This was the sign I had quietly prayed for. A paw of endorsement from my darling Sasha.

It has been over fourteen years since I have reared a pup. Hope has brought back all the memories of nurturing and raising a young dog. She makes me laugh with her antics. She 'talks' in dog language, and 'sings' to boot. If I am rehearsing or singing at home, Miss Hope will sit there and howl along in full voice. Much joy is shared between us. Some things are beyond words, and I feel blessed that Hope entered my life in the most perfect way, via my beloved Sasha, and I treasure each moment I am able to share with her.

Ian, Queensland

Our Black Saturday Survivor

On 21 January 2009, we had to put our beloved family dog, Monty, to sleep. He was twelve-and-a-half and had kidney cancer. We had four days in which to say goodbye to him. How do you say goodbye to your best friend in just four days? The sadness and shock continued soon after, with 7 February 2009 starting out as a normal hot summer's day, but it was to become a day like no other. Now known as Black Saturday, the Victorian bushfires that raged around the state that day devastated the lives of thousands, but from all the horror, a small black dog emerged to bring us hope and a new sense of joy.

A few days after the fires, I read that the Whittlesea vet desperately needed foster carers for injured animals. I promptly rang and left our names as we wanted to help in any way we could. But about two months later we still hadn't heard anything, so I just figured that the vet had found other people to foster dogs and we weren't needed.

Meanwhile, we decided it was time to adopt another dog, and we agreed we wanted to rescue a Staffy mix. We headed out to the Blue Cross Animal Society shelter nearby, and found an older girl who seemed perfect except she didn't like cats, so that wouldn't work with our felines at home. Sadly we had to turn her down and hope another great home came along for her.

The next day I absent-mindedly said aloud to our dog Monty in heaven, 'Oh, Monty, please help us find the right dog at the right time . . . ' Later I was talking to Mum, telling her what the ideal dog for us would be, when I was interrupted by the phone ringing. It was the Whittlesea vet.

They were asking if we'd like to foster a young female Staffy mix!

Almost speechless, I stammered yes, and we headed down straight away. When we arrived, the vet told us that Sheeba had been found wandering the town of Kinglake four weeks after the fires and had recovered at the surgery for a further six weeks. They had no idea what the fate of her owners was, but no one had come looking for her.

As we let Sheeba out of her pen, her eyes lit up with joy and her tail went 100 kilometres an hour. When we led her out to the car she jumped straight in and sat in the driver's seat with a big goofy grin on her face, tail thumping happily beside her. Considering what Sheeba had been through she was in great condition, however her coat still smelt of ash, and she had singed whiskers as well as raw elbows.

Sheeba settled in but two days later she developed a cough. Mum and I were scared that it was to do with the smoke in her lungs. We took her back to the vet that afternoon and they gave her antibiotics as it was a minor infection. The vet then told us they just had someone on the phone that could be Sheeba's owner. He said he was missing a dog that was a Staffy Ridgeback mix. He made a time to come and see her.

When the day arrived, we turned up at the vets with heavy hearts and waited over an hour for her 'owner', who never showed up. After about a month of trying to get in touch with the man again, the vet decided to send him a letter saying if he did not contact them within forty-eight hours they'd assume he had surrendered Sheeba to them. He promptly rang them and said 'Of course I want my bloody dog back.'

It was awful. I didn't want to return Sheeba to a person who spoke of her like that. But divine intervention was to help us again. When the man finally came to see Sheeba, he took one look at her and said she wasn't his dog. Sheeba showed no recognition of him either. The vets agreed we could adopt her. Our relief was huge!

Sheeba has been through so much, and we would never give up on her. Not only did we help her but she has helped us. She's taught me to be a better person and to be more patient. She had significant fear aggression towards other dogs which we worked hard on, and I'm well rewarded when I see the sparkle in her eyes. Sheeba is the epitome of the resilience and love that all animals are capable of.

I'm sure our old dog Monty heard me that day when I asked him to send us the right dog at the right time. Thank you, Monty, and thank you, Sheeba.

Nicole, Victoria

The Day Morrison Found Us

In 2004 our family had to make a very hard decision. It was time for our beautiful old Blue Heeler, Holley, to be put to sleep as she could no longer walk due to crippling arthritis and cancer. My husband, two young sons and I were devastated. The loss was so traumatic we swore we would never get another dog, as the grief was too hard to bear. We eventually moved on but there was a pain in our hearts that would never quite go away and we all cried in our own private space.

One sunny spring afternoon in 2006 as I pulled into our driveway with my eight-year-old son Tristan, we noticed a small, grey, scruffy dog trotting up the footpath towards us. Another dog was with him but that one turned down the side path and out of view. The grey scruffy continued to trot right up our driveway and before we knew it, the dog was sitting on our front mat waiting to be let in, as though he was home from a long walk!

I felt compelled to let him in and so I did. He headed straight to our lounge, jumped up on the couch and settled in.

We were stunned but intrigued. He had no collar on but appeared to be well cared for, so we knew he belonged to someone and they would be worried. Our hearts were falling for this little guy already and Tristan and I knew right then that we wanted to keep him. It was a wonderful feeling having a dog in the house again. I rang my husband Chris and said we had found something that looked just like him: middle-aged and grey! Chris was understandably wary but when he got home he immediately succumbed to this doggie's charm too. Four hours passed, by which time we had given him a name: Smokey.

We knew we should do the right thing and so put a poster up at the local shop: DOG FOUND. But please, no one claim him, I thought to myself! No sooner had I bought a few items when at the checkout I noticed the sign had been removed. It had only been up for ten minutes – where had it gone? Upon asking the shop attendant, she said the owner had already been found. My heart sank very low. Loss was already setting in. Unbeknown to me Smokey's carer, Natalie, had rung home and talked to Chris and yes, it was her dog, but as fate would have it, she was his foster carer and not his owner! She'd had the scruffy eight-year-old for six months as a carer for Save Animals from Euthanasia (SAFE), and no one had applied to adopt him.

We were in luck . . . or was it meant to be? I asked Natalie if he could stay on trial as he seemed too good to be true, and she said yes.

Smokey was perfect. Even our cat Jasper liked him after two weeks of animal negotiations! We could not believe how quickly and positively our lives changed. There was a spark and a smile on our faces that had been missing for two years, that only a dog or perhaps a new baby can bring. We *could* love another dog. It wasn't big, loyal, strong Blue Heeler love; it was a different love: the small, cute, vulnerable Cairn Terrier version. Love does not run out, it is endless for whoever needs it, and in different ways. We were stronger and wiser now and agreed that when the day came that this little dog's life was over, we *would* love again and live with cherished memories, not painful grief.

Smokey turned out to be a Morrison. He had originally come from Gowrie, Victoria, and was lost and never claimed. On death row, he got one last chance. At the time all rescue groups in Victoria were full, and

SAFE in Western Australia ended up saving him. Qantas had been sweet-talked into transporting the scruffy passenger, and so Morrison took to the air. He was collected at the airport by Natalie, who took him to her friendly and busy home in Perth. But Morrie wanted a quiet life and to be an only dog, so when opportunity knocked in the way of an open door, he and his mate took to the neighbourhood. He headed south and found his own family – us. His mate was later collected by a worried Natalie.

I don't know why Morrie was an unclaimed stray and often wonder what his life had been like before us. Last year we fostered some needy dogs and I think Morrison knew what they'd been through. He was a patient guide for them as one was blind and the other deaf.

Our lives have been so enriched and a new dimension found with Morrie. My boys, Lochie and Tris, say, 'Morrison is our brother from another mother.' We rush home to see him, he comes on holidays with us, he has friends, he has toys, he has dreams, we love watching him discover new things, he keeps us fit and makes us feel good – we love him, our Morrison Smokey Crossley.

Janet, Western Australia

Barry and the Little Boy

Barry is a small Border Collie Spaniel mix, with soft black hair and the most gentle of personalities. He came to me as a rescue dog after his original owners 'did a runner' to escape police interest. He had been very, very harshly treated.

Dear Barry is now about fifteen, and despite his past, has a magic way with children and people who are unwell or living with sorrow.

Recently, I was walking Barry and my two other 'scruffy little mutts' in a local park. An older couple and a young boy of about eight approached. The little boy clearly wanted to meet my dogs. He went straight up to Barry and stroked his fur. 'He is a beautiful dog,' said the boy. 'I think he is very gentle and I really like your other two dogs, but this one is gentle.'

The boy began to look sad but he continued patting Barry while he spoke. 'My mother used to live with us and we had a dog then, but she went away, and now I don't have a dog.'

'Oh . . .' Tears welled up in my eyes, and those of his grandparents too.

'But this is a lovely dog,' the little boy continued. Then he looked up at me and asked, most directly and earnestly, as if he really needed the right answer to his question, 'Do you let this dog sleep on your bed? And do you rest your head on him, like a pillow?'

'Yes,' I replied. 'Barry does sleep on my bed. He loves it and sometimes he even lets me rest my head on him, like on a pillow.'

The boy smiled. He continued to pat Barry for a moment longer, then he farewelled my old boy and my other two dogs. He waved as he walked away with his grandparents, but not before we three adults had silently looked at each other during this amazing encounter.

Something very emotive and deep, something beyond words, had touched us all for those few moments. The Sufis say, 'Your angels come in strange disguises.' For a little boy, it may have been a gentle black dog in the park on a sunny day.

Gail, Victoria

Staying Sunny

Dr Michael Bascombe is a vet who has learnt to use alternative or complementary therapies in his work with animals. He's found that Reiki, the Bowen Technique, herbs and cell salts can be successfully applied to pets and lead to dramatic improvements, even when Western methods have been exhausted. In his practice Michael takes into account the physical, emotional and spiritual aspects of the animal's health for the problem's complete resolution. He can also hear the animals talking to him and, by listening, he can help them get well.

Michael has experienced many wonderful miracles with animals, but this one is about how he found Sunny the Pomeranian mix, and their extraordinary working life together. Michael describes Sunny matter-of-factly as a fifteen-year-old dog, veterinary teacher and healer. The vet's first experience of the four-legged guru was in a dream or a vision half a year before they actually met.

'I had an intense and surreal dream, or perhaps a vision. I saw the face of a reddish-orange dog that looked like a fox. It was staring directly into my eyes and I thought it was speaking to me, even though I couldn't hear what it was saying. It was as if the dog was completely familiar and comfortable with me.'

This incident passed and was forgotten until Michael's old Tibetan Spaniel Mr Ewok suddenly died. The grief of his dog's passing was so intense and painful that it took five months before Michael was ready to begin searching for that foxy face he had seen in the dream.

'I found the dog in my vision at Pets Haven Animal Shelter in Woodend, Victoria. I walked in and saw that little face, exactly as in my dream! But the dog was in bad shape. His coat was thin, he was skin and bone, and he had a distant look in his eyes. He even seemed indifferent to my presence. I started to wonder if he was the one after all.'

So Michael drove towards home to think about it, but then turned around, went straight back and adopted him. 'I named him Sunny, because he reminded me of bright sunshine.' When Michael put Sunny into his car, the little dog panicked, apparently traumatised by his past experiences. 'The dog's mind was screaming out in fear. Everything about me and the car was new and foreign to him.'

After six months of concerted effort to treat Sunny's emotional condition, the little one was healed. He put on weight, his coat grew back and he became a relaxed, confident and peaceful dog. Now people mention how calm he is for a Pomeranian!

Sunny goes to work with Michael each day, sitting right beside the clients who come in with their pets. Michael sees Sunny surround everyone with a peaceful aura, and during the consultations, Michael watches him for guidance. 'Sunny goes into a deep meditative state, waking up when the consultation is complete. He always brings something into the room. He is like a little spiritual master. I am blessed that Sunny was sent to me.'

Dr Michael Blascombe, Victoria

Forever and a Day . . .

I'm sure if Princess Doris could speak she would have many stories of her past life and how much it's changed.

Back then, her soon-to-be mummy (that's me) was sitting sadly at home, wishing she could have someone to cuddle, someone who would love her back unconditionally. 'Soon-to-be-Mummy' had often browsed through PetRescue but had always been warned by her family to 'make sure you're ready – a dog is a long and big responsibility'. Now she knew that time had come.

Animals had always been the main focus in my life. On my twentieth birthday, I once again looked longingly through the tens of pictures of deserving dogs on PetRescue. Tears fell down my face; I wished I could save them all. At least I knew I could save one.

I wanted an older girl who loved travelling in the car, who liked other dogs and who enjoyed snuggling. I told Mum what I was looking for and she promised to help me search for a little princess to call my own. I jumped back onto the computer shortly after that phone call, my heart in a flutter. Then I came across the cutest-looking girl in the world. Doris was only two-and-a-half. I sighed, thinking she could be a bit young for me but I read on: 'A couch potato who loves to snuggle, a quiet and friendly dog who enjoys to sleep. The only exercise she feels she needs is from her bed to her bowl and back.'

My heart melted; I was in love. I sent Mum the web link and saved the young girl's page. When I called my mum about the little angel I had seen she replied, 'She's too young, Sheree. You need one a little older.' My heart dropped but I didn't give up hope, following up with my real estate agent about permission to have a dog.

For days I kept looking on PetRescue but the same little Doris kept popping up everywhere. 'That's it,' I said to myself. 'She is mine – I don't care if she is too young. I am young too, and we will be best friends.'

That afternoon I checked my emails and found Mum had sent me a link to a dog she thought would be good for me. 'You have to check this one out,' she wrote. I opened it up, and on my screen sat Doris, my little princess.

It was simply meant to be! I jumped up from the computer and grabbed the phone to call the RSPCA. I began to shake with excitement and nerves. 'Hello, I was wondering if you still have this dog?'

I rambled off the details as tears slid down my face.

'Ah, yes we do,' said a friendly voice at the other end of the phone. Hooray!

Two days later the real estate agent rang and okayed me having a dog. Now, it was a race against time. In just two hours I made a fence for Doris, grabbed my keys, jumped in the car and drove to my sister's house. 'Come with me to pick up my girl!' I called to her as I dialled the RSPCA to tell them I was on my way.

But then came the devastating news. 'Sorry,' said the lady at the shelter, 'someone is here now looking at her.'

I felt my life crash in front of me. No! Doris was meant to be mine! Hanging up, I sat in the car on the side of the road and sobbed. I was too late.

The next minute my phone rang. 'Hello, Sheree? Dakabin RSPCA. Doris is still here – would you like to come down?'

Shaking now, I screamed at my sister to drive, and fast! The moment we pulled up at the shelter I jumped out of the car and ran to the office and just as quickly found Doris's pen. In front of me sat a pudgy white Staffordshire Bull Terrier. Her little eyes seemed to bore into my soul. She came running up to me and as soon as she touched me I knew my soul mate and I had found each other.

Doris, since we met you have helped me overcome many obstacles within myself. You make me smile, laugh and cry with joy. I'll love you forever and a day.

Sheree, Queensland

My Miracle Dogs

I met Brandy after a funny little recurring thought kept popping into my mind that I should adopt an older Staffy. Each time it was quickly dismissed as I didn't think my life was set up for a dog, but the feeling kept at me for a good three months. Before this time I had never considered having a dog. I hadn't had a dog since I was about seven and now I was in my thirties.

I went to the high school where I worked one day and as I was walking along I saw a man leading a stocky brown dog along to a little room full of paints and cleaning products. I went to walk past but then realised what I had just seen and doubled back, asking him about the dog. He was the school caretaker and said he'd found the dog on the grounds. She had no identification, only a tattered brown leather collar on. I knew I should get back to work, but something about her had me riveted.

I knelt down next to her and patted her like I already knew her. I gazed into her eyes, feeling love, compassion and somehow understanding for her, and as I patted her on the head I noticed there was blood on my hand. When I looked at the top of her head closely, I noticed a lot of blood coming out of a small but fairly deep wound. When I found out later that some students had been throwing cans at her and this is how she was injured, I was horrified. The caretaker was going to put her in his room until the ranger could come and collect her.

I walked through the double doors into the school corridor and looked back at the dog through the glass panel. She was sitting there looking so small and scared. A grubby, unwashed dog with an old brown collar, fly-bitten leathery ears and no identification. Her big round eyes stayed glued to mine as I looked through the glass and I felt like she was telling me not to leave her. In my mind I told her I would find out who was coming to collect her and see what I could do.

The ranger took her to the Lost Dogs Home, and when I called them later I said if she didn't have anyone reclaim her, I wanted to adopt her. Eight days later she remained unclaimed, and so she became mine. I often think if I had been ten seconds earlier or later in the school corridor that day I never would have met her.

Another dog, Ziggy, came into my life for all of six months after I decided I wanted a senior dog to be a friend to Brandy. I had been helping Staffy Rescue as a volunteer and as a result I found myself looking on their website to see what dogs were in need. There, I suddenly spotted a beautiful grey angel called Ziggy. She was thirteen and I knew she was the one. Staffy Rescue really wanted the right home for Ziggy and so there were a lot of requirements I had to meet to be able to adopt her. I found out her sad story: Ziggy had been the loyal pet of a man for thirteen years. He'd since met a woman and they were having a baby. Ziggy was no longer wanted.

The first time we met, Ziggy jumped all over me but I could also see how sad she was. She remained very depressed for the first month we were together. She didn't want pats and sat around looking miserable for a long time. Whenever she heard a car she would perk up a little, as though hoping her previous owner was coming to take her home. At the park she would forlornly follow young couples and young men off in the distance and I'd have to call her back to me. It was heartbreaking to see how she suffered because of her abandonment.

She began to pick up a little after a while and would sometimes even run for a moment or play with another dog, but never seemed 100 per cent content. As time went on it got harder for her to get in and out of the car and she stopped wanting to go for walks, so I let her sit in the car with the doors open while Brandy and I stayed close by, playing fetch. These were signs she was developing cancer but I didn't realise. I just put the changes down to old age.

It was on one of our walks when Ziggy suddenly collapsed, vomiting, and she had diarrhoea. I instantly picked her up and carried her back to the car but knew straight away she was dying.

The vet told me her abdomen was riddled with huge lumps and

she also had a lump on her liver. A couple of nights later, she could no longer walk and I had to carry her to the toilet. The vet had told me to give her antibiotics and come back in five days but I knew she was suffering and needed to be put to sleep.

She died in my arms at 2.20 the next afternoon, after spending the entire morning together with me and Brandy. She knew when she was about to go and I sang to her while she passed away in my arms. Devastated, I gathered with my family, friends and some of her doggy pals and buried her under a beautiful old elm tree at my mother's house.

The day after she passed away, still in a daze, Brandy and I went down the street. I wanted to get Ziggy some silk flowers to decorate her grave with so I went to the local florist but they didn't have anything suitable. Then I noticed a funny little secondhand shop with floral decorations outside. When I spoke to the lady inside I ended up telling her about Ziggy, and she shared with me the loss of her own little dog who'd also had cancer. She told me to look at what was on the door as I left, because it was just what I needed at that moment. It was a passage about Rainbow Bridge, where all loved pets go when they pass away. I stood there, reading it, crying.

At that same time, my mum later told me she was at work and a peculiar thing happened. She never sings out loud, but this particular afternoon a funny urge overtook her, and she suddenly blurted out the words to 'I Can Sing a Rainbow'. When we talked about it later, we realised Ziggy had been trying to tell us she was still with us. That night in bed I felt like Ziggy was there with me and I didn't ache so much any more. I just felt I was lucky to have known her and would see her again one day, at Rainbow Bridge.

Only two days later, my good friend Lynda was involved in rescuing some dogs from terrible conditions at the home of a backyard breeder. A Staffy was among them, and as soon as she saw her, she thought of me. They desperately needed foster carers for the dogs, and so she phoned to ask if I could take care of the dog. She knew it was too soon, but they were desperate. I thought about it for a while and then replied that I would. Asking Lynda if she knew what the dog's name was, my friend replied she didn't know, but would find out for me.

I hung up, and as I put the receiver down a thought popped into my head, as clear as day: 'If she doesn't have a name, I'll call her Cassie.' It was strange, though – I had never considered Cassie as a name for a dog before, and yet I was certain that's what I'd call her.

Lynda called me back the next day to talk about bringing the dog in need to me. 'Did you find out her name?' I asked her.

'Yes,' Lynda replied, 'it's Cassie.'

After my stunned silence, I told Lynda Cassie was definitely meant to be with me, whether or not the timing seemed right. And I knew in my heart that I wasn't going to just foster Cassie. I was going to keep her always.

That night Cassie and Brandy were introduced, and it was as though a fog of grief washed off my girl. They got along immediately and to this day it's as though they are twins who were separated at birth! They play for hours and share kisses. It is even more touching because neither of them want to make friends with other dogs. They only want each other.

I have no doubt that Ziggy sent Cassie to me and Brandy, to help us heal. Thank you, my Ziggy.

Yvette, Victoria

Lessons from Tyson

Lesson 1: When you need help, ask for it

They say everyone has a mid-life crisis. Mine came in my forties when I started to question my whole reason for living and slumped into a deep depression. It was one long, dark night of the soul, and when the despair was almost too much to bear, I cried out for help.

A few days later my friend Nicole called out of the blue and suggested I might like to look after a dog. Friends of hers were returning to England and needed someone to mind their pooch, who they had rescued from a pound some time earlier. They hoped the person would look after their pet for six months and then send him over to the UK. Nicole explained that he was a very friendly Rottweiller German Shepherd mix called Tyson. I declined her offer; I wasn't ready for the responsibility of a large dog.

A few days later Nicole rang again. 'Why don't you just meet him? Chloe and Paul leave in a week and they haven't found anyone. He hates cages and won't survive the quarantine. He'll think he's been abandoned again.'

I adore dogs and felt deeply sorry for Tyson but my mind was made up. The next week, with just four days before Tyson's family were to leave, my mobile rang again. The call was from Nicole, of course. 'Something is telling me you have to meet him,' she persisted. I was standing on the street outside a shop on the other side of town from my home. I don't know why I did it, but I heard myself asking where Tyson lived. What Nicole said next made the hairs on my neck stand up and I nearly dropped the phone. I happened to be standing less than two minutes' walk from Tyson's house.

Chloe answered the door and hugged me with excitement. I started to explain I hadn't agreed to look after her dog but my words trailed off when I saw bounding towards me the most strikingly beautiful dog I have ever seen.

Tyson, all big boofy paws and wagging tail, leapt into my arms. He covered me in kisses. I don't know if he knew I was his saviour from the dreaded cage or if he recognised me as his soul mate.

All I know is that it was love at first sight . . . for both of us!

Lesson 2: Live in the moment
From the first day Tyson 'galumphed' his way into our lives with his eternally wagging tail and unquenchable enthusiasm, my girlfriend Dana and I knew it was going to break our hearts to say goodbye to him. We had only six months before the couple in England would ask us to send him over.

Wherever I went, Tyson would walk calmly by my side with no need for a lead or collar. He would stop at roads, obey all commands and wait patiently outside shops until I came out again. Everyone commented on how wonderfully matched we were. When I told them he wasn't my dog, they would say, 'Well, he should be. You're perfect together.'

As the months flew by, Dana and I grew more despondent. Then one day, a light went on in my head. I knew the purpose of life was to learn and grow, so I looked at our predicament from that perspective – and I realised the lesson we were supposed to learn from Tyson was to live in the moment. Rather than spend our lives worrying about dying, we are supposed to enjoy every moment. Our six months with Tyson was a microcosm of that, so we resolved to relish every day we had with him – and as soon as we learnt that lesson, we were rewarded with a miracle.

Two days later, Chloe called from England. I assumed she was making sure Tyson was ready for his big journey, but instead she said, 'Simon – Paul and I are living in an apartment. I know this is a lot to ask, but would you be able to keep Tyson?'

I have never received a better phone call, and I know I never will.

Dana and I whooped and danced and hugged Tyson with tears streaming down our faces. It was without a doubt the best moment of my life.

Lesson 3: Love never has to die
Sadly, my relationship with Dana didn't last. We went our different ways, but today, ten years later, we love each other more than ever, as friends. People ask us how we have stayed so close, and we always give them the same one-word answer: 'Tyson.' You see, after we separated, whatever feelings we had about each other were always secondary to the need to care for our boy. He was a sensitive soul and loved us equally, so it was important that he spend time with both of us.

He stayed with Dana first, and I know how much he helped her by sleeping on her bed and cuddling her through the night. Then, when she moved north, Tyson came to live with me. And that's how he was able to heal both our hearts.

Lesson 4: We don't need to fear death
As Tyson grew older, I knew my nightmare was approaching. His arthritic legs could barely carry him and he had a brain tumour that gave him terrifying seizures. But he never showed a hint of grumpiness. Not once.

Then, one Monday, just after his thirteenth birthday, I took him to the vet to be washed. An hour later, I got a call saying Tyson was having trouble breathing. I raced over and found him in the surgery. Tyson was by now completely unable to move, so we rushed him to the animal hospital where the surgeons shaved him in case he had a paralysis tic. There was no tic, but a brain scan revealed the tumour had ruptured, paralysing him instantly.

For three days, the doctors fought to save him. A nurse told me later that she had never seen them try so hard for a patient. It didn't surprise me – Tyson had that effect on everyone he met. But it was no use. I was told my boy would never sit or stand again.

I asked the doctors for some time alone with Tyson and lay down on the floor, crying and holding him until I plucked up the courage to ask him what he wanted to do. He was drugged, shaved, paralysed, terrified and exhausted, and yet that eternally loving look was still there on his handsome face. It was not a look of pain or self pity but of pure love for me. I will never forget it.

The night before Tyson was to be put to sleep, I asked the spirit of my father, who had passed away, to come for Tyson when it was time and make sure he was okay. I knew Dad was somewhere out there as on several occasions when I needed him, my front door would open without explanation.

The next morning I drove Tyson home from the hospital on his final journey. I carried him into the house and laid him on his bed, and surrounded him with his favourite teddies. He looked so frail without any fur, and although he could move his head a little, his body was broken and motionless.

Dana and her boyfriend had flown back from overseas, cutting the holiday they were on short. Nicole who first brought Tyson into our lives came to say goodbye too. The four of us stroked and kissed Tyson for six hours, feeding him treats and thanking him over and over again for everything he had done to make our lives so happy.

Then the vet arrived and it was time. As she injected the fatal overdose, we held Tyson and told him how much we loved him. He was completely calm and his eyes never flinched as the deadly liquid raced through his veins and towards his heart. Then, at the exact moment that it hit and he slipped away, a miracle happened. The front door swung open with a loud bang . . . and a second later, despite his tail being paralysed, Tyson wagged it several times, and was gone.

It was not physically possible, but it happened. I know it was my father that Tyson saw. And I know that is why he wagged his tail. But best of all, I know that my darling Tyson – the adorable rescue dog who ended up rescuing me – is finally and eternally safe.

Simon, New South Wales

Use PetRescue to Find Your New Best Friend!

Whether it's a dog, cat, guinea pig, or any kind of animal really, we're here to help you find the perfect rescue pet for your family!

How it works
Rescue groups and some pounds and shelters all across Australia use the PetRescue website to list their pets for adoption. We connect families looking for a pet with the organisations. We don't have a shelter ourselves and all these animals are in the care of individual groups across the country.

Getting started
This is the most fun part of using PetRescue! All you need to do is use the Search function (located on the right-hand side of the home page) at PetRescue.com.au. It allows you to search for the type, size and sex of pet you are after. There is also an Advanced Search function which will let you search for interstate pets available for adoption.

Now, the tricky part!
With over 8500 pets listed on PetRescue at any time, the hardest part will be narrowing down the ones that are right for you. Take some time to read their profiles and get to know their personalities – are they cuddly, or more the independent sort? Consider things like size, activity level, grooming requirements, need for training, and so on. Puppies may be super cute, but they require a much bigger time commitment!

You might want to consider writing down the PetRescue ID of the pets you're interested in – this is the 5–6 digit number at the end of the address bar.

Making contact with the rescue group

If you need more information, feel free to contact the rescue group that has the pet in their care. Their details are listed under 'Contact Information' on the pet's page. Generally, shelters prefer to answer calls as they usually have staff rostered on during business hours, while rescue groups prefer emails as they're run by volunteers.

The adoption process

Generally, the adoption process is quite simple, although it may take a bit longer with rescue groups as they are staffed by volunteers.

First contact

This is the initial email you send to the rescue group to register your interest in a particular pet and ask any questions you may have.

Application

The rescue group will then ask that you fill out an application form. While the form may seem quite long, with this information they're better able to help you find the pet that's just right for you. In the event that the pet you were interested in has been adopted, the group might be able to suggest another pet based on the information you've given them.

Meet and greet

If your application sounds like a good match, the rescue group will arrange a time for you and your family to meet the pet. Some rescue groups do a 'housecheck' on your property, too – they're not really interested in checking your house, they just want to make sure the fences are escape-proof and to watch out for any potential dangers your new pet may come across.

Adoption fees

For the most part, the adoption fee reflects the basic medical expenses the group has incurred for the pet. If that pet had any extra medical treatment, it's likely that the fee you are charged won't cover these costs and the rescue group will actually be out of pocket.

Please keep this in mind: The adoption fee for a rescue pet is usually somewhere between $150 and $500. The going rate for a pet-store puppy, that in all likelihood came from a puppy factory, is between $500 and $1500; a kitten from an average of $150 upwards. And you still have to pay for vaccinations, microchipping and desexing on top of that. Rescue pets are a bargain!

Interstate adoptions

Since PetRescue connects you with rescue groups from all over Australia, it's entirely possible that you may fall in love with a pet that's located interstate. Travelling long distances can be stressful for some pets, so not all rescue groups will encourage interstate adoptions. The group may also want to rehome a pet locally so that they are able to provide advice, and in certain cases take the pet back into their care should the adoption not work out.

If you decide to adopt a pet from interstate, bear in mind that the transport costs will most often be borne by you. It's usually not much, and certainly not if you think that particular pet is *perfect* for your family, but it is something to consider.

Well, what are you waiting for?

We wish you all the best in your search for your new best friend. Let us know how you go! Email us at info@PetRescue.org.au.

How Else Can You Help Rescue Pets?

1. Tell your friends

Share PetRescue.com.au with your friends and family, let them know about the wonderful pets waiting for homes at rescue groups, shelters and pounds across Australia. Make sure their next pet is a rescue pet!

2. Foster

Foster carers provide a safe, nurturing environment for a rescue pet until a permanent home can be found. Become part of the community who give these dogs and cats a second chance by opening your heart and home to a foster pet. Visit PetFoster.com.au to find out more.

3. Spread the word

Every pet on PetRescue.com.au has a Facebook and Twitter icon. Use your social media to reach out to animal lovers everywhere by sharing pet profiles and becoming a Facebook fan.

4. Donate

PetRescue relies on donations to continue to offer rehoming programs and tools to over 900 rescue groups, shelters and pounds. Visit our website to make a tax-deductible donation.

5. Share your skills

Are you a knitter, designer, lawyer, photographer, accountant, writer? Can you sizzle a sausage, play with a puppy or cuddle a kitten? To offer your services as a volunteer, visit PetRescue.com.au/get-involved.

6. Become an advocate
Write to your state and federal politicians and let them know that animal welfare issues matter to you. Tell them that the number of healthy pets killed in pounds and shelters each year is not acceptable to you and ask them to take action.

7. Desex!
There are huge advantages to desexing your pet. Desexing reduces territorial aggression in males, making them less likely to fight other dogs. They are also less likely to mark their territories by spraying or cocking their leg in the house. For females, desexing eliminates the possibility of uterine cancer and greatly reduces the possibility of mammary gland (breast) cancer. Oh, and don't forget your council registration fees are considerably cheaper!

8. Make ethical choices
Don't support puppy farms. Shop at pet stores that don't sell animals and let them know why you choose to support them.

9. Read up
Become better informed about the No-Kill Equation sweeping the United States (nokilladvocacycenter.org), and the similar Getting to Zero Model being pioneered by the Animal Welfare League of Queensland (awlqld.com.au/getting-to-zero.html). These programs attest that at least 90 per cent of each community's pets can be saved from euthanasia and be rehomed; that only untreatably ill or vicious animals should be killed. What is your local pound or shelter doing to decrease their kill rates?

10. Howl from the roof tops
Proudly tell everyone you meet that your pet is a rescue pet!